THE ESSENTIAL
John Derbyshire

THE ESSENTIAL

John
Derbyshire

PASSAGE
PUBLISHING

For information, contact support@passage.press.

Hardcover ISBN: 978-1-959403-89-0
eBook ISBN: 978-1-959403-90-6
Audiobook ISBN: 978-1-959403-91-3

Cover design by J.D.M.

Library of Congress Control Number: 2025944663

Passage Publishing
Los Angeles, CA
www.passage.press

Printed in the United States of America

1 3 5 7 9 10 8 6 4 2

Table of Contents

Preface

W RITING, SAID the Roman poet Juvenal, is an incurable disease. I have been a sufferer all my life.

For the first half-century of this life, I obtained relief by occasionally publishing book reviews, opinion pieces, or Letters to the Editor in print outlets. Then in 1996 I published a novel that won many positive reviews, bringing me to the attention of newspaper and magazine editors.

The conservative magazine *National Review* added me to its list of contributors (I was never an employee). For the next fourteen years I graced the pages of that journal and also, as online opinionating took off around the turn of the century, of its internet version. Several other outlets, both print and online, also published my work. When, in 2001, I was given a generous advance by a print publisher for a nonfiction book, I quit my day job—I had been a software developer—to take up writing full-time.

In February 2012 Trayvon Martin, a young black man, was shot dead in Sanford, Florida, during a violent encounter with a white-Hispanic neighborhood watch volunteer. The incident generated nationwide hysteria. One component of that hysteria was a rash of black journalists telling their readers about "The Talk" they gave to their children, warning them of the danger they faced from white aggressors.

In fact, statistics show plainly that of one-on-one assaults where one party is black and the other not, more than eighty percent feature a black assailant. With this in mind I composed an article titled "The Talk: Nonblack Version," sketching the warnings that a nonblack parent might give to his children about the danger they face from black aggressors.

The piece was published in *Taki's Magazine*, a webzine. It was received with widespread outrage as having violated what William F. Buckley Jr. called "the structure of prevailing taboos" about race. *National Review* dropped me from their contributor list.

Peter Brimelow's national conservative webzine *VDARE*.com, to which I had made some occasional previous contributions, invited me on board. I responded with a column titled "Who Are We?" In it I wondered aloud what name would be most appropriate for a faction of conservatism less respectful than *National Review* of that "structure of prevailing taboos." The name I settled on at last was "Dissident Right."

Did I coin that phrase? Possibly, at any rate in the sense now current. Google's Ngram Viewer, which logs the usage of words and phrases in printed matter, shows a curious history for it. Capitalized as "Dissident Right" there are occurrences going back to the 1870s, with a massive spike in 1885 and a lesser one in 1976–79. *Un*-capitalized as "dissident right" there is nothing at all until 1930, then occasional usages spiking moderately in 1960, 1971, 2006. Both spellings, however, show a major and sustained takeoff from low frequency in 2012, so I believe I started, or possibly *re*-started, something.

THE ESSENTIAL

John Derbyshire

CHAPTER ONE:

The
Dissident Right

I Was an Illegal Alien

National Review

MARCH 24, 2003

I MMIGRATION, PEOPLE tell me, is the hot-button political issue of tomorrow. Public anger is swelling. The 9/11 attacks got everyone thinking. Citizens' groups are springing up all over. Congressional and presidential candidates in 2004 are going to face a lot of questions about immigration, had better have well-thought-out positions on the topic. Etc., etc., etc. The tide is turning, my immigration-restrictionist friends tell me. The sleeping giant has woken. Etc., etc., etc.

Well, possibly. Getting Americans to think seriously about immigration, though, is uphill work. There is resistance to be overcome at the deepest level of the national psyche. To the degree that I am entitled to have an opinion on the matter (which, you may understandably say after reading this, is no degree at all), I myself am an immigration restrictionist, and can show published writings to that effect. Still I think we are underestimating the psychological obstacles to firm, strictly enforced immigration laws. I know whereof I speak, for I was once an illegal immigrant in these United States.

When people ask, I say that I came here in 1985. That is quite true. I arrived here in October of that year to work for a Wall Street firm, sucked in by the great mid-1980s financial boom. I entered on an H-1 visa, which is to say a working visa. In the fullness of time, and strictly according to proper legal procedures, I graduated to the fabulous Green Card, and thence to citizenship.

This has, however, been my second spell in the United States. I came here once before, in my feckless youth—in August of 1973, to be precise. On that occasion I bore only a miserable B-2 visa. I was, in other words, a tourist, admitted for no more than six months, with no right to work or settle in this country. One thing led to another, however (*cherchez la femme*) and quite soon I found myself penniless in the streets of New York, without a return ticket to England. I subsisted for a few days on oatmeal cookies, which someone had told me—falsely, I now feel sure—offer the maximum nutrition per dollar. Then I went looking for work.

The guilty flee when none pursueth, and I assumed—so young!, so innocent!—that the I.N.S. had agents lurking in every side alley, liable to leap out and demand to see my papers at any moment. I therefore sought the lowest, least visible kind of work I could think of. Dishwashing seemed about right. I went into a diner—it was Jack's, I recall, on the corner of Delancey and the Bowery—and offered to wash dishes for them. Jack growled that when he needed a dishwasher, he phoned for one. Whom did he phone? I asked. He told me. I phoned them. They gave me their street address. I went there.

The dishwashing agency was one of dozens packed into a grimy building downtown on West Broadway. The deal was, you showed up there as early in the morning as you could and sat with a dozen or so other aspiring dishwashers on wooden benches facing a man at a desk. Every so often the man's phone would ring. He would engage in some grunted exchanges, hang up, and call out something like: "Rockaway eight hours dollar eighty-five." This would mean that there was work in Rockaway for eight hours at $1.85 per hour, subway fares taken care of. If you were first to the desk, off you went for a day's work.

Now, your average New York City dishwasher is not a person with work ethic oozing from every pore. If you showed up at one of the agencies early on a Monday morning, you could often get a week's work all at once. Very few of those who took this option lasted past Wednesday, though. If, after a Monday start, you were still on site that Friday afternoon, the client regarded you with wonder and delight, and offered you a real job at 25¢ extra per hour.

So it went with me. By November I was a permanent full-time employee of a kosher catering firm in New Rochelle, promoted from dishwasher to kitchen porter. I rented a pleasant room in a rooming-house overlooking the harbor, ten minutes' walk from my place of work. By February I had saved enough to buy a car. You see how people fall in love with America? I marveled at the ease of everything here. Job, lodgings, automobile—why, in a few years I might be rich!

I was still, of course, without any legal status, and it weighed on my mind. One day I confessed all to my boss, a genial fellow. He thought it a huge joke. What was this Social Security number I had been giving them for my pay stubs, though? I had made it up, I told him. He frowned. That wouldn't do, might cause trouble for them. He made a phone call to someone he knew in the local Social Security office. I should go up there, he told me, speak to a certain person, fill out the forms. I did so, answering all questions truthfully. Two weeks later I had a Social Security card. I parlayed this into a driver's license and a bank account.

Six months' steady work later, fecklessness kicked in again and I lost my job. By this time, though, I was brazen in crime. I went to an office-work employment agency, got a job as a computer programmer in leafy Westchester County, and sank happily into a middle-class lifestyle. After two years, quite by chance, my new employers found out about my immigration status (which is to say, my utter lack of any such). No problem, they said cheerily, we'll give it to the lawyers. They did so, and for the rest of my time in the United States I would periodically have to go to an attorney's office and sign my name to something, or fill out something. At last, well into the fifth year of my six-month tourist visa, family business called me back to England, my "case" still unresolved.

Despite having committed gross and willful violation of US immigration laws, I had paid no penalty, done no time, suffered no inconvenience. None of the various Americans to whom I had confessed had conveyed the faintest disapproval, none had told me I ought to be ashamed of myself. In the 1970s, I can report, the normal reaction of an American on learning that the person sitting across from him was "undocumented," was puzzlement. They knew, of course, that there was such a thing as illegal immigration. The word "wetback" was then current. It was just that they didn't associate the phenomenon with well-spoken middle-class types with office-worker skill sets.

I am bound to report that I see little difference in attitude between the native-born Americans of today and those of thirty years ago. Nations, like individuals, have their own ineradicable quirks of personality. It is a peculiarity of Americans that they cannot be brought to think seriously about immigration. The two best immigration-restrictionist books of recent years have been by Peter Brimelow, who is an immigrant from England, and Michelle Malkin, daughter of recent Filipino immigrants. If you have been through, or sufficiently close to, the immigration experience, you think about it a lot. Otherwise, you don't think about it at all, and can't be made to. Take it from me, a sometime illegal immigrant: Getting this nation to concentrate on immigration reform is going to be hard work all the way.

No, We Can't

National Review

DECEMBER 1, 2008

I KNOW, I know, we are the land of opportunity. Log cabin to White House! Anyone can be anything! Up by the bootstraps! TV talking heads, motivational speakers, pastors and pedagogues, all want to tell us—and especially our children—that we are each a hissing, throbbing little pressure cooker of potential. If we will only hitch our wagon to a star, we can be all we want to be. Yes, we can!

Here is *New York Times* reporter Deborah Solomon interviewing sociologist Charles Murray, following publication of Murray's latest book *Real Education: Four Simple Truths for Bringing America's Schools Back to Reality* (2008).

> DS: Europeans have historically defined themselves through inherited traits and titles, but isn't America a country where we are supposed to define ourselves through acts of will?
>
> CM: I wonder if there is a single, solitary, real-live public-school teacher who agrees with the proposition that it's all a matter of will. To me, the fact that ability varies—and varies in ways that are impossible to change—is a fact that we learn in first grade.

> DS: I believe that given the opportunity, most people could do most anything.
>
> CM: You're out of touch with reality in that regard.[1]

That little exchange, and some remarks by one of the presidential candidates about special-needs children, stirred some memories. Forty years ago, not long out of college, with a bachelor's degree and a teacher's qualification to my name, I spent a year teaching special-needs children.

"Children" is not quite right. For one thing, this was a secondary school, ages twelve to sixteen. For another, they were all boys, this being England, and English secondary schools of all kinds being single-sex as often as not at that time. And for a third, this was a slum district in Liverpool, a rough port city where slum children grew up fast.

In England there was a system (now defunct) of special schools for students deemed to be in need of unusual attention. There were at least half a dozen official categories: schools for the severely retarded, emotionally disturbed, deaf, "delicate," and so on. Our boys were Educationally Sub-Normal. Without having any known physical, mental, or emotional abnormality, they had finished their primary schooling still unable to read or do basic arithmetic.

That year of teaching a class of ESN boys was a total-immersion course in the nature/nurture controversy. The administrator at the city Education Office who offered me the job was a nurturist of Ms. Solomon's stripe. "They're not bad boys," he assured me. "They just missed out on too much of their primary schooling. Not enough truant officers . . . And they come from bad homes, many of them."

That last part at any rate was true. The school was in Edge Hill, not far from the city center. (The local railroad stop was the last before the main Liverpool terminus. Liverpudlians, who cherish a pawky style of wit, used "getting off at Edge Hill" as a synonym for *coitus interruptus*.) The streets were all nineteenth-century terraced row houses. The district might have had a shot at being poor-but-cozy, except that "urban renewal" was under way, the old row houses being demolished street by street, the inhabitants relocated to soulless distant "estates." Edge Hill wasn't just a slum, it was a demoralized slum.

The stories we heard from the school nurse (who went to boys' homes) and the local police station's Juvenile Liaison Officer (frequently at the school) were grim. Was it really the case, in prosperous late-1960s England, that a father would supplement the family's supply of firewood by removing alternate boards from the stairs? Or that a twelve-year-old boy should not know the function of toilet paper? My colleagues, the nurse, and our policeman, assured me that such things were quite normal.

Though rough, the boys were surprisingly easy to handle. In part this was because, as my colleagues said bluntly, they were so slow-witted, it was easy to outfox them. They were given tests every year, including a frank IQ test, on which most scored in the 70s or low 80s. There was nothing wrong with any of them, and many were cheerful and pleasant boys, but there was no mistaking the fact of their being . . . dim. Dimness also helped weed out the really hard cases, who would embark on a criminal career at age thirteen or fourteen. Too clueless to evade detection, they would be caught at once and whisked off to Juvenile Hall to be someone else's problem.

Why were they so dim, though? We discussed this endlessly in the staff room. A young idealist, I very much wanted it to be nurture. Such awful environments! And missing so much primary schooling, as most of them had! My colleagues—dedicated men all, and a couple of them close to saintly in their determination to find what could be found in these lads, and to do what could be done for them—were pretty solidly for nature. In the pungent Liverpool manner, the topic was discussed as: "Does the pig make the sty; or the sty, the pig?"

It was depressing work, with little to show for months of effort. Perhaps the most depressing thing of all was that none of the boys was very capable at anything. To play soccer, for example, needs a modicum of thought as well as some minimal physical fitness. Our boys could not rise to it. The masters–boys soccer match was a rout of them, strapping fifteen- and sixteen-year-olds, by us, wheezy desk-wallahs with a median age around forty. Up to that point I had assumed that even seriously un-intellectual people must have *some* ability at *something*. That this is not necessarily the case is one of the saddest true things I ever learned.

Charles Murray is right. Ability varies, and not much can be done to change it. By no effort of will, applied from no matter how young an age, could I come to play the violin like Yehudi Menuhin, or golf like Tiger Woods. And yet, of course, this bleak fact is dispiriting and destructive, while Ms. Solomon's airy fiction is affirmative and inspiring. Tragic truth, or festive falsehood? The will needs a goal, said Nietzsche, *er braucht ein Ziel*, and we'd rather will Nothingness than not will, rather believe than know. Nietzsche was right, too.

Who Are We?

VDARE

MAY 10, 2012

This article was published shortly after John Derbyshire was dropped from *National Review*.

S O THIS is the other side of the Right, eh? Not bad; though of course nothing like as classy as the hushed, oak-paneled, Chambers-of-Commerce-financed precincts of Conservatism Inc., whose entrance is now barred against me by an angel with a flaming sword. The furnishings are a bit cheesy in fact, if you look too closely, which of course you shouldn't. Do those drapes really match that carpet?

Nice people, though—most of whom, truth be told, I've known for a decade or more. And after watching Conservatism Inc. for a quarter of a century running along behind History's great rumbling juggernaut squealing, "Would you mind slowing down just a teeny bit, please?", there is always the faint hope that this other crowd might actually turn us back some way toward liberty, sovereignty, science, constitutionalism.

But who are they—I mean, we? What do we call ourselves?

For a special-interest website like *VDARE*.com this is not really a problem: "Immigration Patriot" is sufficiently accurate.

VDARE.com occupies a corner of the non–Conservatism Inc. spectrum, though, and publishes commentary from other corners thereof, and it would be nice to have a definitive name for the whole shebang—something a little less defined-by-exclusion than "non–Conservatism Inc."

"Alternative Right" has been snaffled by Richard Spencer, all good luck to him. "Paleoconservative" has come to have a whiff of incense and cassocks about it, at least to me. I have tried to float "Oppositional Right," but it's a bit of a mouthful.

The enemies of conservatism are eager to supply their own nomenclature. "White Supremacist" seems to be their current favorite. It is meant maliciously, of course, to bring up images of fire hoses, attack dogs, pick handles, and segregated lunch counters—to imply that conservatives, especially nonmainstream conservatives, are cruel people with dark thoughts.

Leaving aside the intended malice, I actually think "White Supremacist" is not bad semantically. White supremacy, in the sense of a society in which key decisions are made by white Europeans, is one of the better arrangements History has come up with. There have of course been some blots on the record, but I don't see how it can be denied that, net-net, white Europeans have made a better job of running fair and stable societies than any other group.

Even nonwhites acknowledge this in unguarded moments, for example, an American high school student in this exchange with his teacher:

> One day I asked the bored, black faces staring back at me: "What would happen if all the white people in America disappeared tomorrow?"
>
> "We screwed," a young, pitch-black boy screamed back. The rest of the blacks laughed.[2]

Non-white supremacy is after all the rule over much of the world, from entire continental spaces such as sub-Saharan Africa to individual black-run or mestizo-run municipalities in the United States. I see no great floods *into* these places by refugees desperate to escape the horrors of white supremacy.

We should not let our enemies dictate vocabulary to us, though. In any case, the Whatever Right contains many separatists—who, far from wanting to lord it over nonwhites, just want to get away from them.

No, "White Supremacist" really won't do, even in an owning-the-insult spirit.

"White Nationalist," which has a fairly healthy currency here on the Whadda-We-Call-Ourselves Right, strikes me as even more problematical.

What is the nation to which "nationalist" is the referent? "White" isn't a nation, nor likely to become one.

I am of course aware of the much chewed-over distinction between nationalism and patriotism, first aired I think by Orwell,[3] then taken up by Russell Kirk, the bloke who is supposed to have said—and you can register a skeptical background harrumph from me here—that "I am deeply patriotic, but I don't have a nationalist bone in my body."

I don't mind the word "white" in either of those expressions. Conservatism Inc. or otherwise is a white people's movement, a scattering of outliers notwithstanding.

Always has been, always will be. I have attended at least a hundred conservative gatherings, conferences, cruises, and jamborees: Let me tell you, there ain't too many raisins in that bun. I was in and out of the *National Review* offices for twelve years, and the only black person I saw there, other than when Herman Cain came calling, was Alex, the guy who runs the mail room. (Hey, Alex!)

This isn't because conservatism is hostile to blacks and mestizos. Very much the contrary, especially in the case of Conservatism Inc. They fawn over the occasional nonwhite with a puppyish deference that fairly fogs the air with embarrassment. (Q: What do you call the one black guy at a gathering of 1,000 Republicans? A: "Mr. Chairman.")

It's just that conservative ideals such as self-sufficiency and minimal dependence on government have no appeal to underperforming minorities—groups who, in the statistical generality, are short of the attributes that make for group success in a modern commercial nation.

Of what use would it be to them to embrace such ideals? They would end up even more decisively pooled at the bottom of society than they are currently.

A much better strategy for them is to ally with as many disaffected white and Asian subgroups as they can (homosexuals, feminists, dead-end labor unions), attain electoral majorities, and institute big redistributionist governments to give them make-work jobs and transfer wealth to them from successful groups.

Which is what, very rationally and sensibly, they do.

So it's not the "white" that bothers me. Heck, conservatives might just as well be honest about it, since it's so almighty bleeding obvious.

It's that "supremacy" and "nationalism" are poor fits for the spectrum of views out here on the To-Be-Determined Right.

(Whether "white" will become a poor fit too once I get the Arctic Alliance going, I shall discuss another time.[4])

What else have we got?

American Renaissance's Jared Taylor, who has himself used "White Nationalism" in the past, seems to have settled on "race realist." Again, though, Jared is working his own particular furrow. I'm all for race realism—it sure beats race denialism—and it's a key concept underpinning the Who-The-Heck-Are-We Right. But it's just one concept sharing space with others (the aforementioned liberty, sovereignty, science, constitutionalism) and I don't think it should be privileged.

So what do we call ourselves? I'm going to make a pitch for "Dissident Right."

The word "dissident" has its roots in Latin *dis-*, meaning "apart," and *sedere*, "to sit." Dissidents sit apart from the main crowd, don't join in the community singing,[5] and refuse to applaud the Emperor's new clothes.[6]

Dissidence is a very honorable estate, made so by the brave dissidents of the great totalitarian empires. Here is the gold standard:

> [Wang Ruowang] was jailed by all the major Chinese despots of that era: by Chiang Kai-shek in the 1930s, by Mao Tse-tung in the 1950s, and again in the 1960s, and then by Deng Xiaoping after the student movement of 1989, which Wang—then aged 71—vigorously supported . . . Wang enjoyed the distinction of having been expelled from the Party *twice* . . .[7]

The sensational courage and integrity of those dissidents from totalitarianism in fact gives me pause. There might, I mean, be something a bit *impertinent* in comparing our occasional inconveniences with the horrors that they, and often their families and friends, faced up to.

There is also the air of loserdom that hangs over dissidence: what I once described in a column as "the futility of dissidents."[8]

All right; I was obviously on a downer at the time. I've put in hundreds of hours with Soviet and Chinese dissidents, though, and they really are a shabby and depressing lot. (I'll except Wang Bingzhang, who was always smartly turned out.)

Still and all, we need a name. And I suggest that "Dissident Right" is as good as any.

For a fallback position—considering the pusillanimity and careerism of Conservatism Inc., its eagerness to fall into line with any leftist doctrine that does not involve higher taxation or being beastly to embryos—how about just . . .

(drumroll!) . . .

"Conservatism"?

The National Question: Race, Ethnicity, and Identity in the 21st Century

VDARE

Originally intended to be a speech delivered to a student group at Williams College on February 22, 2016. The speech was canceled by the college's president on the grounds of "hate speech" and then published on *VDARE*.

M Y NAME is John Derbyshire. I am a freelance writer. My principal outlet nowadays is the online web magazine *VDARE*. com (which is why it is such a worthy cause), though I do occasional reviews for print publications. *VDARE*.com hosts my weekly podcast, *Radio Derb*.

VDARE.com mainly concerns itself with what we call the National Question, which we approach from a conservative position.

What is the National Question, and how does one approach it from a conservative position? Let me take those in turn.

THE NATIONAL QUESTION

WHAT IS THE National Question? I have a handy answer to that here: a book written in 2004 by the late Professor Samuel Huntington of Harvard. Title of the book: *Who Are We? The Challenges to America's National Identity.* That is the National Question: Who are we?

The answer is of course that we are Americans. But what does that mean? That's the National Question re-phrased: What does it mean to be an American?

THE CONSERVATIVE APPROACH

HOW ABOUT A conservative approach to the National Question? What does that mean?

Let me come at my answer indirectly by stating the *un*-conservative approach.

This un-conservative approach says: We, Americans, are a proposition nation. That is to say, we are a nation by virtue of our agreement on a set of propositions about the place of individuals in society, the relationship of the individual to government, and the proper scope of governmental powers.

It's rather easy to mock this concept of a proposition nation. Suppose I were to trek up into the highlands of Ethiopia, get myself invited into the hut of some illiterate Amhara goatherd, and explain our founding documents to him; and suppose he were to respond with enthusiastic agreement. Did he thereby instantly become an American?

Conversely, here is a US citizen every one of whose forebears arrived here before the Revolution, and whose male forebears fought with distinction in our country's wars. He strongly disagrees with the principles of the Founders, and would have preferred we become a Christian theocracy. Should he be stripped of his citizenship?

Well, it's easy to make fun. The proposition nation is not actually a completely absurd concept. It is not what the Founders intended, though; and, as the wisest of them would have told you, it ignores important features of our human nature in its social context. Both those features—contradicting the Founders and ignoring human nature—betray its *un*-conservative character.

So there is an answer, or the beginnings of one, to the question: What is a conservative approach to this topic? A conservative approach is one that rejects the merely propositional definition of Who We Are, or at least considers it inadequate.

We have, in fact, waded some way here into waters that get very deep indeed. What is a nation?

Let me work my way round the back of that by proceeding to the next few words in the title of my talk.

RACE, ETHNICITY, IDENTITY

THE THREE NOUNS "race," "ethnicity," and "identity" name three concepts that overlap considerably; whose main difference in fact is not so much in meaning as in provenance—where they come from.

The word "race" comes from biology; the word "ethnicity" comes from sociology; the word "identity" comes from psychology. What they all have in common is the notion of an individual belonging to a group.

In the matter of race, most individuals actually do belong to an actual group that can be objectively defined.

Race is a feature of the natural world. Members of any sexually reproducing species mate predominantly with nearby individuals. Thus, if the species is widely distributed, localized and mostly inbred groups develop over time, isolated from other groups. Each group has a distinctive menu of genetic variations, shaped by founder effect, genetic drift, and natural selection. These localized varieties are races.

Ethnicity describes the social behavior of individuals who perceive themselves as belonging to a group.

Identity is the interior view of that: the group membership as felt and understood by an individual.

ETHNICITY AS PERCEIVED KINSHIP

ETHNICITY DOES NOT of course describe just any kind of group. Most of us belong to several groups. You may belong to a church, a basketball team, a bridge club, the Republican Party, and the Royal Antediluvian Order of Buffaloes. None of those is an ethny.

A good thumbnail definition of ethnicity is *perceived kinship*. The sociologist Pierre van den Berghe, in his 1981 book *The Ethnic Phenomenon* describes ethnic sentiments as "extended forms of nepotism—the propensity to favor kin over nonkin."

That's the "kinship" side of my thumbnail definition. The other side is the word "perceived." People belong to an ethny when they believe they do. That's why the word "ethny" belongs to sociology, not to biology. To quote Professor van den Berghe again:

> Descent . . . is the central feature of ethnicity. Yet, it is clear that, in many cases, the common descent ascribed to an ethny is fictive. In fact, in most cases it is at least partly fictive.

Let me give an example. This is from a different author, also a professor, but this time of political science: Walker Connor. I've taken it from his 1993 book *Ethnonationalism*. He is speaking about the American Revolution and the Declaration of Independence.

> The political elite of the period did not believe that they were leading an ethnically heterogeneous people. Despite the presence of settlers of Dutch, French, German, Irish, Scottish, and Welsh extraction—as well as the presence of native Americans and peoples from Africa (the latter accounted for one of every five persons at the time)—the prevalent elite-held and mass-held self-perception of the American people was that of an ethnically homogeneous people of English descent.

Connor proceeds to give many examples taken from the words of our Founders. The Declaration, for instance, speaks of "our British brethren," and grumbles that "[t]hey . . . have been deaf to the voice of justice and of consanguinity."

THE WEALTH OF MANKIND

THE UNITED STATES is by no means alone in having had to invent a partly fictive ethnicity for itself. As nations go, in fact, this has been rather the rule than the exception. One of the leaders of the Risorgimento, the movement for Italian unity in the middle nineteenth century, famously said: "Having made Italy, we must now make Italians."

Likewise, modern Greeks boast themselves the descendants—the kin—of Homer, Pericles, and Aristotle. In fact Greece was massively invaded by Slavs in the Middle Ages, and modern Greeks have a large Slavic component in their ancestry. If you point this out to a Greek patriot, he'll sock you on the jaw.

And come to think of it, you can even take that ethnic identifier "British" that I just quoted the authors of the Declaration having used. As Princeton historian Linda Colley showed in her 1992 book *Britons*, British ethnicity was rather new at the time of the Declaration, a product of the wars with France in the earlier eighteenth century.

To this day, it has not altogether "taken." For the English and Scots, at least, the older national loyalties—which, after all, went back several centuries—persist. When making out envelopes for the Christmas cards I send home to relatives over there, under the name of the city, I write England. It would never occur to me to write Britain; let alone the United Kingdom, an even more recent creation.

(The lady who described the intimate side of her marriage as, "I close my eyes, open my legs, and think of England" may not actually have existed; but the legend would likely never have gained currency at all if she had been quoted as saying " . . . of Britain.")

Citizens in many nations nurse these subnational loyalties—ethnicities. They don't invalidate the concept of a nation-state, any more than the fictive element in ethnic loyalties invalidates the emotional power of the ethny.

A human society must be administered under agreed rules. Its members need a common language in which to discuss their affairs. Laws must be written and approved by agreed procedures. Armies must be raised for the common defense.

Localized populations have, over many generations, come to common understandings, different from one population to another, about these arrangements. Each population, by long fellowship, cherishes customary traditions and observances. These are our nations.

Attempts to manage these things on a supranational scale have, in the modern age, always failed at last. We see the European Union failing before our eyes right now. Before that, we saw the Soviet Union fail.

Aleksandr Solzhenitsyn, who was a citizen of that latter supranational entity expressed a great truth in his famous commencement speech at Harvard in 1978. He expressed it in religious language, but the underlying fact about human sociality is independent of one's spiritual outlook.

> The disappearance of nations would impoverish us no less than if all peoples were made alike, with one character, one face. Nations are the wealth of mankind, they are its generalized personalities: the smallest of them has its own peculiar colors, and embodies a particular facet of God's design.

LONGING FOR MEANINGFUL COMMUNITY

HOMO SAPIENS IS a social animal. We long to bond with other people, at many levels. We enlist the emotions aroused by blood ties rather carelessly, sometimes unscrupulously, to aid that bonding.

I have mentioned Professor Huntington's book *Who Are We?* Here is a quote from that book:

> People are not likely to find in political principles the deep emotional content and meaning provided by kith and kin, blood and belonging, culture and nationality. These attachments may have little or no basis in fact but they do satisfy a deep human longing for meaningful community.

Note please that second sentence: "These attachments may have little or no basis in fact." We live by myths and fictions. I don't say that flippantly: It is an important sociological truth.

It is also of course a *psych*-ological truth. If ethnicity generally has some fictive component, identity may be entirely fictive. Does the name Rachel Dolezal mean anything?

THE PRESENT SITUATION: SHAPING FORCES

SO HOW IS this all playing out in the twenty-first century?

Today's world has been shaped by two big clusters of events in the last century.

The first cluster consists of the two world wars and the Cold War. At the heart of this cluster was a flow and a counterflow of ideas about human society. The flow was Marxist-Leninist universalism, "the proletariat has no country." The counterflow was despotic ethnonationalism, most prominent in Italy, Japan, and Germany in the second quarter of the century.

That was the first cluster. The second cluster you could file under the heading "Rise of the Third World."

There was a political rise across the third quarter of the century, as former colonial possessions became independent and took up self-government.

There was also a demographic rise, in many cases a very spectacular one. Here's one of my favorite illustrations of that.

In 1922 the British Isles had a population of 47.31 million. The territory called British West Africa, for contrast, had a population of 22.48

million. So the British Isles had over twice the population of British West Africa ninety-four years ago.

Forward to today. The British Isles are still here, now the United Kingdom plus Ireland: total population 68.97 million. British West Africa is nowadays the independent nations of Nigeria, Ghana, Sierra Leone, and Gambia: total population 215.74 million. That's over three times Britain's number.

Once again:

* In 1922 the British Isles had over twice the population of British West Africa.
* In 2016 British West Africa has over three times the population of the British Isles.

This happened very quickly as history goes. Ninety-four years ago, my father was a young adult, a war veteran and a failed businessman. If demography is destiny, the shape of our destiny has been changing very fast these past few decades.

Universalism, ethnonationalism. These two clusters I've identified—one, the world wars and the Cold War; two, the rise of the Third World—worked together in complex ways.

What, for example, brought about the end of colonialism?

Well, in Japan's case it was simply defeat in World War Two. For the European powers, it was in part a response to the Cold War.

Later Marxist-Leninism appealed directly to the colonized peoples. In many cases—Vietnam, for example, and the Portuguese colonies in Africa—it armed their insurgent groups.

There was a feeling on our side of the Cold War that we needed a universalist appeal of our own.

The phrase "of our own" needs some qualifying. Much of the Western intelligentsia was sympathetic to Marxist-Leninism, so the universalism came naturally to them. "The intelligentsia has no country!" . . . as it were.

Universalism was widespread beyond the intelligentsia, though. Seek out old copies of *Reader's Digest* from around 1960. Yearning for the Brotherhood of Man long predated the arrivals of Marx and Lenin.

There is a pleasant symmetry here. If antinational universalism found a ready market in the West, ethnonationalism had plenty of customers on the other side. The official Soviet name for World War Two was "the Great Patriotic War."

In Asia, where ethnonationalism is stronger, the Communists were even more frank. Mao Tse-tung referred to the Chinese Communist Party not as the Vanguard of the Proletariat but as, quote, "the vanguard of the Chinese nation and the Chinese people." Ho Chi Minh argued against the division of Vietnam thus, quote: "We have the same ancestors, we are of the same family." The press in communist North Korea frequently scolds South Korea for allowing mixed marriages, which, say the Norks, dilute the purity of the Korean race.

Note how, in all these ethnic appeals, the speakers harness those human emotions related to kinship. "We are brothers and sisters," they say. "This is our fatherland [or motherland; or in Chinese, ancestor-land.]"

HITLER'S REVENGE

THESE PARADOXES ASIDE, the despotic ethnonationalism of the Axis powers in World War Two was widely understood, at any rate by governing and academic elites in the postwar West, to have delegitimized ethnonationalism altogether.

The logical fallacy is plain: "Since despotic ethnonationalism generated such cruelty and destruction, ethnonationalism is an evil force." The second thing does not follow from the first.

Absolute monarchy has a fairly long rap sheet, but that is not an argument against monarchy. Constitutional monarchy has proved one of the more benign forms of government.

Logic is not a major determinant in human affairs, though, nor even much in evidence. Those generalized, partly fictionalized emotions of ethnic kinship that had been normal and socially healthful components of national identity before fascism came up, were now seen as shameful, the very concept of the nation-state as illegitimate.

My colleague, *VDARE*.com editor Peter Brimelow, calls this "Hitler's revenge."

UNIVERSALISM IN AMERICA: CIVIL RIGHTS

UNIVERSALISM AS THUS shaped by the world wars and the Cold War was at work in the two great revolutionary upheavals of the United States in the 1960s: the civil rights movement and the 1965 Immigration Act. Both arose during the deepest depths of the Cold War. That is not a coincidence.

The civil rights movement was of course much more than a Cold War phenomenon, but the Cold War was a factor.

For example, in the later Soviet Union, there was a strain of cynical underground humor aimed against the system. Its productions were known as "Radio Armenia jokes." Here is a Radio Armenia joke I recall from my college days in the early 1960s:

> Question from a listener to Radio Armenia: "Tell me, comrades, is it true that an engineer in America earns four times as much as one in the USSR?"
>
> Radio Armenia's reply: "In America they lynch negroes!"

Part of the desire among white Americans to get right with blacks came from awareness of being the target of that sort of critique: not only from the Soviets, but also from Europeans.

American elites have always been susceptible to the "cultural cringe" vis-à-vis Europeans; and midcentury Europeans, as soon as they had shaken off the dust of their colonies—in some cases, before—were striking poses of lofty moral superiority to the gap-toothed hillbillies of North America.

UNIVERSALISM IN AMERICA: IMMIGRATION

SIMILARLY WITH THE 1965 Immigration Act.

After some order had been brought to the US immigration system in the early 1920s, permanent settlement was granted in limited numbers and based on national origin, with preference for settlers from north and west Europe.

This was grounded in a commonsense approach to ethnonationalism. If subnational ethnies became too numerous and strong, it was believed, the core of American nationhood, what Professor Huntington called our "Anglo-Protestant culture," would be threatened. This belief was perfectly rational.

By the early 1960s, however, with universalism in the ascendant, selection of immigrants by national origin was being seen, at any rate by key sections in our elites, as shamefully racist, a sort of border-guard Jim Crow. The 1965 Act was a response to this perception.

There has been much discussion about the motives of those who gave us the Immigration Act. Edward Kennedy, the floor manager for the Act in the Senate, famously said:

> First, our cities will not be flooded with a million immigrants annually. Under the proposed bill, the present level of immigration remains substantially the same. . . . Secondly, the ethnic mix of this country will not be upset . . .

In fact, levels of legal immigration have been over a million a year since 1989; and the ethnic mix of 1960—eighty-nine percent white, ten percent black, one percent other—is a fading memory.

What accounts for the huge discrepancy between declared intent and actual consequences of the 1965 Act? Malicious dishonesty, or blank stupidity?

There are cogent arguments on both sides. I am personally inclined to the view stated by Professor Huntington, that there was a deliberate intent on the part of our elites to move the governance of our country from a national to an imperial model.

Let me quote the relevant passage from Professor Huntington's book. It is rather long, I'm afraid, but I believe it strikes to the heart of the matter.

> In the past, imperial and colonial governments provided resources to minority groups and encouraged people to identify with them, so as to enhance the government's ability to divide and rule. The governments of nation-states, in contrast, attempted to promote the unity of their people, the development of national consciousness, the suppression of subnational regional and ethnic loyalties, the universal use of the national language, and the allocation of benefits to those who conform to the national norm. Until the late twentieth century, American political and governmental leaders acted similarly. Then in the 1960s and 1970s they began to promote measures consciously designed to weaken America's cultural and creedal identity and to strengthen racial, ethnic, cultural, and other subnational identities. These efforts by a nation's leaders to deconstruct the nation they governed were, quite possibly, without precedent in human history.

I should say there is also a line of thought that applies a Marxist analysis to these changes. In the Western world, these post–World War Two decades saw the opening of a great new age of consumerism. Business was humming; and whole new types of business came up, especially in the services sector, that were outside the entrenched protections of labor union power.

Why not bring in willing workers from abroad who would accept lower wages than natives? Sure, they would incur social costs—housing, roads, energy, schooling, policing, healthcare, native unemployment—but government expenditures could take care of that. Privatize profits, socialize costs!

You can see the appeal to Capital. A school of economists came up to assure us that, yes, mass immigration would make us all richer.

Curiously, the fastest-developing nations of that era were the "tigers" of East Asia: Japan, South Korea, Taiwan. These nations held firm to their ethnic nationalism and shunned mass immigration; but they got rich anyway.

Nowadays of course they are having their comeuppance. Japanese people today are huddled under threadbare blankets as icy winds blow through their disintegrating houses. They subsist on tree bark, insects, and the flesh of their family pets. So, at any rate, I am given to understand by economists.

UNIVERSALISM TRIUMPHANT

BY THE LATE 1980s, antinational universalism was triumphant in the West. Immigrants from all over the world were pouring into our countries: not just the United States but Britain, France, Germany, Australia . . .

One of the crowning achievements of this peak universalism was the European Union. A Marxist analysis can be applied here, too; but there is no doubt that the EU came up at least in part as a reaction against the despotic ethnonationalism that had brought such horrors to the continent in the 1940s.

Away with all ethnonationalism, then! There will be no more Spaniards and Dutchmen and Frenchmen and such men, only Europeans!

So barriers came down all over Europe. The Third World poured into the First World.

Then two things happened: one suddenly, one gradually.

NATIONS MAKE A COMEBACK

THE FIRST THING that happened was the end of the Cold War in 1991.

I assume I am speaking to an audience of millennials here, persons with no direct recollection of the Cold War. To you people—and I don't mean to be patronizing, I'm sure some of you know about this: but it can't be said often enough—to you people, just let me say: the Cold War was a very big deal.

Here's one data point at random. Time: about fifteen years ago, before 9/11. Place: the Manhattan town house of a very senior figure, an elder statesman, in the American conservative movement. *Dramatis personae:* ten or a dozen conservative writers and policy intellectuals ranging in age from thirties to seventies, seated around the elder statesman's dinner table.

We were discussing the state of the world. The discussion lapsed for a minute or two. Then one of the older persons present said, with what I recall as a perfectly genuine-sounding sigh of nostalgia: "How I miss the Cold War!"

Two or three others of the same generation murmured agreement. "Oh, yes!" One of the younger members of the company laughed, a bit nervously—the way you laugh when you're not sure if you should laugh. The others just looked baffled.

Well, the Cold War ended, and policy intellectuals bent their attention to prognostications about the shape of things to come. What would the *post*–Cold War world look like?

Think-tanker Francis Fukuyama was first off the starting blocks. In fact he jumped the gun: His landmark essay "The End of History" was published in 1989, when the Soviet Union was still intact, though plainly tottering. Fukuyama foresaw a world in which Western-style liberal democracy would triumph everywhere.

It quickly became apparent that in defiance of Dr. Fukuyama, History intended to go on for a while longer. The first Gulf War and more especially the violent breakup of what had once been Yugoslavia showed that ethnonational passions had by no means been extinguished by decades of Marxist-Leninist universalism.

The liberation of Eastern Europe likewise. Here is a story I heard from one of the participants.

> After the Soviet troops withdrew from Hungary following the end of the Cold War, there was a political faction in the new Hungarian government clamoring for war against Romania. The Treaty of Trianon in 1920 had stripped Hungary of much of its territory, for example giving Transylvania to Romania, and Hungarian patriots had been seething about it ever since. (Some of them still are.) "Here's our chance to get back Transylvania!" they clamored.

The US ambassador had to talk them down off the ledge. If Hungary attacked Romania, he told them, they could kiss goodbye their chances of joining the EU. The Hungarians very much wanted to join the EU for economic reasons, so they came off the ledge.

That was Europe after the Cold War.

I should add, by the way, that the years after the Cold War ended were a Golden Age of geopolitical speculation. Francis Fukuyama kicked it off, but many fine minds followed. Professor Huntington was one of them: His 1993 essay, later a book, "The Clash of Civilizations" is still well worth reading. So is Benjamin Schwarz's 1995 essay "The Diversity Myth" in the May 1995 issue of *The Atlantic*, which ties together American and European developments. So are many others: It was, as I said, a Golden Age for geopolitical policy eggheads.

The resurgence of ethnonationalism was in any case too obvious to ignore. Francis Fukuyama's End of History thesis became what Wall Street calls a distressed security. One wag, I forget who, proclaimed "the end of the End of History."

THE COLLAPSE OF UNIVERSALISM

I SAID THAT two things happened at the end of the twentieth century: one suddenly, one gradually. The end of the Cold War was the sudden event. The gradual one—it is in fact still underway—was the collapse of universalism.

Let's just go back to the 1950s and 1960s, when the old colonial empires of Europe and Japan had fallen or were in the process of being dismantled. What had once been colonies were emerging as independent nations under self-government. What were the expectations for these new nations?

Again, you have to see this situation in the context of the Cold War, with much jostling for favors, East versus West. Overall, though, for persons of a universalist mindset, there were good reasons to hope.

These ex-colonies had experienced First World–grade government. They'd seen how it was done. Many of their elites had studied in Western universities.

Human beings are a very imitative species. Since human beings everywhere have common hopes, desires, and abilities, why should not

Africa, Asia, Oceania, the Caribbean, and the Middle East have nifty little parliamentary democracies up and running in no time?

A few of them did. A few more, especially in Asia, slipped into autocracy then came out at the other end after a decade or three into properly constitutional government.

Others, especially in Africa and the Islamic world, fell under the control of gangster-despots. Still others got some semblance of rational government, but were plagued by corruption, crime, poor human capital, and demographic pressure.

The result in these latter cases—Africa and Islamia—has been despair.

A young Third Worlder of fifty years ago—a citizen of newly or recently independent Nigeria, Pakistan, or Algeria, for example—could reasonably hope that his nation would develop into a comfortable welfare democracy like those of the First World; that his children and grandchildren, and he himself in his old age, could live in security and prosperity, as Australians and Japanese and Norwegians do.

Young Nigerians, Pakistanis, and Algerians no longer think like that. The hope proved an illusion. All over the Third World today, young people understand that their only hope for a decent, secure life is to get themselves into a First World country by any means possible.

REVEALED PREFERENCE

FORTIFYING THE PULL of First World living standards is technology: the comparative ease of modern travel, and the worldwide communications revolution, bringing pictures of those living standards into Third World hovels.

Another pull factor is what systems analysts call "the installed base": communities of one's fellow nationals or ethnics already settled in the First World by half a century of generous immigration policies.

And then there's the push factor of demography. To repeat my earlier illustration:

- In 1922 the British Isles had over twice the population of British West Africa.

- In 2016 British West Africa has over three times the population of the British Isles.

Hundreds of millions of Third Worlders see no hope in their own countries. This is why you see boatloads of them crossing the Mediterranean, scaling the border fences of Spain's African territories, crowding into the "Jungle" camp at Calais.

I'm sorry to say that when I see pictures of those boatloads, the phrase that comes into my mind is one from economics: "revealed preference." The idea here is that if you want to know what people truly desire and believe, watching what they do is a much surer guide than listening to what they say.

The revealed preference of those boat people is to live in a First World country. Their hope—an entirely reasonable one—is to improve their lives thereby.

The fear of many First Worlders is that the boat people, if they settle in sufficient numbers, will reduce the host nations, or significant enclaves within them, to the wretched condition of the nations they're fleeing. This fear is also entirely reasonable.

DESPAIR, AMERICAN-STYLE

AS IN THE world at large, so within the United States fifty years ago—I was there, I was active, I remember it—it was assumed by almost everyone that with legalized segregation struck down, black Americans would soon rise and merge into the uniform American population as most other ethnies had done, and race would no longer be a significant social issue.

That hasn't happened. Smart, capable, and well-socialized blacks—the "talented tenth"—have indeed merged as promised, but a huge black underclass remains, exhibiting spectacular levels of crime and social dysfunction. The underclass is proportionally much larger, and the social pathologies more intense, than is the case with any other race.

Revealed preference is in play here, too. Fifty years ago there was a faction among black civil rights activists who argued that blacks could never be happy or fulfilled in white society. Stokely Carmichael settled in Guinea; Maya Angelou lived in Ghana for a while.

You never see that now. Can you imagine Al Sharpton going to live in Guinea, or Ghana, or Haiti? What would he do there? To be sure, Ta-Nehisi Coates, the current darling of gentry white liberals, has left America. He has gone to live in . . . France.

Sharpton or Coates would starve to death in a black society. They are, in the plain ecological sense, parasites on their nonblack fellow citizens.

The revealed preference of blacks everywhere today is to live in white societies, an implicit admission that they can't create pleasant societies of their own and are dependent on other races for a decent living standard.

The orthodox explanation for black failure, at both the national and subnational level, is that it is the fault of whites. The peculiar success of East Asians at both these levels, despite past white colonialism and discrimination, suggests that this orthodox explanation may need work.

LOOKING FORWARD

HOW MAY WE expect nationality, race, and ethnicity to play out in years to come?

One thing we may reasonably expect is better understanding. A human society is the vector sum of many human personalities, past and present. Everything that we can quantify about the human personality—intelligence, extraversion, neuroticism, aggressiveness, and so on—is heritable to some degree, typically at around the fifty percent level.

This suggests that the human personality, and the societies it forms, are shaped to some degree by human genetics, the only known mechanism of heredity. It would therefore not be very surprising to learn that the different menus of genetic variation that characterize different races might tend to result in different societies.

At present we can't do much more than speculate about these matters, but the fog is clearing fast. Almost every week I read something new out of the human sciences bearing on these topics. As one of Shakespeare's characters says: "The future comes apace." Or as Charles Murray likes to say: "There's a locomotive coming down the tracks."

And in the caboose of that locomotive of understanding will come technology. It is already the case today that no one in a First World country need give birth to a Down syndrome child, unless she wants to. If my knowledge of current science is correct, it will be the case ten years from now, perhaps less, that no First-Worlder will need to give birth to a stupid child unless she wants to; or an ugly child, or an un-athletic or un-musical child, or an antisocial child.

Supposing this is right, how will this technology be made available? Who will be the decision-makers? Individual citizens, exercising their own volition under constitutionally protected liberties? Or overbearing governments with grand plans of social engineering?

That will depend on which nation, which one of Solzhenitsyn's "generalized personalities," you find yourself living in.

Thank you, ladies and gentlemen.

Race Realism Has a Past. Does Race Denialism Have a Future?

VDARE

AUGUST 8, 2017

Originally a PowerPoint presentation delivered to the American Renaissance conference on July 29, 2017. Then published as a text essay on *VDARE* shortly afterward.

INTRODUCTION

WITH ALL the chatter about the Alt Right that came up in last year's election season, Jared Taylor has been doing some interviews recently. The interviewer generally opens by asking: "What is your organization, this American Renaissance, all about? What do you stand for?"

Jared commonly gives a two-part answer.

First, he says, we are a white advocacy group, speaking up on behalf of the collective interests of white Americans and pushing back against the antiwhite rhetoric that pervades our culture.

Second, we are race-realist, seeking to promote honest, open discussion about race differences and their implications for social policies, especially immigration, education, and law enforcement.

You have heard, or will be hearing, white advocacy from Jared himself and from other speakers at this conference. In this talk I am going to turn my plow into the other field. I am going to talk about race realism, and about the opposite thing: race denialism.

DEFINITIONS

LET ME DEFINE these two positions: race realism and race denialism.

Race realism is the point of view that *homo sapiens*, like any other widely distributed species, is divided into local varieties—races—that differ in their biology.

Where races show different statistical profiles on heritable traits— physiognomy, metabolism, disease susceptibility, and the BIP traits (Behavior, Intelligence, Personality)—it is reasonable to infer that biological differences are causal factors. Biological race differences work together with adscititious factors (history, geography, epidemiology) to shape social outcomes.

The opposite of race realism is race denialism.

Race denialism is the point of view that observed group differences between local varieties of *homo sapiens* are superficial and inconsequential, like the hair color of individuals.

The different statistical profiles of races on BIP traits and social outcomes are entirely caused by historical and social factors. Biology plays no part.

My approach here will be chronological. I'm going to take a look at the present of both race realism and race denialism; then at the past; then I'll offer some speculations about the future.

THE PRESENT SITUATION, WEST AND EAST

THE INTELLECTUAL CLIMATE in the West today is one of guerrilla race realism.

The commanding heights of Western societies—media, schools, politics—are held by race denialists. Race denialism is a social dogma. All respectable people are required to affirm it.

Meanwhile, in the maquis, the biological and human sciences (especially genetics, psychometry, paleoanthropology) uncover ever more race-realist facts—"hatefacts."

Ever more educated, thoughtful citizens observe persistent patterns in group social outcomes that contradict official dogma. (The thoughtcrime of Noticing.) They conclude that the race-denialist Emperor has no clothes.

The guardians of race denialism are obliged to conduct counter-guerilla operations. Here is a representative one from—yes!—the *Guardian*. The occasion here was the publication of Nicholas Wade's race-realist 2014 book *A Troublesome Inheritance*.

Guardian reviewer Adam Rutherford cracked the race-denialist whip.

> We now know that the way we talk about race has no scientific validity. There is no genetic basis that corresponds with any particular group of people, no essentialist DNA for black people or white people or anyone. . . . There are genetic characteristics that associate with certain populations, but none of these is exclusive, nor correspond uniquely with any one group that might fit a racial epithet. . . . Race doesn't exist, racism does. But we can now confine it to opinions and not pretend that there might be any scientific validity in bigotry.[9]

Indeed. Some sub-Saharan Africans, of entirely local ancestry, have white skin. They are albinos. So white skin is certainly not exclusive to non-Africans. So . . . there is no such thing as race?

Rutherford here is retailing an argument put forward by Marxist ideologue Richard Lewontin in 1972, an argument since debunked so often and comprehensively that it commonly appears in reference sources as "Lewontin's Fallacy." Wade deals with it in his book (chapter 5).

So much for the Western world of today. What about the East?

The advanced nations of East and South Asia are broadly race-realist. Race denialism is not a social dogma in China, India, Japan, or Korea.

These nations are, however, monoracial (or in India's case long, long accustomed to the racial mix they have), and apparently wish to remain so.

Race realism and race denialism are therefore not salient topics in the current intellectual climate of Eastern Civilization.

THE SALIENCE OF RACE

WHEN DISCUSSING THE past of race realism and race denialism, as always with historical topics, some effort of imagination is necessary.

From the beginnings of science in the seventeenth century to the rise of the United States in the late nineteenth, the center of Western intellectual activity was in Europe. For Europeans of this period, race in the modern understanding was not salient. It occupied very little space in their minds.

"Race" to them generally meant "nationality." A character in Benjamin Disraeli's 1847 novel *Tancred* says: "All is race, there is no other truth."

He was referring to the Anglo-Saxon Celts of the British Isles, in the context of the rise and fall of nations within Europe.

Similarly with Winston Churchill's 1964 (!) book *The Island Race*, also about the British. The race referred to in the title of Madison Grant's 1916 bestseller *The Passing of the Great Race* was the Nordics, a subset of white Europeans.[10]

As a dabbler in the history of mathematics, my favorite in this line comes from a speech with the title "Mathematics Knows No Races" (*Die Mathematik kennt keine Rassen*) prepared by David Hilbert for the International Congress of Mathematicians in Bologna, 1928.

> If we look—even superficially—at the history of our science, we see all nations and peoples, the big as well as the small, taking a successful and equal part in it. Let us think of Descartes, Fermat, Pascal, Huygens, Newton, Leibniz, Bernoulli, Euler, d'Alembert, Lagrange, Monge, Laplace, Legendre, Fourier, Gauss, Poisson, Möbius, Chasles, Lamé, Steiner, Abel, Jacobi, Dirichlet, Hamilton, Riemann, Clebsch, Cantor, Poincaré, Darboux, Klein—these names are thrown wildly among the nations, as a dice-cup couldn't do more thoroughly and less biased [*gründlicher und unparteiischer*].

My photomontage[11] makes my point: "race" in this usage is distinctly monochromatic.

For one more example of the weak salience of race in Europe until recent decades I bring forward my grandfather's 1922 *Atlas-Guide to the British Commonwealth of Nations and Foreign Countries*. From which:

1922 populations

- British Isles: 47.31 million.
- British West Africa: 22.48 million.
- Ratio: 2.10.

2015 populations

- United Kingdom + Irish Republic: 68.97 million.
- Nigeria + Ghana + Sierra Leone + Gambia: 215.74 million.
- Ratio: 0.32.

"Numbers are of the essence"—Enoch Powell.

RACE REALISM HAS A PAST

BEFORE THE SEVENTEENTH-century scientific revolution, ideas about race were inchoate and unsystematic—"Folk anthropology." To the degree they included notions we would now consider biological, those notions came from:

- The obsession, in aristocratic societies, with ancestry and lineage.

- Practical knowledge obtained from millennia of experience in selective breeding of crops and livestock.

From these, by the time methodical science arrived on the scene, civilized peoples had a fair, but unorganized, stock of knowledge about inheritance and genetic similarity.

With the Enlightenment, systematic biological classification was attempted, most persuasively by Linnaeus.* Philosophers also took an interest—Kant,† for example.

Race in the modern sense was salient in the eighteenth-century Americas and the Caribbean, which had long made use of black African

---

*   Carolus Linnaeus (1707–1778), in his *System of Nature* (1758), describes four racial categories. 1) Amerind: Obstinate, contented, free. Ruled by custom. 2) European: Active, clever, inventive. Ruled by law. 3) East Asian: Severe, haughty, desirous. Ruled by opinion. 4) sub-Saharan African: Crafty, slow, foolish. Ruled by caprice.

†   Twenty years after Linnaeus, Immanuel Kant (1724–1804), in his "Of the Different Human Races" (1777), checked in with a different schema. 1) The white race. 2) The Negro race. 3) The Hun race (Mongol or Kalmuck). 4) The Hindu or Hindustani race. Kant's typology was mainly physical. He didn't have much to say about the BIP traits, although he did note of the Negro that, "because he is so amply supplied by his motherland, he is . . . lazy, indolent, and dawdling."

and (to a much smaller degree) local indigenous peoples as slave labor. It was salient, too, for the small minority of Europeans who had first-hand experience of Europe's overseas empires.

This did not lead to much scientific theorizing, but it did cause a lot of *noticing*. Thomas Jefferson can be taken as representative. In his *Notes on the State of Virginia* (1781), Jefferson writes:

> I advance it therefore as a suspicion only, that the blacks, whether originally a distinct race, or made distinct by time and circumstances, are inferior to the whites in the endow-ments both of body and mind. It is not against experience to suppose, that different species of the same genus, or varieties of the same species, may possess different qualifications.

The "long" nineteenth century (that is, to 1914) saw the end of race slavery in the civilized world, and the rise and acceptance of evolution-ary biology. There was much theorizing about race, most of it not very scientific. Charles Darwin was of course an outstanding exception—a great scientist. In *The Descent of Man* (1871), he writes:

> The races differ also in constitution, in acclimatisation and in liability to certain diseases. Their mental characteristics are likewise very distinct; chiefly as it would appear in their emotional, but partly in their intellectual faculties. Every one who has had the opportunity of comparison, must have been struck with the contrast between the taciturn, even morose, aborigines of South America and the light-hearted, talkative negroes. There is a nearly similar contrast between the Malays and the Papuans, who live under the same physical conditions, and are separated from each other only by a narrow space of sea.

The twentieth century saw the rise of population genetics (Wright, Fisher, Haldane[*]), the neo-Darwinian synthesis in evolutionary biology

---

[*] In the years between the two World Wars, Sewall Wright (1889–1988), Sir Ronald Fisher (1890–1962), and J. B. S. Haldane (1892–1964) built the modern theory of pop-ulation genetics, using advanced statistical methods to show how genetic variation arises and changes over time. Their subject can be taught without direct reference to race (the word "race" does not occur in the index of the standard textbook, *Principles of Popu-lation Genetics*: "local population" is the preferred term), but race realism is plainly implicit in their discoveries.

(Dobzhansky, Mayr), the molecular structure of DNA (Watson & Crick), and rigorous psychometry (Burt, Eysenck, Jensen[*]).

All these developments had implications for the understanding of race as a feature of the human world.

RACE DENIALISM HAS A PAST, TOO

RACE DENIALISM HAS a past at least as long and respectable as race realism's.

Premodern civilizations often had race-denialist themes. Most interpretations of Christianity have been race-denialist. Missionary endeavors by white Christians among other races were usually inspired by race-denialist ideas about the Brotherhood of Man. There were similar strains in the other big old religions.

(This didn't stop the premoderns practicing race slavery, however. At least one medieval Pope accepted a gift of African slaves as tribute to the Holy See. Devoutly Muslim Saudi Arabia did not abolish slavery until 1962.)

The European Enlightenment brought a new style of moral universalism that was implicitly race-denialist.

You see this in, for example, Dr. Johnson's preface to Father Jerome Lobo's *Voyage to Abyssinia* (1735):

> The reader will . . . discover, what will always be discovered by a diligent and impartial inquirer, that, wherever human nature is to be found, there is a mixture of vice and virtue, a contest of passion and reason.

Johnson famously remarked at the time of the American Revolution: "How is it that we hear the loudest yelps for liberty among the drivers of negroes?" He employed a black manservant, Francis Barber, whom he treated kindly and to whom he left a bequest in his will. Barber's descendants still farm in Staffordshire.

The most important legacy of Enlightenment universalism today is found in college departments of Economics (in some ways the quintes-

---

[*] In his April 1969 essay in *Harvard Educational Review,* "How Much Can We Boost IQ and Scholastic Achievement?" Arthur Jensen (1923–2012) writes: "There is an increasing realization among students of the psychology of the disadvantaged that the discrepancy in their average performance cannot be completely or directly attributed to discrimination or inequalities in education. It seems not unreasonable, in view of the fact that intelligence variation has a large genetic component, to hypothesize that genetic factors may play a part in this picture."

sential Enlightenment discipline), where human beings and human populations are treated as perfectly interchangeable units without biological essence.

There has been, though, some low-level guerilla activity in those departments in recent years. Presumably Behavioral Economics will at some point have to seek terms from Behavioral Genetics; but that point is a couple of decades away, at least.

As the Enlightenment made room for the Romantic era, a strain of "romantic primitivism" came up, with the Noble Savage as a stock figure. Jean-Jacques Rousseau is generally blamed here; but in fact some related notions can be traced all the way back to the pastoralism of ancient poets (Hesiod, Vergil), and are present in other civilizations (for example, in Taoism).

Enlightenment universalism did not always get on well with romantic primitivism, its illegitimate offspring. When James Boswell ventured an admiring remark about Polynesians, Johnson slapped him down with: "Don't cant in defence of savages."

Romantic primitivism evolved naturally into phenomena of our own time: white ethnomasochism and reverence for the "magic Negro."

RACE DENIALISM'S PAST, CONTINUED: AFTER THE ENLIGHTENMENT

DURING THE "LONG" nineteenth century, elite Protestant universalism in the United States was implicitly race-denialist. Most Abolitionists were race-denialists.

Harriet Beecher Stowe, for example, closed out her 1852 novel *Uncle Tom's Cabin* with a plea to fellow Christians to educate and improve freed slaves so that when shipped to Liberia (as most white Americans, including most Abolitionists, wanted), they could build a successful modern country over there.

The subsequent history of Liberia suggests that either the author's plea was not heard—remarkable, for such a colossally bestselling book—or that the race-denialist premises underlying it are false, or both.

A more consequential development in race denialism was the anthropology of Adolf Bastian and his acolytes.

In 1859, the year Darwin published *On the Origin of Species*, Bastian coined the phrase "the psychic unity of mankind" (*die psychische Einheit des Menschen*).

Bastian's most important follower, in the next generation, was Franz Boas. Boas brought Bastian's universalism to the United States, where it took over the social and human sciences in the decades after World War One.

"Culture" became the standard rationale for group differences—a sort of all-explanatory phlogiston or luminiferous aether.

This modern race denialism got a mighty boost from World War Two—what Peter Brimelow calls "Hitler's Revenge."

Yet at the same time, biology was staging something of a recovery in the human sciences, at least at the guerilla level. Carl Degler tells the story in his 1991 book, *In Search of Human Nature*. Degler tracks the beginnings of the revival to post-WWII psychologists, dissatisfied with the cold mechanics of Behaviorism.

A key event was the publication in 1975 of E. O. Wilson's *Sociobiology*, which, as its title plainly tells, sought to apply biological principles to human society.

Forty-two years on from that, you can still get yourself into major trouble by mentioning sociobiology in an academic journal of the Humanities, as Professor Raymond Wolters discovered recently.[*]

So the revival of biology in the social and human sciences remains at the guerilla level. Carl Degler, writing in 1991, did not foresee this. Indeed, the 1990s proved to be a time of remarkable openness in those sciences. I had a go at quantifying this once.[12] Peter Brimelow calls that period an "interglacial."

The ice-sheets have since returned.

RACE REALISM'S FUTURE

WHAT THEN IS the future of race realism?

At the level of research into the rigorous sciences, race realism is established fact.

The human genome and its many varieties are now the subject of massive, lavishly funded research. A person's self-identified race can be read off from the genome with ninety-nine percent accuracy.

China is a big player here, but genomic research is happening all over: in Ireland, for example, whose government announced a major island-wide genomic study in 2016.

---

[*] The late Raymond Wolters got into trouble with the academic Left for a review he wrote in *American Historical Review* in 2017. His account of the fuss is here.

Deeper understanding of the genetic architecture of BIP traits, and of race differences in that architecture, will inevitably emerge as a by-product of this research.

Mapping that genetic architecture is, however, harder than we thought twenty years ago. Thousands of genes are involved, each with a tiny effect (and possible side-effects).

That is no excuse for race denialism: "You don't need to know the name and job description of every worker in the factory to know that the factory produces widgets." It does, though, mean that race denialism has plenty of life in it yet.

RACE DENIALISM'S FUTURE

IT MAY WELL be that while race denialism disappears from the rigorous sciences, it maintains its grip on the social sciences, and on the liberal-arts elites who control the cultural heights of Western nations.

Understandings from the rigorous sciences can take an awfully long time to be accepted outside the labs. As I have written myself:

> More important, especially in this supremely un-PC area, is the power with which the human mind resists science. When the boffins deliver some irresistible amenity—a drug, a plane, a light switch—there is grudging acceptance that the underlying principles must have some epistemic content. In other cases, nobody much is convinced. Forty-six percent of Americans deny the truth of evolution.
>
> The collective death wish that seized the European-derived civilizations sometime in the second half of the twentieth century has hardened from mere wish to near-fanatical determination. The dogma of utopian egalitarianism, which has been used to justify the opening of white nations (with a very few exceptions) to mass immigration from regions with very different civilizational attainment, or none, waxes stronger by the hour.[13]

And if you doubt that race denialism can persist in the teeth of obvious fact and proven science, consider sex denialism.

Here was Nicholas Matte, Lecturer in History at the University of Toronto, speaking on *The Agenda* (a Canadian TV program), October 2016:

Basically, it's not correct that there is such a thing as biological sex. And I'm a historian of medicine; I can unpack that for you accurately at length if you want, but in the interests of time I won't. So that's a very popular misconception.

Once again: That is a licensed, credentialed academic in the Humanities speaking.

If we can deny the reality of sex, what aspect of human biology can we not deny?

The White Queen, speaking to Alice in *Through the Looking-Glass* (1871): "Why, sometimes I've believed as many as six impossible things before breakfast."

That's what human beings are like—other than the few freaks and misfits who take the empirical sciences seriously. As a very wise man once wrote:

The ordinary modes of human thinking are magical, religious, social, and personal. We want our wishes to come true; we want the universe to care about us; we want the approval of those around us; we want to get even with that s.o.b who insulted us at the last tribal council. For most people, wanting to know the cold truth about the world is way, way down the list.[14]

Let's not get our hopes up. Race denialism will be around for a while yet.

The De-Rehabilitation of Charles Murray

Academic Questions

DECEMBER 2018

W HEN CHARLES Murray's book *Human Accomplishment: The Pursuit of Excellence in the Arts and Sciences, 800 B.C. to 1950* was published in 2003, I was assigned to review it. Forming my thoughts after reading the book, I recalled an earlier exchange I had had with the author. (We had some slight personal acquaintance by way of a private email discussion group we both belonged to.) I recorded that exchange in my review.

> I once suggested to Charles Murray that the true object of his intellectual passion is not sociology, or psychology, or psychometry, but statistics. Murray: "If you had said 'data,' you would have been nearer to the truth." That was when he was still at work on *Human Accomplishment*. Reading the book now, I see the wisdom of his reply. Murray is a master mariner of data—a datanaut, as it were. The science of statistical analysis supplies his tool kit—his sounding line and sextant—but his passion is for the numbers, and the truths that lie hidden in their dim green depths.[15]

That is a key insight into Murray the public intellectual. I should say before proceeding, though, that it sells him short as a writer. The book about the Apollo Program that Murray and his wife Catherine Bly Cox wrote together, *Apollo: The Race to the Moon* (1989), is straight reportage with very little number-crunching. It is beautifully done, a small masterpiece of journalism, and rightly received rave reviews. (Murray: "The one in the *Washington Post* is the stuff of authors' fantasies."[16]) With the fiftieth anniversary of the first Moon landing coming up, *Apollo* is still well worth reading, if you can find a copy.

However, it is that passion for data that most characterizes Murray as a public intellectual. Looking back on his life in a podcast conversation with science writer Sam Harris in April last year, Murray recalled the writing of *Human Accomplishment* very fondly. The five years he had spent on the book were, he said, "one of the great intellectual adventures of my life . . . a great memory."[17]

That intellectual adventure must also have been something of a refuge. In 1994 Murray had published *The Bell Curve: Intelligence and Class Structure in American Life*, co-written with psychologist Richard Herrnstein, who died of cancer in the month the book was published. *The Bell Curve* was of course extraordinarily controversial. I shall enlarge on the reasons for the controversy further along in this article, but a key one was some passing references in the book to race differences in IQ.

Murray is a sociable and articulate man, but a private one, by no means a publicity hound. The obloquy heaped on him by detractors of *The Bell Curve* must have been vexing to him at the very least, perhaps distressing. It is easy to understand the pleasure he felt, working away on *Human Accomplishment* those five years, secluded with graphs, tables, and spreadsheets—a datanaut sailing the ocean of numbers, the howling of the mob only a distant murmur far across the waves, beyond the walls of his study.

In the years following 2003 Murray published five more books: two offering libertarian approaches to social policy,[18] one on education,[19] one of life advice,[20] and a big one—*Coming Apart: The State of White America, 1960–2010*, published in 2012—revisiting the theme of *The Bell Curve* but restricting its attention entirely to white Americans. By mid-2016, Murray told Sam Harris, he believed he had been "pretty much rehabilitated, that the viciousness and the anger and so forth had disappeared."

Then came the election of Donald Trump to the US presidency and the rise of the "Resistance" movement and its street-fighting vanguard,

Antifa. Quite suddenly the political temperature went up twenty degrees. In the nation's intellectual life, the dull schoolmarmish conformism of the Bush and Obama years in matters relating to the human sciences gave way to a fierce, angry intolerance of all dissent from socially approved dogma. Viewpoints that had formerly been countered with a disapproving tongue-click and a roll of the eyes were now denounced from academic pulpits with passionate zeal.

As in Mao Tse-tung's Great Proletarian Cultural Revolution of 1966–76, persons demoted or blacklisted years before and left to vegetate in silent ignominy were dragged out from their places of banishment to be "struggled" anew for the edification of the masses. Murray encountered this new atmosphere of zealotry when, six weeks into the Trump presidency, he showed up at Middlebury College, a small liberal-arts school in Vermont, to give a talk about his book *Coming Apart* at the invitation of a conservative club at the college. More than a hundred shouting, chanting protesters prevented him from speaking. He was eventually able to give his talk, in the form of an interview with Middlebury professor Allison Stanger, by video from a closed room, while the protesters set off fire alarms in the corridors outside. However, when Murray and Professor Stanger were escorted out from the back of the building by college officials,

> several masked protesters, who were believed to be outside agitators, began pushing and shoving Mr. Murray and Ms. Stanger, Mr. Burger [a spokesman for the college] said. "Someone grabbed Allison's hair and twisted her neck," he said.
>
> After the two got into a car, Mr. Burger said, protesters pounded on it, rocked it back and forth, and jumped onto the hood. Ms. Stanger later went to a hospital, where she was put in a neck brace.[21]

Sixty-seven Middlebury students were subsequently disciplined for the fracas, but the penalties were as light as they could be. No student was expelled nor even suspended. None of the masked assailants who put Professor Stanger in the hospital were identified, and there were no arrests. "It was more of a scrum," shrugged Middlebury's police chief. "There wasn't any assault *per se*."[22]

An irony of the Middlebury event is that Charles Murray, a small-government libertarian-conservative, was a fierce Never Trumper during the 2016 election campaign. This irony is, however, only visible from outside the political cauldron. In the unlikely event the protesters bothered to apprise themselves of it, it would have done nothing to cool their anger. In their eyes Murray had been sufficiently exposed twenty years before in the *Bell Curve* controversy. He was a counter-revolutionary, an enemy of the people. *Denounce! Denounce!*

I should add that while he personally dislikes Trump, Murray the social scientist soon understood very well what had happened in November 2016. As he told Sam Harris: "The working-class guys I know would hate Trump if he lived next door . . . What I didn't get was the extent to which they were looking on Trump as the murder weapon . . . He was a guy who was not acting like the Establishment elite." Trump as the murder weapon! I know of no better five-word encapsulation of Trump's appeal.

One more footnote to that March 2017 event. The protesters needed no encouragement to their obscurantism and bad manners. What they needed was *dis*-couragement, but discouragement came only very feebly and equivocally from the college authorities. Murray told Sam Harris that:

> The president of the college was there and she made a statement beforehand . . . to the effect that: "We have to let this awful person speak on behalf of the values of freedom of speech" . . . I wish she'd been a little less willing to feed the preconceptions of the crowd . . .

The source of those preconceptions was of course Murray's (with Herrnstein) 1994 book *The Bell Curve*; or rather, a loud and well-publicized subset of the responses to that book.

Since the middle of the last century much of the academic world—the humanities and most of the soft sciences (especially anthropology)—has been in thrall to a strong ideology. It is a curious thing that this ideology has no fixed name, although several have been suggested and enjoy limited circulation: the Standard Social Science Model, Blank Slate Theory, Neo-Lysenkoism,[23] and a few others. Seeing nothing much to prefer among available options, I shall refer to it just as "the Ideology."

The essence of the Ideology is that the "BIP" traits (behavior, intelligence, and personality) of a developed human being are shaped entirely by postnatal experiences, with various small allowances generally made for events in the womb. So far as potential development of the BIP traits is concerned, all human zygotes are identical. Charles Murray himself came face to face with the Ideology—by no means for the first time, I am sure—in 2008, following the publication of his book *Real Education*.

The book argues, among many other things, that people have different innate abilities, and that a rational education system ought to acknowledge the fact. Murray gave an interview about the book in 2008 to Deborah Solomon of the *New York Times*. It included the following exchange between Murray and Ms. Solomon.

> DS: Europeans have historically defined themselves through inherited traits and titles, but isn't America a country where we are supposed to define ourselves through acts of will?

> CM: I wonder if there is a single, solitary, real-live public-school teacher who agrees with the proposition that it's all a matter of will. To me, the fact that ability varies—and varies in ways that are impossible to change—is a fact that we learn in first grade.

> DS: I believe that given the opportunity, most people could do most anything.

> CM: You're out of touch with reality in that regard.[24]

As Ms. Solomon's remarks illustrate, the Ideology was by that point the default outlook on human nature among cultural elites outside the hard sciences. (Ms. Solomon's credentials are in Art History and Journalism.) It still maintains that position ten years later.

It follows from the fundamental axioms of the Ideology that IQ tests do not measure any intrinsic, immutable quality of a person. They only record the consequences of a person's post-conception environment acting on his original zygote, whose potential for development of BIP traits is the same as all other human zygotes'. "Given the opportunity, most people could do most anything." For the general public, this outlook was presented most influentially in a 1981 book, *The Mismeasure of Man*, by paleontologist and science popularizer Stephen Jay Gould. The observations and speculations about the current and future evolution of American society that form the real matter of *The Bell Curve* depend heavily on analysis of large-scale IQ testing. From the point of view of the Ideology, therefore, that means they depend on nothing, so the book is worthless.

Murray and Herrnstein mightily compounded their offense against ideological orthodoxy by including a section—it comprises 48 of the 687 pages of main text in my 1996 edition—dealing directly with race differences in IQ. (A further 72 pages discuss related social consequences.) Large-scale testing of Americans consistently turns up different mean IQs by ancestry group: Ashkenazi Jews highest, northeast Asians next highest, non-Ashkenazi whites lower, blacks lower still. The Ideology is even more fiercely hostile to the reality of race than it is to the reality of innate intelligence. Race and intelligence (and now, most recently, sex) are mere "social constructs." To say otherwise, declare the ideologues, is tantamount to approving race slavery and the Holocaust. Hence the furious reactions to *The Bell Curve*. One of the most hysterical was offered by sociologist Steven Rosenthal at a website belonging to Montclair State University:

> *The Bell Curve* is a vehicle of Nazi propaganda wrapped in a cover of pseudo-scientific respectability. It is an academic version of Adolph Hitler's *Mein Kampf*. . . . The voices of millions should be raised in condemnation of the authors of *The Bell Curve* and their circle of Nazi-admiring friends.[25]

(The attitude of actual Nazis toward IQ testing was inconsistent, with no strong party line. IQ tests were used in Germany up to the mid-1930s as they were everywhere else, for identification of the "feebleminded" and for military selection, but later fell out of favor for reasons unclear to me. That the Nazis banned IQ testing because of the high scores of Jews is an urban legend; there was no formal ban. The party ideologues just seem not to have found psychometry very interesting. In the USSR, disapproval of IQ testing was stronger and more official, as contradicting Marxist theory about human nature; but again, there does not seem to have been any formal ban.)

These intensely negative responses were already, by the mid-1990s, in the nature of a rearguard action. From the 1960s to the 1980s, while the Ideology was enjoying its glory days, key developments were accumulating to undermine it. IQ testing was improved and refined. Studies of genetics at the "output" end—the BIP-trait consequences of genetic similarity and difference, as revealed by sibling and twin studies—gave birth to Behavioral Genetics[26] as a legitimate field of inquiry. Databases of test results became ever larger and ever more accessible to datanauts thanks to the advent of cheap computing power. While there are always, in any field of science—and in the human sciences more than most—disputes and disagreements among researchers on particular points, the science of intelligence presented in *The Bell Curve* was as mainstream for 1994 as science gets. A collective statement to that effect by experts in psychometry was organized by Linda Gottfredson, a professor of psychology at the University of Delaware, and published in the *Wall Street Journal* later that year. In a postscript added slightly later, Professor Gottfredson wrote:

> The mainstream shifted slowly but steadily in recent decades as accumulating research evidence changed our understanding of the nature, measurement, origins, and consequence of differences of intelligence. The press and public have yet to catch up to the new mainstream.

The Middlebury College incident of March 2, 2017, brought Murray back to the attention of the American public in general, and of ideological enforcers in particular. By the time the aforementioned podcast with Sam Harris was published on April 22 that year, Murray's hopes of rehabilitation had been dashed. The influential Ideology-compliant website Vox.com had already, on March 28, published a 1,700-word tirade against Murray and *The Bell Curve* by political scientist Nicole Hemmer. She called the book "racist" and "social Darwinist" and linked it to, yes, Donald Trump.[27]

The podcast with Sam Harris itself then inspired a more thoughtful piece, also on Vox.com, co-authored by three academic psychologists: Eric Turkheimer, Kathryn Paige Harden, and Richard Nisbett, hereinafter THN. The title of the piece is "Charles Murray is once again peddling junk science about race and IQ." Authors are not necessarily responsible for the titles under which their words are published, so we should make allowances. It is the case, however, that all three co-authors are on the political Left. (And then some, in Dr. Harden's case: In a *New York Times* op-ed published July 24, 2018, she quoted Lenin with approval![28])

The science in the THN piece is, to borrow a favorite cant word of the ideologues, problematic. "[N]o self-respecting statistical geneticist would undertake a study based only on self-identified racial category as a proxy for genetic ancestry measured from DNA."[29] Really? Without trying hard I turned up a 2005 study out of Stanford University Medical Center finding that in a sample "consisting of 3,636 people who all identified themselves as either white, African-American, East Asian or Hispanic . . . only five individuals had DNA that matched an ethnic group different than the box they checked at the beginning of the study. That's an error rate of 0.14 percent."[30] THN's statistical geneticist, as well as respecting himself, would surely respect an accuracy level of 99.86 percent; and presumably twelve further years of research pushed that level higher.

More telling from the THN piece was this:

> The new DNA-based science has also led to an ironic discovery: virtually none of the complex human qualities that have been shown to be heritable are associated with a single determinative gene! There are no "genes for" IQ in any but the very weakest sense. Murray's assertion in the podcast that we are only a few years away from a thorough understanding of IQ at the level of individual genes is scientifically unserious.

Concerning that first sentence, with its take-*that!* exclamation point at the end: Who thinks otherwise? Monogenic traits (hairy elbows, crumbly earwax) are exceptional—that's Genetics 101. Any trait as complex as intelligence can safely be assumed to be polygenic. Scientifically literate citizens have understood this for decades. What did THN take us for? (And why is this long-held assumption "ironic"?)

And "scientifically unserious"? As I write, in July 2018, the latest news in this field concerns a genome-wide association study of educational attainment in 1.1 million individuals.[31] The study found 1,271 significant SNPs. (A SNP, pronounced "snip," is one of the few million—out of three billion—basic components of the genome that regularly vary among individuals.) As genetics blogger Razib Khan notes: "This is a big achievement, considering that five years ago a paper with ~125,000 individuals identified just 3 SNPs that were significant for this trait!" From 3 to 1,271 in five years is a compounding annual rate of 335 percent. With that rate of progress, Murray's assertion doesn't look so "unserious."

Neuroscientist Richard Haier did a full professional critique of THN at the invaluable website Quillette.com, June 21, 2017. He identified one particular notion as the fundamental sticking-point separating THN from Murray: *Whatever factors influence intelligence differences among individuals will also influence average differences among groups.* Haier calls this "the Default Hypothesis." THN, he says, reject it—prematurely, as it is not inherently preposterous, only unproven. The worst possible interpretation of the Murray-Harris podcast is, says Haier, that they prematurely endorse it.[32]

I think an alternative name for the Default Hypothesis would be "the Last Ditch." THN actually concede most of what Murray and Herrnstein wrote in *The Bell Curve*. With evidence on the genetic architecture of intelligence accumulating ever faster, the long rearguard action to defend the Ideology against the advance of reality has retreated at last to this one earthwork. But the jig may be up on the Last Ditch stratagem. This past March, Harvard geneticist David Reich took to Last Ditch home field, i.e., the *New York Times*, to write:

> So how should we prepare for the likelihood that in the coming years, genetic studies will show that many traits are influenced by genetic variations, and that these traits will differ on average across human populations? It will be impossible—indeed, anti-scientific, foolish and absurd—to deny those differences.[33]

Meanwhile Charles Murray has informed me via private email that he is hard at work on a new book with the working title *Human Differences: Gender, Race, and Genes*. Yes, the datanaut is back on the high seas with compass, sextant, and sounding line. To judge by that working title, his spirit is in the best nautical tradition: Damn the torpedoes!

CHAPTER TWO:

Conservatism Inc.

A Frigid and Pitiless Dogma

New English Review

JUNE 2006

The following is a review of Ramesh Ponnuru's *Party of Death: The Democrats, the Media, the Courts, and the Disregard for Human Life* (2006).

C AN RIGHT to Life (hereinafter RTL) fairly be called a cult? This is a point on which I cannot make up my mind. Some of the common characteristics of culthood are missing—the *Führerprinzip*, for example. On the other hand, RTL has the following things in common with every cult in the world: to those inside, it appears to be a structure of perfect logical integrity, founded on unassailable philosophical principles, while to those outside—among whom, obviously, I count myself—it seems to some degree (depending on the observer's temperament and inclinations) nutty; to some other degree (ditto) hysterical; and to some yet other degree (ditto ditto) a threat to liberty. My own ratings of RTL on those three degrees are two, six, and four out of a possible ten each.

The second of those ratings would have been lower before the grotesque carnival surrounding the death of Terri Schiavo last year, when a motley menagerie of quack doctors, bogus "Nobel Prize nominees," emoting relatives, get-a-life monomaniacs, keening mobs of religious fanatics, death-threat-hissing warriors for "life," dimwitted TV presenters straining to keep their very best my-puppy-just-died faces on while speaking of "Terri" as if they had known her personally from grade school, pandering politicians, and shyster lawyers all joined forces in a massive effort to convince the American public that RTL was a thing no sane citizen ought to touch with a barge pole while wearing triple-ply rubber gloves.

On the other hand, the first of those ratings would have been a couple of ticks higher before I read *Party of Death*. Ramesh Ponnuru is one of the best advocates that a cult—cause, movement, whatever—could hope for; so much so that (just to complete the set) the third of my ratings went up by a corresponding amount after setting down his book. With polemical skills and intellectual firepower of this order, it is possible that RTL might break out from its natural habitat in student chapters of the Confraternity of the Immaculate Conception to attain real influence in the land. A general reduction of our liberties would indeed follow, since RTL is, in its essence, an authoritarian movement, whose ultimate desire is to boss the rest of us around.

Whether it is a cult or not, RTL is made as presentable as possible in *Party of Death*, with writing that is engaging and lucid. Will Ponnuru's book make any converts to the RTL whatever-it-is? That depends on how much exposure it gets outside RTL circles. Just to be on the safe side, the mainstream media are studiously ignoring the book—a sad reflection on the current state of public debate, and of respect for rhetorical virtuosity. RTL-ers are welcoming *Party of Death* very joyfully, though, and they are right to do so, as it is an exceptionally fine piece of polemical writing in support of their . . . cause.

The word "polemical" needs emphasizing. Some people would say that a writer who refers to embryos as "the young," to Mrs. Schiavo as "disabled," or to the framers of the Fourteenth Amendment as having carefully pondered its implications for abortion, is just plain dishonest. There are matters of taste involved here. In the case of this reviewer, there is some fundamental transatlantic disagreement, too, I think. A great British opinion journalist once described his skill set as "the vituperative arts." This attitude, which I share, is widely held across the Pond, but is not very popular here in what Florence King calls the Republic of Nice. Personally I don't mind rhetorical sleights of hand in a polemical work. They keep you on your toes, which is where you should be when reading a book like this. Readers of a more nervous disposition, or too much afflicted with the middle-class American terror of strong opinions, might take offense at them, though. (The absurd hyper-ventilating from some quarters over the book's title also comes within the scope of this paragraph. I think the title is perfect—just the one I would have chosen myself in Ponnuru's place.)

Party of Death is organized in three parts, their lengths in approximate ratio 3:2:2. The first and longest part deals with abortion; the second with the other RTL issues; the third with the treatment of RTL matters in the public sphere—in the media and in politics (but not in the courts, as RTL jurisprudence is pretty thoroughly covered in Part One). To a person coming to the book from outside the RTL mentality, I think the second part will have the most interest, and will be found to make the most telling points. An exception there is the major point made in Part One, that the US Supreme Court's 1973 *Roe v. Wade* decision is lousy jurisprudence, an assertion that seems to me indisputable. Since the Constitution has nothing to say about abortion, this is a matter for the states, and the Supreme Court should have left it there. What else is there to be said?

Ponnuru manages to find a great deal else, and presents it all in Part One of his book. He shows that *Roe v. Wade* (buttressed by later decisions such as the 1992 *Planned Parenthood v. Casey*), as well as being jurisprudentially preposterous, is very widely misunderstood, to the disadvantage of the RTL point of view. Commentators one would expect to be well-informed—Ponnuru quotes several—believe that *Roe* greatly restricts second- and third-trimester abortions (it does not), or that overturning it would criminalize abortion nationwide (it would not). He gives a mordant account of the contortions engaged in by politicians seeking to straddle the issue, or to hold together coalitions whose components are fundamentally at odds on RTL topics—old-school white Roman Catholics plus feminist intellectuals, for example. Democratic office-seekers who are themselves Roman Catholic are in a particularly nasty bind here, and Ponnuru's scathing exposure of their agonized wrigglings and tongue-forkings left me almost—almost—feeling sorry for Ted Kennedy, Mario Cuomo, and (later in the book) John Kerry.

The author then takes us through the grisly business of partial-birth abortion, presents some basic ethical arguments, with counter-rebuttals of the most common rebuttals, and concludes Part One with a historical survey that I found very interesting. What was the Common Law jurisprudence on abortion? How did people in premodern times regard the issue? I had never given a moment's thought to any of this, and all I know now is what this author has told me. His coverage might, for all I know, be highly selective; but this section is extensively footnoted with references to books and journals, so the reader who has more time and interest than I can check the soundness of the author's case. Nobody, at any rate, can complain that Ponnuru has left them short of further reading matter.

(Here, however, I should like to register a grumble about the book's numbering of footnotes. The numbers start again at 1 for each chapter, so that you have to flip back to see which number chapter you are reading to get to the right footnote. It is *much* better to number the footnotes from 1 to *n*, all through the book, without regard to chapter breaks. This is harder for the author, because the addition of a footnote at a late stage in the preparation of the manuscript means that all subsequent ones, and their in-text tags, must be renumbered. As always in writing, however, what is harder for the author is easier for the reader, and the reader should come first. This is not particularly a complaint against *Party of Death*, as ninety percent of footnoted books follow this highly irritating practice. My own books are of course exceptions.)

Part Two opens with a discussion of euthanasia, with several references to the Schiavo case. To Ponnuru's credit, even he seems a little embarrassed by the freak show that surrounded Mrs. Schiavo's last days, and he spares us most of the details (which are anyway thoroughly covered, from both sides, in at least five recent books). Not that his embarrassment prevents the author from engaging in a dense flurry of those rhetorical sleights of hand I noted earlier. He tells us, to take one example from many, that Michael Schiavo won a $1.1 million settlement in a negligence suit against his wife's doctors, without also telling us that Mrs. Schiavo's parents fought like cats to get their hands on their daughter's estate; or that Mr. Schiavo offered (in writing, in documents deposited with officers of the court) to sign over that estate—which was anyway much diminished by legal bills—to a registered charity if his in-laws would withdraw their lawsuits; or for that matter that Mr. Schiavo was a well-paid working professional well able to support himself, while his in-laws were chronically broke, at least until the big RTL foundations showed up with checkbooks a-flapping. And of course Ponnuru does not mention the few seconds of misleading videotape, carefully selected from over four hours' worth, released (in violation of a court order!) by the in-laws to the media, and endlessly replayed on sensationalist TV news programs.

In fact, Ponnuru has nothing to say at all about the monstrous character assassination, carried out by utterly unscrupulous RTL propagandists, of a decent man who coped humanely and well with a terrible life calamity. Well, not quite nothing: "It cannot be denied that pro-lifers were guilty of some excesses," Ponnuru murmurs. *Some excesses?* I would say. Here the author sounds like nothing so much as a Soviet Communist Party apparatchik, circa 1960, offering a grudging admission that Stalin and his cronies might, just once or twice, have been a tad overzealous in dealing with class enemies. Perhaps I should add here that after reading three of the abovementioned five-or-so books,[34] I came away more convinced than ever that Michael Schiavo is a good man criminally traduced by brutal, unprincipled RTL fanatics, from whose number, on the evidence of this chapter, Ponnuru cannot with certainty be excluded.

The balance of Part Two deals with eugenics, embryonic stem cell research, the market in human organs, and infanticide. For me this was, as I have said, the most interesting part of the book, and it seems to me to offer some of the strongest ground for RTL-ers to fight from. I had not thought until reading *Party of Death*, for example, that there was much need to construct arguments against infanticide in modern America. Ponnuru persuades me that I was mistaken, though not that his arguments are necessarily the right ones. The taboo on infanticide, he made me reflect, is not a particularly universal one, even among civilized peoples. Infanticide was widely, lawfully, practiced in China within living memory; and the ancient Athenians, a very civilized people, exposed unwanted infants on the Acropolis. Could infanticide make a comeback? After reading *Party of Death*, I wouldn't rule out the possibility, though I think it remote.

In the matter of modern bioethics, Ponnuru could have made an even stronger case than he has done. Medical people—I write as a person who grew up surrounded by hospital gossip—naturally, from their daily exposure to suffering and death, develop a rather peculiar attitude to these matters, an attitude that might seem callous to outsiders. It isn't really, and medical professionals can be loving and kindhearted people in their private lives, while yet dealing in a briskly unsentimental way with matters of life or death in their working hours. (Possibly some similar remarks might even apply to priests, who are also overfamiliar with death and pain. See the court testimony of Father Gerard Murphy in Michael Schiavo's book.) For example: In my mother's time it was common practice on geriatric wards, if a patient died near the end of the ward sister's shift, to pack hot water bottles round the corpse, to keep him warm till the relief sister came on. Then your shift would not be prolonged by all the paperwork, the summoning of doctors, and so on, required when a death had occurred under your supervision. As my mother said, with logic that always seemed impeccable to me: "It makes no difference to *him*, poor soul." Similarly with doctors, who were of course quietly and humanely euthanizing patients for centuries, until the modern culture of relentless litigation, and the rise of the RTL busybodies, scared them off the practice, to a general increase in human suffering.

The RTL case to be made here, I think, is that this widespread medical mentality—cold-eyed and unillusioned, though rarely inhumane—is magnified and distorted by the bureaucratic superstructure of present-day medicine. The higher you go up the health-care bureaucracy, the further from the actual patient, the worse is the distortion, so that unspeakable things—the killing of people who wish to live—might indeed become more possible as health care becomes ever more bureaucratized. Doctors and nurses would still have to carry out the bureaucrats' decisions, of course; but I am not altogether confident, given the great financial and bureaucratic pressures involved, that they would be able to hold on to the humane good-sense for which their professions, justly in my experience, have always been respected. There has never been a health-care system quite like the modern insurance-and-litigation-driven behemoths of today, and there is no telling where they may carry us.

Party of Death makes pretty free use of slippery-slope arguments, to varying effect. Not every slope is slippery. Most of our social taboos are in fact surprisingly robust, even when perfectly arbitrary. Anglo-Saxon cultures are, I believe, in a minority in having a taboo against the eating of horseflesh; yet our regular consumption of pork, lamb, and beef does not seem to be pushing us down a slippery slope toward hippophagy, even though nobody much (except Bo Derek) would care if it did. Given the abovementioned pressures on the medical profession, though, I think the euthanasia slope actually might be slippery, at least in potential. That is not in itself an argument against euthanasia, only an argument for great vigilance and care in that area. Ponnuru makes it an argument, of course, and I think it's a pity, from the RTL point of view, he didn't do more with this. He didn't because he has other arguments that he prefers, arguments from abstract principles, which he *much* prefers to the untidy, relativistic, and hypocritical realities of human social life. "[Terri] Schiavo's death was surrounded by euphemisms," Ponnuru complains. Good heavens!—people are using euphemisms when talking about death? Whatever next?—the euphemizing of sex?

Ponnuru also fails to tackle one of the hard bioethical questions RTL-ers face. He of course deplores embryo-destructive stem cell research, and leaves the reader with the rather strong impression that such research is anyway pointless, that there is no prospect of it turning up any of the much-advertised "miracle cures." *But what if it does?* There is no reason why this research might not yield a sensational cure for some widely feared disease or condition. Ponnuru of course hopes that it won't, and points out correctly that there is no immediate prospect of it doing so. *But what if it does?* If embryo-destructive stem cell research is, as Ponnuru plainly believes, a serious issue, then wishful thinking doesn't cut it as a serious response.

Part Three of *Party of Death* rounds off the discussions of RTL in the public (media, political) sphere, bits and pieces of which were covered earlier in the book as occasion demanded. Ponnuru is a seasoned observer of the Washington scene, and here he dons steel-capped boots and brass knuckles to give several current or recent political figures a thorough working-over. This is very entertaining for anyone who despises politicians, which is to say, for pretty much anyone. The book concludes with a stirring call—which I endorse!—for the reversal of *Roe v. Wade.* As the author says:

> The end of *Roe* would not hand pro-lifers victory in all the political debates over abortion policy. It would give them the right to have those debates in the first place.

Nothing wrong with that, so far as I can see. Even cults have a right to be heard. I would not like to see RTL views prevail; but I would rather see them prevail than see them stifled.

The best thing in this third part of the book is chapter 17, which deals with public opinion about abortion, and offers telling insights. This chapter also shows Ponnuru the intellectual at his best. His purpose is to make the case that support for abortion is trending downward. The actual evidence he offers, however, paints an ambiguous picture—largely because of the admirable honesty with which he offers it. He takes his pluses where he can find them ("characters in prime-time television shows almost never have abortions") while frankly admitting the minuses ("there isn't a pro-life majority . . . exactly").

What the poll numbers suggest to me is that the moral philosophy of the people of the United States is—as is, I would guess, that of people pretty much anywhere else—basically pagan, with a couple of thin coats of vague religiosity painted over it. We no longer smash sick people on the head with a rock, as I suppose our remote ancestors did, but invalids remain just as unpopular as they were back in the Paleolithic. Anyone who has endured a long confining illness knows this. Our preferred method for dealing with the unpleasant side of life, including topics such as abortion and euthanasia, is to think about them as little as possible. In the fuss over Mrs. Schiavo, it was not hard to detect a general public irritation at having had the whole unsightly business forced on our attention. Perhaps this is not humanity at its most noble, but:

> Show me what angels feel.
> Till then I cling, a mere weak man, to men.[35]

A corollary, though Ponnuru seems unaware of it, is that people who are obsessively interested in these topics seem, to the rest of us, a bit creepy. We may even find ourselves wondering which side, really, is the Party of Death. Ponnuru says that it is unjust to regard some instances of the human organism as less alive than others based on how we feel about them. (Another RTL-er once derided this approach to me, in conversation, as "Barry Manilow ethics"—the worth of another human life judged by our own feelings, wo wo wo feelings . . . I offer this designation for Ramesh Ponnuru's future use, free of charge.) Unfortunately most of us do so judge; and feelings, wo wo wo feelings, are a much more common foundation for our social taboos than are Natural Law principles, or indeed any abstract principles at all. Why, if a woman's husband dies, should she not use his corpse for garden mulch, or serve it up with mashed potatoes and collard greens for dinner? I cannot think of any reason well rooted in pure philosophy, though there might be a public health issue to be addressed. We do not do such things because of the disgust we feel—we *feel*—at the mistreatment of human corpses.

We likewise feel that an adult woman's life, even a few months of it, is worth more than that of a hardly formed fetus; and that the vigorous, usefully employed, merrily procreating Michael Schiavo has a life, a *life*, more worthy of the name than had the incurably insensate relict of his spouse. Those like Ponnuru who think differently are working against the grain of human nature, against our feelings—yes, our feelings—about what life *is*. The life of a newly formed embryo, or of a brain-damaged patient who has shown no trace of consciousness for fifteen years, is worth just as much as the life of a healthy adult, Ponnuru insists. Well, most of us instinctively but emphatically disagree, and no amount of argumentative ingenuity is likely to change our minds. Hearts, whatever.

I mentioned Natural Law there because one very striking feature of *Party of Death* is that it barely mentions religion at all. Ponnuru is not, he insists, arguing from religious grounds, but from the Lockean principles on which our nation was founded. The key passages here are in chapter 8 ("Silencing Dissent"), and I think this chapter is the one that needs to be read with closest attention. Ponnuru is subtle here—I think I will go ahead and say "jesuitical"—and it is plain that he has thought, and read, deeply in ethical philosophy. Listen:

> Liberals tend to assume, without realizing it, that the rational view of any controversial moral issue is likely to be the one that most nonreligious people take. The idea that a religious tradition could strengthen people's reason—could help them reach rationally sound conclusions they might not otherwise reach, and stick to them when there may be reasons of emotion or self-interest not to do so—rarely occurs to them.

That is very well said, and true. Nobody even glancingly acquainted with the history of the last quarter-millennium would assert that you can arrive at a rational social order by dumping religion overboard. My own estimate of the power of reason in human affairs is, I am willing to bet, a lot smaller than Ponnuru's—it is, I think, smaller than that of anyone I have ever met—and I am sure that poor beleaguered reason needs all the help it can get. A sophisticated religious belief (I am not speaking of shamanism or voodoo) can indeed supply an organizing principle within which reason might usefully operate, "might" being of course the key word there.

Yet it remains the case that our Constitution does not permit the framing of laws based on the peculiar tenets of any religion or sect, and *Party of Death* is obviously inspired by religious belief. The philosophical passages strictly follow the Golden Rule of religious apologetics, which is: The conclusion is known in advance, and the task of the intellectual is to erect supporting arguments. It would be an astounding thing, just from a statistical point of view, if, after conducting a rigorous open-ended inquiry from philosophical first principles, our author came to conclusions precisely congruent with the dogmas of the church in which he himself is a communicant. Yet that is the case, very nearly, with *Party of Death*. Remarkable! What if, after all that intellectual work, all that propositional algebra, all those elegant syllogisms, the author had come to the conclusion that abortion was not such a bad thing after all? I suppose he would have been plunged into severe psychic distress. Fortunately there was never the slightest chance of this happening.

Ponnuru's distancing himself from religion is, in fact, a bit disingenuous. It is certainly the case, as he tells us, that RTL includes some committed and energetic agnostics, though they are usually working one particular narrow aspect of the portfolio. Diane Coleman of the anti-euthanasia group Not Dead Yet is an instance—there is a good interview with her in Jon Eisenberg's book *Using Terri*. The indisputable fact remains, though, that whenever one finds oneself in a room full of RTL-ers they turn out to be a well-nigh solid phalanx of devout Christians, a mix of Roman Catholics and evangelical Protestants. (Ponnuru does one of his rhetorical card-flips here, telling us that "[t]he opponents [of embryo-destructive research] are often evangelicals and Catholics." Aye, and men who come home drunk to their wives are often those with a fondness for liquor.) The same thing applies, incidentally to the "Intelligent Design" movement, though there the proportions in the mix are somewhat different. The ID-ers likewise proudly advertise the odd non-believer who has wandered into their ranks. When tested to courtroom standards of evidence, however, "Intelligent Design" has been unmasked as a religious movement, the token agnostic or two notwithstanding. I am sure the same would happen with RTL. Protestations such as Ponnuru's, that the movement is not innately religious at all, should in fact be viewed with suspicion, as tactical attempts to inoculate RTL against courtroom defeats on church-state grounds. The open glee with which pro-lifers greeted the recent elevation of two practicing Roman Catholics to the US Supreme Court suggests that however much Ramesh Ponnuru might affirm the not-essentially-religious nature of the RTL thingummy, pro-lifers in general see matters otherwise.

And while it is true that Natural Law philosophy has been a key source for US constitutional jurisprudence, it by no means follows that Natural Law arguments will, or should, invariably win our public debates, even our Constitutional debates. If, from the principles of Natural Law, it ineluctably follows that women who discover that they are bearing Down syndrome fetuses should not be allowed to abort those fetuses, then I can assure Ramesh Ponnuru that Natural Law principles will be tossed out of the window by every juridical authority in the land, so long as we remain a democracy. And that is as it should be.

I wonder again: Who, actually, is the Party of Death? Here I see a woman who, having missed her period and found herself pregnant, has an abortion, comes home, downs a stiff drink, and gets on with her life. With her *life*. Here I meet a man whose loved wife has gone, never to return, yet her personless body still twitches and grunts randomly on its plastic sheet, defying years of care and therapy. *Let her go*, everyone begs him, and his own conscience cries; and at last he does, whichever way the law will permit. Here I find a couple who want a lively, healthy child, but who know their genes carry dark possibilities of a lifetime's misery and an early death. They permit multiple embryos to be created, select the one free from the dread traits, and give over the rest to the use of science, or authorize their destruction.

The RTL-ers would tell me that these people, and the medical professionals who help them, are all moral criminals, who have destroyed human lives. They support their belief with careful definitions, precise chains of reasoning, and—I do not doubt it—sincere intentions. Yet how inhuman they seem! What a frigid and pitiless dogma they preach!—one that would take from the living, without any regard to what the living have to say about it, to give to those whom common intuition regards as nonliving; that would criminalize acts of compassion; and that would strip away such little personal autonomy as is left to us after the attentions of the IRS, Big Medicine, the litigation rackets, and the myriad government bureaucracies that regulate our lives and peer into our private affairs.

For RTL is, really, just another species of political correctness, just another manifestation of the intellectual pathology, the hypertrophied and academical egalitarianism, the victimological scab-picking, the gaseous sentimentality that has afflicted our civilization this past forty years. We have lost our innocence, traded it in for a passel of theorems. The RTL-ers are just another bunch of schoolmarms trying to boss us around and to diminish our liberties. Is it wrong to have concern for fetuses and for the vegetative, incapable, or incurable? Not at all. Do we need to do some hard thinking about the notion of personhood in a society with fast-advancing biological capabilities? We surely do. (And I think *Party of Death* contributes useful things to that discussion.) Should we let a cult of theologians, monks, scolds, grad-school debaters, logic-choppers, and schoolmarms tell us what to do with our wombs, or when we may give up the ghost, or when we should part with our loved ones? Absolutely not! Give me liberty, and give me death!

I think at last it is largely a matter of temperament. Ponnuru has given his chapter on euthanasia the title "The Doctor Will Kill You Now." I imagine the author meant this to have shock value. He plainly finds atrocious the notion of a doctor—a healer!—killing someone. I can't say I agree. I can all too easily imagine circumstances in which I would respond to "The doctor will kill you now" with "Thank God!" either on my own behalf or a loved one's. I suppose this, by Ponnuru's standards and definitions, puts me in the Party of Death. It depends what you look for from life, and from the great cold cosmos—as I said, just a matter of temperament, really. Some of us are RTL absolutists: "You can't do *that* to a living human being!" Some of us are personal autonomy absolutists: "Don't tell *me* what to do with my own body!" Most of us are too unintellectual to be consistently absolutist about anything. We just favor one side or the other, more or less strongly. America would be a happier and freer nation if the accursed intellectuals would just leave us alone with our lives, our blunders, our tragedies, and our deaths.

Not Your Father's Conservatism

The American Conservative

FEBRUARY 12, 2007

A response to Paul M. Weyrich's & William S. Lind's "The Next Conservatism" in the same issue of *TAC.**

WELL, PAUL Weyrich and William Lind have certainly offered a comprehensive program. Trade policy, military reform, urban aesthetics, ballot initiatives. Our authors have boxed the compass. Much of what they offer is hard to disagree with. Term limits? Yes, please. Ideologies as "armed cant"? Too true. Tax and spending cuts? Control of our borders? The power of example? Bring them on.

For all that, and with real and proper respect to these two battle-scarred veterans of American conservatism, there is a musty odor rising from their pages: the odor of nostalgia. The general tenor of this piece is a sort of geezer conservatism. Now, I am trembling on the brink of geezerhood myself and not altogether out of sympathy with the authors

---

* Paul M. Weyrich and William S. Lind, "The Next Conservatism," *The American Conservative*, February 12, 2007.

in their affection for 1957, which I can just about remember, and when, as best I recall, things went along pretty well. I am sorry to tell them, though, that 1957 is past and gone and will not come back.

The business of conservatism is not to get us all riding streetcars again or working on family farms. (When were farmers conservatives? Were not small farmers key components of the Progressive movement? Is there anyone more tenaciously attached to his federal subsidy than a farmer?) The business of conservatism is not to chase Walmart out of town or to bring back men's hats. The business of conservatism is not to "recover the America we knew as recently as the 1950s," even if that was "the last normal decade." (What does that mean? Top personal income tax rates of ninety-one percent? Four-pack-a-day habits and four-martini lunches? European abortions for the rich, back-street abortions for the poor? Lobotomies and the psychoanalysis cult? The draft? Are those things normal?)

The business of conservatism is to conserve essential values and principles as future becomes present and present, past. The principles to be conserved are those our Republic was founded on: personal liberty, autonomy, and choice; self-sufficiency and self-support; limited government, loose federalism, and the rule of subsidiarity; freedom of speech, belief, assembly, and enterprise. There are now dire threats to all of these principles, and we ought to be busy fighting those threats, not yearning for a lost idyll—an idyll in which, in fact, though many present evils were absent, many different evils were present that have since been overcome.

In public, as in private life, a degree of fatalism and resignation is appropriate. The old must ever give way to the young; new technologies must be weighed and welcomed if they bring convenience without harm; present evils must be vanquished but always with the understanding that new—though, one may always hope, lesser—evils will rise up in their place.

The future is always open and unpredictable. The great blind currents of technology and economics will never deliver what we expect. Those Americans of 1950 who, buying their first TV, imagined a future in which citizens would come home from their work at the factory to watch symphony concerts and lectures on metaphysics in their living rooms, could not have foreseen *American Idol* or the flight of our factories to China.

On the other hand, they could not have foreseen Rush Limbaugh or *South Park* either—wonderful new growths of the fine Anglo-American tradition of ribald social satire and scorn for authoritarian pieties. Nor could they have foreseen a China where state terror is no longer the dominating fact of people's lives and where a declared determination to overthrow American capitalism has given way to utter dependence on American consumer power.

Certainly our popular culture presents an unattractive sight. When did it not, though? Is Paris Hilton intrinsically more deplorable than Jayne Mansfield? Bette Midler than Mae West? Johnny Depp than Fatty Arbuckle?

I will certainly agree with what I think is Weyrich and Lind's objection here: that the zone of decorum has shrunk, that the coarse and ribald has advanced inward from the periphery of popular culture to nearer the everyday center. I deplore that development as much as the next conservative. Even there, though, compensations must be weighed. We knew far more about the 42nd president's intimate life than we knew about the 35th's, more than many of us would have wished to know. With which set of knowledge were we—we, the people—better equipped to estimate the character of our chief executive?

The state of our republic today is pretty dire. Calls to rectify the situation by means of *Kulturkampf* seem to me misguided, however. The central problem of the United States today is not that people's brains are encrusted with filth but that they have been scrubbed so clean by puritan Left ideology that we have lost the ability to talk, even to think, about what ails us. This is as true over large parts of the conservative movement as it is in the popular culture at large. We cannot discuss what needs discussing, and we have stripped away defenses that will protect us when the coming tsunami of new understandings in the human sciences makes landfall.

The horrors and cruelties of our present political culture, from the million-page tax codes to our university speech codes, all have their origins in this turning away from reality. Rather than facing straightforward truths about our nature and condition and seeking to deal with them according to our customs and traditions, we have handed over our powers of judgment to that dark power Tocqueville spoke of so unforgettably, the power that:

> . . . every day renders the exercise of the free agency of man less useful and less frequent; it circumscribes the will within a narrower range and gradually robs a man of all the uses of himself. The principle of equality has prepared men for these things; it has predisposed men to endure them and often to look on them as benefits.[36]

We have lost the will even to expel lawless intruders from our territory or to smite our enemies with appropriate hatred and ruthlessness. We pretend to believe that one child's abilities in any sphere of activity are just the same as another's. We have persuaded ourselves that there is no deeper wickedness than to use our ordinary powers of discrimination in selecting those with whom we will associate or live amongst or trade with or employ. While we have surrendered our individual judgments to schoolmarms and scolds, we have surrendered our collective judgments to legions of avaricious lawyers and mediocrities in black robes.

Things are, in short, pretty bad for America, and for that native vigor, that creative liberty, that thrusting irreverence to old hierarchies and dogmas that so dazzled and charmed mankind when Uncle Sam first strode onto the world stage a century and a quarter ago, knocking over the props, hooting irreverently at the management, and offering the audience strange new visions of possibility.

Perhaps we can salvage some of that old vitality to fortify us in the coming storms. I certainly hope so. The salvaging won't be accomplished, though, supposing it can be accomplished, by turning us into a flock of hat-wearing, church-going, streetcar-riding, home-schooling, natural-produce-eating, *Lawrence Welk Show*–watching brownstone-dwellers.

Indeed, the more I look at the Weyrich-Lind vision of a reconstituted American culture—and setting aside their many excellent political prescriptions already noted—the less I see to distinguish it from the drab enforced rectitude of lefty-*völkisch* "communitarianism." The world is what it is and will become what it unguessably will become. It's pleasant to think of what it once was but not relevant to this fight. Geezer conservatism? Not for this geezer.

How Radio Wrecks the Right

The American Conservative

FEBRUARY 23, 2009

YOU CAN'T help but admire Rush Limbaugh's talent for publicity. His radio talk show is probably—reliable figures only go back to 1991—in its third decade as the number-one-rated radio show in the country. And here he is in the news again, trading verbal punches with the president of the United States.

Limbaugh remarked on January 16 that to the degree that Obama's program is one of state socialism, he hopes it will fail. (If only he had said the same about George W. Bush.) The president riposted at a session with congressional leaders a week later, telling them, "You can't just listen to Rush Limbaugh and get things done." Outsiders weighed in: Limbaugh should not have wished failure on a president trying to cope with a national crisis; Obama should not have stooped to insult a mere media *artiste*, the kind of task traditionally delegated to presidential subordinates while the chief stands loftily mute. Citizens picked sides and sat back to enjoy the circus.

For Limbaugh to remain a player at this level after twenty-odd years bespeaks powers far beyond the ordinary. Most conservatives—even those who do not listen to his show—regard him as a good thing. His fourteen million listeners are a key component of the conservative base. When he first emerged nationally, soon after the FCC dropped the Fairness Doctrine in 1987, conservatives for the first time in decades had something worth listening to on their radios other than country music and bland news programs read off the AP wire. In the early Clinton years, when Republicans were regrouping, Limbaugh was perhaps the most prominent conservative in the United States. *National Review* ran a cover story on him as "The Leader of the Opposition."

Limbaugh has a similarly high opinion of himself: "I know I have become the intellectual engine of the conservative movement," he told the *New York Times*.[37] This doesn't sit well with all conservatives. Fred Barnes grumbled, "When the GOP rose in the late 1970s, it had Ronald Reagan. Now the loudest Republican voice belongs to Rush Limbaugh."[38] Upon discovering that Limbaugh had anointed himself the successor to William F. Buckley Jr., WFB's son Christopher retorted, "Rush, I *knew* William F. Buckley Jr. William F. Buckley Jr. was a father of mine. Rush, you're no William F. Buckley Jr."[39]

The more po-faced conservative intellectuals have long winced at Limbaugh's quips, parodies, slogans, and impatience with the starched-collar respectability of the official Right. American conservatism had been a pretty staid and erudite affair pre-Limbaugh, occasional lapses into jollification on *Firing Line* being the main public expression of conservatism's lighter side.

Now the airwaves are full of conservative chat. *Talkers* magazine's list of the top ten radio talk shows by number of weekly listeners also features Sean Hannity, Michael Savage, Glenn Beck, Laura Ingraham, and Mark Levin. Agony aunt Laura Schlessinger and financial advisor Dave Ramsey are both in the top ten too, though their conservatism is more incidental to the content of their shows.

Liberal attempts to duplicate the successes of Limbaugh and his imitators have fallen flat. Alan Colmes's late-evening radio show can be heard in most cities, and Air America is still alive somewhere—the Aleutians, perhaps—but colorful, populist, political talk radio seems to be a thing that liberals can't do.

There are many reasons to be grateful for conservative talk radio, and with a left-Democrat president and a Democratic Congress, there are good reasons to fear for its survival. Reinstatement of the Fairness Doctrine is generally perceived as the major threat, but may not in fact be necessary. Obama is known to have strong feelings about "localism," the FCC rule that requires radio and TV stations to serve the interests of their local communities as a condition of keeping their broadcast licenses. "Local community" invariably turns out in practice to mean leftist agitator and race-guilt shakedown organizations—the kind of environment in which Obama learned his practical politics. Localism will likely be the key to unlock the door through which conservative talk radio will be expelled with a presidential boot in the rear.

With reasons for gratitude duly noted, are there some downsides to conservative talk radio? Taking the conservative project as a whole—limited government, fiscal prudence, equality under law, personal liberty, patriotism, realism abroad—has talk radio helped or hurt? All those good things are plainly off the table for the next four years at least, a prospect that conservatives can only view with anguish. Did the Limbaughs, Hannitys, Savages, and Ingrahams lead us to this sorry state of affairs?

They surely did. At the very least, by yoking themselves to the clueless George W. Bush and his free-spending administration, they helped create the great debt bubble that has now burst so spectacularly. The big names, too, were all uncritical of the decade-long (at least) efforts to "build democracy" in no-account nations with politically primitive populations. Sean Hannity called the Iraq War a "massive success," and in January 2008 deemed the US economy "phenomenal."

Much as their blind loyalty discredited the Right, perhaps the worst effect of Limbaugh *et al.* has been their draining away of political energy from what might have been a much more worthwhile project: the fostering of a middlebrow conservatism. There is nothing wrong with lowbrow conservatism. It's energizing and fun. What's wrong is the impression fixed in the minds of too many Americans that conservatism is always lowbrow, an impression our enemies gleefully reinforce when the opportunity arises. Thus a liberal such as E. J. Dionne can write, "The cause of Edmund Burke, Leo Strauss, Robert Nisbet and William F. Buckley Jr. is now in the hands of Rush Limbaugh, Sean Hannity. . . . Reason has been overwhelmed by propaganda, ideas by slogans."[40] Talk radio has contributed mightily to this development.

It does so by routinely descending into the ad hominem—Feminazis instead of feminism—and catering to reflex rather than thought. Where once conservatism had been about individualism, talk radio now rallies the mob. "Revolt against the masses?" asked Jeffrey Hart. "Limbaugh is the masses."

In place of the permanent things, we get Happy Meal conservatism: cheap, childish, familiar. Gone are the internal tensions, the thought-provoking paradoxes, the ideological uneasiness that marked the early Right. But however much this dumbing down has damaged the conservative brand, it appeals to millions of Americans. McDonald's profits rose eighty percent last year.

There is a lowbrow liberalism, too, but the Left hasn't learned how to market it. Consider again the failure of liberals at the talk-radio format, with the bankruptcy of Air America always put forward as an example. Yet in fact liberals are very successful at talk radio. They are just no good at the lowbrow sort. The *Rush Limbaugh Show* may be first in those current *Talkers* magazine rankings, but second and third are National Public Radio's *Morning Edition* and *All Things Considered*, with thirteen million weekly listeners each. It is easy to mock the studied gentility, affectless voices, and reflexive liberalism of NPR, but these are very successful radio programs.

Liberals are getting rather good at talk TV, too. The key to this medium, they have discovered, is irony. *I don't take this political stuff seriously, I assure you, but really, these damn fool Republicans . . .* Bill Maher, Jon Stewart, and Stephen Colbert offer different styles of irony, but none leaves any shadow of doubt where his political sympathies lie. Liberals have done well to master this trick, but it depends too much on facial expressions and body language—the double-take, the arched eyebrow, the knowing smirk—to transfer to radio. It is, in any case, not quite populism, the target audience being mainly the ironic cohort—college-educated Stuff White People Like types.

If liberals can't do populism, the converse is also true: Conservatives are not much good at gentility. We don't do affectless voices, it seems. There are genteel conservative events—I've been to about a million of them and have the NoDoz pharmacy receipts to prove it—but they preach to the converted. If anything, they reinforce the ghettoization of conservatism, of which talk radio's echo chamber is the major symptom. We don't know how to speak to that vast segment of the American middle class that lives sensibly (indeed, conservatively), wishes to be thought generous and good, finds everyday politics boring, and has a horror of strong opinions. This untapped constituency might be receptive to interesting radio programs with a conservative slant.

Even better than NPR as a listening experience is the BBC's Radio 4. One of the few things I used to look forward to on my occasional visits to the mother country was Radio 4, which almost always had something interesting to say on the ninety-minute drive from Heathrow to my hometown. One current feature is *America, Empire of Liberty*, a thumbnail history of the United States for British listeners. The show's viewpoint is entirely conventional but pitched just right for a middlebrow radio audience. Why can't conservatives do radio like that? Instead we have crude cheerleading for world-saving Wilsonianism, social utopianism, and a cloth-eared, moon-booted Republican administration.

You might object that the Right didn't need talk radio to ruin it; it was quite capable of ruining itself. At sea for a uniting cause once the Soviet Union had fallen, buffaloed by master gamers in Congress, outfoxed by Bill Clinton, then seduced by the vapid "compassionate conservatism" of Rove and Bush, the post–Cold War Right cheerfully dug its own grave. And there was some valiant resistance from conservative talk radio to Bush's crazier initiatives, such as "comprehensive immigration reform" and the Medicare prescription-drug extravaganza.

But there was not much confrontation with other deep social and economic problems. The unholy marriage of social engineering and high finance that ended with our present ruin was left largely unanalyzed from reluctance to slight a Republican administration. Plenty of people saw what was coming. There was Ron Paul, for example: "Our present course . . . is not sustainable. Our spendthrift ways are going to come to an end one way or another. Politicians won't even mention the issue, much less face up to it."[41]

Neither will the GOP pep squad of conservative talk radio. And Ron Paul, you know, has a cousin whose best friend's daughter was once a dog-walker for a member of the John Birch Society. So much for him!

Why engage an opponent when an epithet is in easy reach? Some are crude: Rather than debating Jimmy Carter's views on Mideast peace, Michael Savage dismisses him as a "war criminal." Others are juvenile: Mark Levin blasts the *Washington Compost* and *New York Slimes*.

But for all the bullying bluster of conservative talk-show hosts, their essential attitude is one of apology and submission—the dreary old conservative cringe. Their underlying metaphysic is the same as the liberals': infinite human potential—Yes, we can!—if only we get society right. To the Left, getting society right involves shoveling us around like truckloads of concrete; to the Right, it means banging on about responsibility, God, and tax cuts while deficits balloon, Congress extrudes yet another social-engineering fiasco, and our armies guard the Fulda Gap. That human beings have limitations and that wise social policy ought to accept the fact—some problems insoluble, some Children Left Behind—is as unsayable on *Hannity* as it is on *All Things Considered*.

I enjoy these radio bloviators (and their TV equivalents) and hope they can survive the coming assault from Left triumphalists. If conservatism is to have a future, though, it will need to listen to more than the looped tape of lowbrow talk radio. We could even tackle the matter of tone, bringing a sportsman's respect for his opponents to the debate.

I repeat: There is nothing wrong with lowbrow conservatism. Ideas must be marketed, and right-wing talk radio captures a big and useful market segment. However, if there is no thoughtful, rigorous presentation of conservative ideas, then conservatism by default becomes the raucous parochialism of Limbaugh, Savage, Hannity, and company. That loses us a market segment at least as useful, if perhaps not as big.

Conservatives have never had, and never should have, a problem with elitism. Why have we allowed carny barkers to run away with the Right?

One Cheer for Conservatism Inc.

VDARE

JULY 12, 2012

This was a speech originally delivered to the Council of Conservative Citizens on July 7, 2012, and published in *VDARE* shortly after.

G OOD AFTERNOON, ladies and gentlemen. I am very flattered to have been invited here today to address you. I thank the organizers for their consideration, and congratulate you all on the success of the conference.

My name is John Derbyshire. As you can probably tell, I was born and raised in England. I have lived much of my adult life here in the United States, though—more than thirty years—and became a US citizen in 2002.

My claim on your interest is that I have been writing as a freelancer for Mainstream Conservative outlets here in North America since the 1990s, and for similar publications elsewhere for a decade before that.

The easiest way to clarify the term "Mainstream Conservative" is just to list those American outlets. My opinion columns and reviews have appeared in the following Mainstream Conservative periodicals:

- *The American Enterprise*
- *The American Spectator*
- *Claremont Review of Books*
- *The National Post (Canada)*
- *National Review*
- *The New Atlantis*
- *The New Criterion*
- *The New York Sun*
- *The Wall Street Journal*
- *The Washington Times*
- *The Weekly Standard*

I have also attended innumerable conferences, forums, cruises, and other kinds of gatherings organized by these outlets and by organizations affiliated with them.

Putting those experiences together with my publication list, I'm going to hurl modesty to the winds and offer myself to you as an expert on Mainstream Conservatism—and to submit a defense, though a tepid and qualified one, of Mainstream Conservatism.

First, just a word about nomenclature. "Mainstream Conservatism" is a bit of a mouthful, but there isn't much out there in the way of alternative names for the phenomenon.

The term "Neocon" had its moment in the sun as a snappy way to refer to aggressively internationalist types who didn't mind multiculturalism and the welfare state but who wanted a vigorous capitalist economy to pay for it all.

I think that moment has passed, though. With capitalism stagnant, public finances bumping up against limits—in the case of some municipalities here in the United States, more like *crashing* up against limits—and public enthusiasm for world-saving military adventures at a low ebb, the Neocon brand has passed its sell-by date.

VDARE.com has coined the term "Conservatism Inc." I like it: It is at just the right point on the line from gentle mockery to snarling contempt. It's new, though, and you have to be constantly explaining its meaning to people who haven't yet heard it, which is a bit tiresome. I hope "Conservatism Inc." catches on. But until it does, I'll prefer the more self-explanatory "Mainstream Conservatism."

– ◆ ◆ ◆ –

WITH THAT OUT of the way, let's take a look at Mainstream Conservatism and see whether there is anything to be said in its favor.

I began by offering a list of eleven current American magazines of opinion that I've written for, and that, according to me, define Mainstream Conservatism. If you look into those magazines, what do you find?

Well, you *do* find oppositional talk. I *don't* believe it is the case, as Larry Auster has said, that Mainstream Conservatism "is now . . . dead."

The principal elements of American Conservatism have always been:

- mistrust of government power, especially federal power;
- respect for traditional social arrangements centered on the biological family and the free association of citizens;
- property rights and the encouragement of free commerce;
- patriotism;
- demographic integrity and continuity;
- religion—or at least, in the case of the temperamentally irreligious, respect for religion; and
- individual liberty, with a willingness to accept a price in inequality.

Conservatism stands in opposition to an establishment that *favors* federal power, *mocks* traditional arrangements, *infringes* property rights when it can and cumbers commerce with taxes and regulations, *disdains* patriotism as uncouth and defers to international organizations, *seeks* demographic replacement, *wars against* popular religion, and always, *always* privileges equality over liberty.

In their promotion of those elements I just listed, Mainstream-Conservative publications do a good job overall; but they do better on some of my bullet points than on others, and are fatally weak on the fifth, on demographic integrity and continuity.

This weakness exists in part because Mainstream Conservatism is yoked to the Republican Party and its business sponsors. The dire effect of this relationship on demographic integrity was clearly seen following the 1986 Immigration Reform and Control Act, when the Act's punitive and protective (i.e., of American workers) clauses soon went unenforced as businesses dependent on illegal labor made angry phone calls to their GOP congressmen.

Because of their bonds with the GOP-business axis, Mainstream Conservatives are shy of demographic issues. Their shyness is compounded by the atmosphere of cultural Marxism we all live in, with its insistence on the perfect interchangeability of all human groups.

So I say that Mainstream Conservatism is doing valuable and useful work, acting at least as a brake on the relentless downhill slide into globalism, socialism, mass dependency, and enforced uniformity of thought. I hope I was able to make some small contribution to that work myself via the words I published in those periodicals.

It's uphill work, of course. The American public, just like the public in any advanced country, wants incremental socialism, and does not see where socialism inevitably leads.

To quote from Igor Shafarevich's book *The Socialist Phenomenon* (1980):

> The death of mankind is not only a conceivable result of the triumph of socialism—it constitutes the goal of socialism.

It's hard, though, to get the sense of that into John Q. Public's head when there's a demon whispering in his other ear: "They want to take away your Medicare!"

Mainstream Conservatism is, though, missing in action on what we would, if we were not so terrified of the topic, refer to frankly as population policy. As I noted in my book *We Are Doomed* (2009), a nation can't *not* have a population policy:

> To *not* have any laws at all concerning immigration and settlement, for example, to train yourself and your fellow citizens never to think about such matters at all, *would itself be a population policy*—in the case of a rich and stable nation like ours, it would be a policy of very fast and unlimited population growth.

– ◆ ◆ ◆ –

LET'S REMEMBER, TOO, that Mainstream Conservatism, like any other kind of conservatism, is up against a very formidable foe. Because of my own professional background as a systems analyst, I think of that foe as "the installed base."[42]

Imagine you are hired in with a team of computer specialists to give a bank a computerized system for running its books. The job would be pretty easy if you could start from scratch, with a bank that had nothing but paper record-keeping—or better still, with a new-founded bank that had no established system of record-keeping at all.

Unfortunately things are rarely like that. The bank you are contracted to already has a computer system. It's been in use for years, and it's a mess. The databases are festooned with redundancies and contradictions, the code is unreadable, and the users have to do time-wasting work-arounds to deal with all the anomalies.

Everyone's used to this creaking, leaking old system, though, and comfortable with it. They know its faults, but they know how to cope with them, like an old married couple. They resent you coming in and imposing new methods on them.

Their resentment, their *conservatism* in clinging to the familiar, blinds them to the fact that they don't have a choice. The manufacturer no longer supports their software, the hardware's blowing fuses, and the regulators are frowning. Gotta have a new system. Without a new system, the bank will sink into ruination.

That old system is called "the installed base." Ancient systems analysts' joke:

Q: How was God able to create the world in just six days?

A: No installed base!

Mainstream Conservatism is up against an installed base.

Who installed the installed base? Well, you could argue that it was installed by the Great Depression, by FDR, by WW2, by the postwar consensus, by Walter Cronkite and John F. Kennedy and Arthur Schlesinger and the Hollywood studio bosses and the broadsheet newspapers, and any number of other events and names.

The truth is, it was installed by the American people, pursuing comfort and security for themselves—not very deplorable pursuits, surely—and by our business establishment pursuing profits, which is what a business establishment ought to do.

I've mentioned the unhappy effects of business pressure on Mainstream Conservatism in the context of the 1986 Immigration Act. To illustrate the other half of the problem, the consequences that flow from our pursuit of comfort and security, here's another data point from that same year.

In some discussions of Obamacare I was engaged in recently, the subject of EMTALA came up. That's the Emergency Medical Treatment and Active Labor Act of 1986, a law requiring practically all hospitals to provide unreimbursed care to anyone needing emergency treatment regardless of citizenship, legal status, or ability to pay.

Pure socialism. Yet EMTALA was signed into law by . . . Ronald Reagan!—another block of concrete set into the installed base, by a man generally acknowledged to be as conservative a president as modern Americans can reasonably hope for.

So this installed base of socialism, inevitably accompanied by a suitable conceptual apparatus of liberal egalitarianism, is what Mainstream Conservatism is constantly dashing itself against. It's like watching the Charge of the Light Brigade.

I often think in fact that modern American Conservatism has a Tennysonian character to it—hopeless charges into the enemy's guns. Perhaps that's why it's strong in the South: another Lost Cause to lament.

When I find myself in this mood, I am encouraged to remember that the Light Brigade actually reached its objective and did considerable damage to the enemy, killing many and forcing them back from their positions. The officer who led the charge made it back to his own lines unscathed.

You don't win wars with operations like the Charge of the Light Brigade, but there are satisfactions to be found nonetheless, and minor triumphs in making the enemy squeal and run . . . unless, of course (ahem), you're unlucky enough stop a cannonball.

– ◆ ◆ ◆ –

AS YOU CAN tell by now, I am not ill-disposed to Mainstream Conservatism. I know and like too many of these people. To be sure, I also know some who, in my opinion, ought to be tarred and feathered and run out of town; but I am a poor hater, and if the decision came to me, I'd probably let even the worst of them off with an appearance ticket.

There are qualifications and subtractions to be stated, though—most seriously, those relating to Mainstream Conservatism's self-inflicted impotence on population policy. I have pegged that impotence on two factors: subservience to business interests unrestrained by thoughts of demographic harm, and the collection of widespread popular notions and sentiments known as "political correctness" that accompany socialism.

Mainstream Conservatism suffers from two built-in weaknesses. Like any other large political movement, it needs money to support its operations; and it needs rewards to offer to its functionaries.

In a capitalist country the *money* must come ultimately from commerce. Commercial enterprises always seek to maintain—and, they hope, increase—their market share by presenting their wares to the public in an appealing way.

The *rewards* for Mainstream Conservatives are political—access to those in power, and in the case of writers for conservative publications, actual positions in the government apparatus: presidential speechwriters, press secretaries, and so on. There are more of these jobs than is commonly known. The vice president's wife, for example, has a press secretary. *The vice president's wife!*

Both sides of this equation, the money coming in and the rewards going out, are restraining and sometimes corrupting. Both rest ultimately in the quicksands of public taste. You can't get money from a firm that's fallen out of favor with consumers; you can't get a job as presidential speechwriter if your guy didn't get elected by the voters.

And public taste is saturated with socialism and egalitarianism. It won't do to say that this is because the general public are helpless puppets of malign forces. In some sense, to some degree, socialism and egalitarianism are what the mass of people want.

Out here in the *non*–Mainstream Conservative movement you will hear the word "sheeple." The implication is that the great mass of citizens are like sheep, a flock easily directed this way or that by wily politicians, media barons, the Jews, etc., etc.

I don't believe any of that, and I don't like this word "sheeple." In well over a million words of opinion commentary this past thirty years, I have never used it once.

The worst charge that can be laid against the general public, in my opinion, is that it prefers not to think much about big social and political issues, and wants accredited experts to do its thinking for it.

But what do you expect? Most of us exhaust our powers of thinking in dealing with our families, our jobs, our associations, our hobbies. Who has mental energy left over to wrestle with remote abstractions such as educational policy or international diplomacy?

In this regard, political correctness is an ideal social dogma. It is full of bogus fellowship and warmth—see how much its propagandists like the word "community." It offers easy formulas and taboos that obviate the need to think for more than a few seconds.

It also offers status markers by which we can easily and quickly calibrate ourselves against our fellow citizens.

For example, what is happening when someone calls you a racist? What is happening is, the accuser is claiming moral purity: "My soul is pure and spotless, washed in the blood of the Lamb. *Your* soul, on the other hand, is dirty—stained, blotched, sticky, and icky. Eiuw!"

Anti-racism is really an infantile conceit, a childish vanity: But what are we, most of us most of the time, but great children?

- ◆ ◆ ◆ -

SO MAINSTREAM CONSERVATISM must work not only against the installed base of liberal egalitarianism in the mainstream media, the universities, the bureaucracy, business, the churches, the international organizations to which we are yoked; it must also swim against mighty currents of public taste and perceptions.

In part, yes, that taste and those perceptions are shaped for us by elites, but we are not sheeple. Often enough, *we* dictate to the elites. There *is* a dialectic, even if it is less well-balanced than the ideal. If a race-guilt movie or a feminist-triumph TV show goes unwatched by the public, the producers take note and change tack.

And regrettable to report, these kinds of products *do* get watched. The book and movie *The Blind Side,* and the book and movie *The Help*—both of which belong to a genre that a friend of mine calls "white guilt porn"—were quite commercially successful.

(And both, I can't help noticing, were created by Southerners: Michael Lewis is from Louisiana, Kathryn Stockett from Mississippi. Hey, Southrons: Stop calling down fire on your own positions!)

The mass of people subscribe to political correctness not out of intellectual conviction. The mass of people are not much inclined to intellectualizing. They subscribe because political correctness offers them simple formulas and taboos that relieve them of the need for thinking, and as a bonus give them the gratification of basic social emotions.

- ◆ ◆ ◆ -

THAT'S WHAT MAINSTREAM Conservatism is up against, while it strives to keep money coming in from mass-pleasing commercial supporters, and simultaneously strives to keep alive the hope of political rewards for its functionaries from mass-pleasing candidates.

That's why Mainstream Conservatism is timid to the point of spinelessness, especially in the area of human differences, and especially when trying to capture a mass audience, as in the case of Fox News or the Tea Party movement.

It doesn't help that the escape hatch from the suffocating false doctrines of political correctness bears the label SCIENCE.

The sciences, particularly the biological sciences, have never been in much favor with conservative Americans. This allows our enemies an easy win by claiming to be, as Barack Obama at his inauguration claimed the Democrats to be, the "party of science," even as they turn a blind eye to the exciting new discoveries pouring out of the human sciences.

The gist of those discoveries is that the traditional conservative image of human nature is closer to the truth than the traditional left-liberal conception.

To quote novelist Tom Wolfe: "We now live in an age in which science is a court from which there is no appeal."[43]

At some point, both liberals and conservatives will have to accept the judgment of that court. Acceptance will be easier for conservatives: We have been right all along about human nature—about the limitations on human reason, about associative preferences, about intractable sex and race differences.

That is why, of all the many individuals and associations contributing to *non*–Mainstream Conservatism, I most particularly admire and appreciate my friend Jared Taylor here, who constantly strives to root his own ideas and prescriptions in good science.

If Mainstream Conservatives could shed their timidity and embrace our new understandings, they would be able to speak frankly and forcefully on issues of population policy, as we do here in the nonmainstream Right.

Then those desperate charges into the guns might become real, effective assaults on key enemy positions; and the nation we know and love might be conserved for our descendants, instead of falling into ruination. Isn't conserving what conservatives are supposed to do?

Thank you, ladies and gentlemen.

CHAPTER THREE:

The Blacks

Race on Wall Street

National Review

JANUARY 5, 2001

EMPLOYEES TO SUE MICROSOFT FOR DISCRIMINATION

By D. Ian Hopper, Associated Press Writer
Jan 3, 2001—12:12 AM

WASHINGTON (AP)—Seven current and former Microsoft Corp. employees are planning to sue the computer software maker for discrimination, citing racial bias, the plaintiffs' lawyers said Tuesday. The suit, to be filed in US District Court for the District of Columbia on Wednesday, asks for $5 billion, the lawyers said in a statement. This is the second bias suit against the Redmond, Wash., company in the past three months . . .

- ◆ ◆ ◆ -

HERE IS a Wall Street story. Through most of the 1990s I worked for a big Wall Street investment bank. I wasn't a hot-shot trader or a high-flying executive, just a back-office worker bee. Most of my work was in a small department—twelve to sixteen people—that kept tabs on the credit-worthiness of the firms we did business with. It was a pretty stable department, with a happy workforce under a good boss. Some of the people who were there when I arrived were still there when I left.

My department had a small legal section attached. The firm had originally been a bond brokerage, so most of our business concerned setting up deals with other banks or big institutional investors to buy, sell, borrow, or lend different kinds of bonds, or to arrange complex cross-bets with these other counterparties on the movement of interest rates or currency exchange rates. All of these deals needed careful legal documentation to ensure that every party to a deal understood things in the same light, and that the firm's hindquarters were adequately covered if for some reason a deal ended up in a courtroom, as occasionally happened.

In 1991 the head of this legal section, with three or four administrators and paralegals working under him, was an African American who I shall call Jason. At the time he was the only black person in the department. This was, I repeat, a friendly department, under a boss much loved by his employees—an old Wall Street hand who knew everybody and had seen everything, and who took good care of his people at bonus time. There was a high level of banter in the department, some of it politically incorrect—the black humor and rough manners of the trading floor percolate up to the back offices in these places. It was all understood to be in good fun, though, and I never saw anybody take offense.

Here is an example of what I mean. At the time of the Rodney King riots, management let it be known that people could leave early if they chose, since there was some fear that New York City might erupt. We put on our coats and headed for the elevator. While we were waiting, I turned to Jason and said: "Oh, by the way, Jason. If you're planning to go out this evening, I could really use a new VCR." Everybody, including Jason, laughed. OK, it wasn't in the best of taste, but it was nothing compared with the kinds of exchanges you hear on the trading floor. Certainly it wasn't particularly out of line with our normal departmental banter. (Jason's predecessor had been Jewish, and at one point had had two out of three Jewish assistants. The rest of the department used to refer to the legal section as "the ghetto.")

After a while I began to hear things about Jason and our boss. The boss wasn't satisfied with Jason's work. He took too much time off. (Yes, he did take rather a lot.) He didn't understand some of the complicated deals we were doing. He was lazy and cut corners. Jason, contrariwise, seemed to have a low opinion of the boss. He was crude and insensitive. He made impossible demands. He was short-tempered. Jason, I should note, had graduated from law school in the early 1980s, and had taken in all the psycho- and socio-babble of early political correctness. Our boss had graduated from business school in the 1950s, and regarded PC as a bit of a joke, though—out of the context of the banter mentioned above—he was wise enough to watch his tongue when sensitive topics came up. Fundamentally the whole thing was, as far as I could see, just a clash of personalities. It ended with Jason resigning. Soon afterward I heard that he was suing the firm for "racial discrimination."

The case dragged on for a couple of years, then was settled out of court. The firm paid Jason $250,000 for the "discrimination" he had suffered.

Fast forward four years. Same department, same boss. The legal team, however, had moved out of our department, had placed themselves under the control of the firm's legal department. The lawyer who ran the team—Jason's successor, a Jewish white man—no longer reported to our boss, and was located at the other end of the building. We still had some necessary dealings with them, though, and I knew the whole team very well. One recent hire was an African American woman I shall call Margaret. Margaret had grown up dirt poor in one of the Deep South states, come to New York, improved herself through night school, and landed this job performing minor clerical functions for our firm. She had done well: Wall Street firms, even at the low level I am discussing here, are exceptionally good to their back-office people. They are very good employers, if you don't mind hard work.

Margaret was rather shy, a bit sensitive about her background, I think, but good-natured and cheerful, with no chip on her shoulder that I could detect. You wouldn't have called her the sharpest knife in the drawer; but then, her duties didn't require her to be. Her boss, the guy who had replaced Jason, was, to tell the truth of the matter, not blessed with a very agreeable personality, but he was lawyer all the way through—the kind of person who, if you asked him what time it was, would give you an answer broken out in sections, subsections, and paragraphs, with footnotes for clarification.

My original boss, the one who had failed to get on with Jason, retired. Shortly afterward I myself left the firm. About a year after the latter event I happened to be talking to my old boss—we had kept in touch. "Oh, by the way," he said, "I found myself sitting on the bus the other day with guess who? Margaret, from the legal section." Was she still with the firm? I asked. "No. Matter of fact, she's suing them." For what? "What d'you think?" Margaret, it turned out, had a suit for racial discrimination going against her boss, the lawyer.

Now, I worked with those people—the credit department and their legal section—for eight years, during which time three African American employees had come and gone. Two of them had ended up with a lawsuit against the firm for racial discrimination, citing a different boss in the two cases. Furthermore, in daily interaction with these people across some two thousand days, I had witnessed nothing—setting aside the harmless kind of banter I mentioned above—that struck me as offensive, inflammatory, or discriminatory. Two out of three: sixty-seven per cent.

I know a couple of very senior people at the firm—managing directors—and broached the subject with one of them. He shrugged. "Cost of doing business." But did these people have any actual case? "No, of course not. It's just a shakedown." Why didn't the firm fight these cases? (They are invariably settled out of court.) "Are you kidding? The publicity! Think of Texaco!"[44] Couldn't they vet potential employees for these tendencies at hiring time? "It's not the employees, it's the civil-rights attorneys. Whole firms of them. They go trawling around Wall Street looking for black employees, tell them how much money they can get them for a discrimination complaint. It's hard to resist, you know. Could *you* resist it?" But wasn't the result of all this that Wall Street firms would become reluctant to hire African Americans? "Don't be silly. Imagine if we *stopped* hiring them—think what the civil rights crowd would make of that! No, it's just a cost of doing business. Like employee pilferage in a supermarket. You make a certain allowance for it."

Perhaps I am naive, but this all seems very shocking to me. *Like employee pilferage in a supermarket.* Yes, but that is illegal, and also immoral. Suppose you are a supermarket worker, and you see a fellow-worker sneaking off with some merchandise—how do you feel about that person? What my ex-colleagues were doing was obviously not illegal, but surely it was immoral. Wasn't it?

It is easy to understand, and even to sympathize, with the point of view of everyone concerned here. The employee: Some civil-rights lawyer invites him to lunch and explains that he can get five times his annual salary, in cash, for signing a couple of depositions. The lawyer: "Hey, gotta make a living. And these are the *laws*!" The firm: "Cost of doing business. We are 'deep pockets,' got to expect this sort of thing. Our shareholders wouldn't like a lot of publicity over something like that, so we settle."

Yes, everybody's making a rational choice . . . but it's *wrong*.

You may say: Well, perhaps there really was some discrimination going on there that you just didn't see. To which I reply: Gimme a break. I worked in that department for years, and knew those people as well as I know some of my own family members. All of them, without exception, were decent middle-class Americans. Which is to say, they lived in terror of being thought "intolerant," "divisive," "discriminatory," or "mean-spirited." They all chirped "Have a nice day!" when colleagues got off the elevator. They all said "Hangin' in there!" when you asked them how they were coping. That dash of Wall Street black humor aside, these were citizens of what Florence King calls "The Republic of Nice," who would no more have committed an act of racial insensitivity in the workplace than they would have pushed their grandmothers downstairs. Like practically all late-twentieth-century middle-class Americans, they had standards of manners and etiquette that would have put the courtiers of Louis XIV to shame.

Perhaps the firm had, for racial reasons, failed to promote those African Americans as quickly as other employees? Gimme another break. Every big corporation in the United States is desperate to get African Americans into senior positions. This especially applies in Wall Street firms, which have further to go than most. In my firm the pattern was: Mail room, approximately ninety percent black. Cafeteria: one hundred percent Hispanic. Maintenance staff: looks like America— better yet, like New York City. Back offices: my department was probably pretty representative, usually one black face in twelve or sixteen. Trading floor: the same, a black face every dozen desks or so. Senior management: practically all white. Now, these people are not fools. They know this won't do. They are pathetically anxious to get some "diversity" into their annual reports. Discrimination? Sorry, don't believe it.

If I'm right and it's all just a shakedown driven by avaricious lawyers, how upset should we be about this? My own answer is: quite upset. As I pointed out above, everybody involved is acting from rational, if not entirely respectable, motives. The real problem is that our laws encourage this sort of immorality. This means there is something wrong with our laws. Doesn't it?

The Case for Racial Profiling

National Review

FEBRUARY 19, 2001

"RACIAL PROFILING" is now one of the shibboleths of our time. Anyone who wants a public career in the United States must place himself on record as being against it. Thus, former senator John Ashcroft, on the eve of his confirmation hearings: "It's wrong, inappropriate, shouldn't be done." During the vice-presidential debate last October, Bernard Shaw invited the candidates to imagine themselves black victims of racial profiling. Both made the required ritual protestations of outrage. Lieberman: "I have a few African American friends who have gone through this horror, and you know, it makes me want to kind of hit the wall, because it is such an assault on their humanity and their citizenship." Cheney: "It's the sense of anger and frustration and rage that would go with knowing that the only reason you were stopped . . . was because of the color of your skin . . . " In the strange, rather depressing, pattern these things always follow nowadays, the American public has speedily swung into line behind the Pied Pipers: Gallup reports that eighty-one percent of the public disapproves of racial profiling.

All of which represents an extraordinary level of awareness of, and hostility to, and even *passion* against ("hit the wall . . . ") a practice that, up to about five years ago, practically nobody had heard of. It is, in fact, instructive to begin by looking at the history of this shibboleth.

To people who follow politics, the term "racial profiling" probably first registered as a large issue when Al Gore debated Bill Bradley at New York's Apollo Theater last February. Here is Bradley, speaking of the 1999 shooting of African immigrant Amadou Diallo by New York City police: "I . . . think it reflects . . . racial profiling that seeps into the mind of someone so that he sees a wallet in the hand of a white man as a wallet, but a wallet in the hand of a black man as a gun. And we—we have to change that. I would issue an executive order that would elimi-nate racial profiling at the federal level."[45]

Nobody was unkind enough to ask Senator Bradley how an execu-tive order would change what a policeman sees in a dark lobby in a dan-gerous neighborhood at night. Nor was anyone so tactless as to ask him about the case of LaTanya Haggerty, shot dead in June 1999 by a Chicago policewoman who mistook her cell phone for a handgun. The policewoman was, like Ms. Haggerty, black.

Al Gore, in that debate at the Apollo, did successfully, and famously, ambush Bradley by remarking: "You know, racial profiling practically began in New Jersey, Senator Bradley." In true Clinton-Gore fashion, this is not true, but it is *sort of* true. "Racial profiling" the *thing* has been around for as long as police work, and is practiced everywhere. "Racial profiling" the *term* did indeed have its origins on the New Jersey Turn-pike in the early 1990s. The reason for the prominence of this rather unappealing stretch of expressway in the history of the phenomenon is simple: The Turnpike is the main conduit for shipment of illegal drugs and other contraband to the great criminal marts of the Northeast. If Canada, instead of Mexico, were a major drug entrepôt, we should be talking about the New York State Thruway in this context.

The career of the term "racial profiling" seems to have begun in 1994, but did not really take off until April of 1998, when two white New Jersey state troopers pulled over a van for speeding. As they approached the van from behind, it suddenly reversed toward them. The troopers fired eleven shots from their handguns, wounding three of the van's four occupants, who were all black or Hispanic. The troopers, James Kenna and John Hogan, subsequently became poster boys for the "racial profiling" lobbies, facing the same indignities, though so far with less serious consequences, as were endured by the Los Angeles policemen in the Rodney King case: endless investigations, double jeopardy, and so on.

And a shibboleth was born. News-media databases list only a scattering of instances of the term "racial profiling" from 1994 to 1998. In that latter year the number hit double figures, and thereafter rose quickly into the hundreds and thousands. Now we all know about it, and we are, of course, all against it.

Well, not quite all. American courts—including (see below) the US Supreme Court—are not against it. Jurisprudence on the matter is pretty clear: So long as race is only one factor in a generalized approach to questioning of suspects, it may be considered. And of course, *pace* candidate Cheney, it always *is* only one factor. I have been unable to locate any statistics on the point, but I feel sure that elderly black women are stopped by the police much less often than are young white men.

Even in the political sphere, where truth-telling and independent thinking on matters of race have long been liabilities, there are those who refuse to mouth the required pieties. Alan Keyes, when asked by Larry King if he would be angry with a police officer who pulled him over for being black, replied: "I was raised that everything I did represented my family, my race, and my country. I will be angry with the people giving me a bad reputation."

Practically all law-enforcement professionals believe in the need for racial profiling. In an article on the topic for the *New York Times Magazine* in June 1999, Jeffrey Goldberg interviewed Bernard Parks, chief of the Los Angeles Police Department. Parks, who is black, called racial profiling "playing the percentages," and added: "It's common sense."[46] Note that date, though. It was pretty much the last point at which it was possible for a public official to speak truthfully about racial profiling. Law-enforcement professionals were learning the importance of keeping their thoughts to themselves on this issue. Four months before the *Times* story saw print, New Jersey State Police superintendent Carl Williams, in an interview, said that certain crimes were associated with certain ethnic groups, and that it was naive to think that race was not an issue in policing—both statements, of course, perfectly true. Superintendent Williams was fired the next day by Governor Christine Todd Whitman.

Like other race issues in the United States, racial profiling is a "tadpole," with an enormous black head and a long but comparatively inconsequential brown, yellow, and red tail. While Hispanic, "Asian American," and other lesser groups have taken up the "racial profiling" chant with gusto, the crux of the matter is the resentment that black Americans feel toward the attentions of white policemen. By far the largest number of Americans that are angry about racial profiling are law-abiding black people who feel that they are stopped and questioned because the police regard *all* black people with undue suspicion. They feel that they are the victims of a negative stereotype.

They are. Unfortunately, a negative stereotype can be correct, and even useful. I was surprised to find, when researching this article, that within the academic field of social psychology there is a large literature on stereotypes, and that much of it—an entire school of thought— holds that stereotypes are essential life tools, are accurate much more often than not, and that we do not use them as much as, from cold practical considerations, we should. On the scientific evidence, the primary function of stereotypes is what researchers call "the reality function." That is, stereotypes are useful tools for dealing with the world. Confronted with a snake or a faun, our immediate behavior is determined by generalized beliefs—stereotypes—about snakes and fauns. Stereotypes are, in fact, merely one aspect of the mind's ability to make generalizations, without which science and mathematics, not to mention, as the snake/faun example shows, much of everyday life, would be impossible.

At some level, everybody knows this stuff, even the guardians of the "racial profiling" flame. Jesse Jackson famously, in 1993, confessed: "There is nothing more painful to me at this stage in my life than to walk down the street and hear footsteps and start thinking about robbery, then look around and see somebody white and feel relieved."[47] Here is Sandra Seegars of the Washington DC Taxicab Commission:

> Late at night, if I saw young black men dressed in a slovenly way, I wouldn't pick them up. . . . And during the day, I'd think twice about it.[48]

Pressed to define "slovenly," Ms. Seegars elaborated thus: "A young black guy with his hat on backwards, shirttail hanging down longer than his coat, baggy pants down below his underwear and unlaced tennis shoes." Now *there's* a stereotype for you! Did I mention that Ms. Seegars is black?

Law enforcement officials are simply employing the same stereotypes as you, me, Jesse, and Sandra, but taking the opposite course of action. What we seek to avoid, they pursue. They do this for reasons of simple efficiency. A policeman who concentrates a disproportionate amount of his limited time and resources on young black men is going to uncover far more crimes—and therefore be far more successful in his career—than one who biases his attention toward, say, middle-aged Asian men. It is, as Chief Parks said, common sense.

Similarly with the tail of the tadpole—racial profiling issues that do not involve black people. China is known to have obtained a top-secret warhead design. Among those with clearance to work on that design are people from various kinds of national and racial backgrounds. Which ones should investigators concentrate on? The Italians? The answer surely is: They should first check out anyone who has family or friends in China, who has made trips to China, or who has met with Chinese officials. This would include me, for example—my father-in-law is an official of the Chinese Communist Party. Would I then have been "racially profiled"?

It is not very surprising to learn that the main fruit of the "racial profiling" hysteria has been a decline in the efficiency of police work. In Philadelphia, a federal court order now requires police to fill out both sides of an 8½ by 11 sheet on every citizen contact. Law enforcement agencies nationwide are engaged in similar statistics-gathering exercises, under pressure from federal lawmakers like US Representative John Conyers, who has announced that he will introduce a bill to force police agencies to keep detailed information about traffic stops. ("The struggle goes on," declared Representative Conyers. The struggle that is going on, it sometimes seems, is a struggle to prevent our police forces from accomplishing any useful work at all.)

The mountain of statistics that is being brought forth by all this panic does not, on the evidence so far, seem likely to shed much light on what is happening. The numbers have a way of leading off into infinite regresses of uncertainty. The city of San Jose, California, for example, discovered that, yes, the percentage of blacks being stopped was higher than their representation in the city's population. Ah, but patrol cars were computer-assigned to high-crime districts, which are mainly inhabited by minorities. So that over-representation might actually be an under-representation! But then, minorities have fewer cars . . .

Notwithstanding the extreme difficulty of finding out what is actually happening, we can at least seek some moral and philosophical grounds on which to take a stand either for or against racial profiling. I am going to take it as a given that most readers of this piece will be of a conservative inclination, and shall offer only those arguments likely to appeal to persons so inclined. If you seek arguments of other kinds, they are not hard to find—just pick up your broadsheet newspaper or turn on your TV.

Of arguments *against* racial profiling, probably the ones most persuasive to a conservative are the ones from libertarianism. Many of the stop-and-search cases that brought this matter into the headlines were part of the so-called "war on drugs." The police procedures behind them were ratified by court decisions of the 1980s, themselves mostly responding to the rising tide of illegal narcotics. In *United States v. Montoya De Hernandez* (1985) for example, Chief Justice Rehnquist validated the detention of a suspected "balloon swallowing" drug courier until the material had passed through her system, by noting previous invasions upheld by the Court:

> [F]irst class mail may be opened without a warrant on less than probable cause. . . . Automotive travelers may be stopped . . . near the border without individualized suspicion *even if the stop is based largely on ethnicity* [italics added] . . .[49]

The chief justice further noted that these incursions are in response to "the veritable national crisis in law enforcement caused by smuggling of illegal narcotics."

Many on the political Right feel that the war on drugs is at best misguided, at worst a moral and constitutional disaster. I do not myself agree with this point of view, though this is not the place to argue the matter.[50] I do, however, think it is naive to imagine that the "racial profiling" hubbub would go away, or even much diminish, if all state and federal drug laws were repealed tomorrow. Black and Hispanic Americans would still be committing crimes at rates higher than citizens of other races. The differential criminality of various ethnic groups is not only, nor even mainly, located in drug crimes. In 1997, for example, blacks, who are thirteen percent of the US population, comprised thirty-five percent of those arrested for embezzlement. (It is not generally appreciated that black Americans commit higher levels not only of "street crime," but also of white-collar crime.)

Even without the drug war, diligent police officers would still, therefore, be correct to regard black and Hispanic citizens—other factors duly considered—as more likely to be breaking the law. The Chinese government would still be trying to recruit spies exclusively from among Chinese-born Americans. (The Chinese Communist Party is, in this respect, the keenest "racial profiler" of all.) The Amadou Diallo case— the police were looking for a rapist—would still have happened.

The best nonlibertarian argument against racial profiling is the one from equality before the law. This has been most cogently presented by Randall Kennedy. Professor Kennedy concedes most of the points I have made. Yes, he says:

Statistics abundantly confirm that African Americans—and particularly young black men—commit a dramatically disproportionate share of street crime in the United States. This is a sociological fact, not a figment of the media's (or the police's) racist imagination. In recent years, for example, victims of crime report blacks as the perpetrators in around twenty-five percent of the violent crimes suffered, although blacks constitute only about twelve percent of the nation's population.[51]

And yes, says Professor Kennedy, outlawing racial profiling will reduce the efficiency of police work. Nonetheless, for constitutional and moral reasons we should outlaw the practice. If this places extra burdens on law enforcement, well, "racial equality, like all good things in life, costs something; it does not come for free."

There are two problems with this. The first is that Professor Kennedy has minimized the black-white difference in criminality, and therefore that "cost." I don't know where his twenty-five percent comes from, or what "recent years" means, but I do know that in Department of Justice figures for 1997, victims report sixty percent of robberies as having been committed by black persons. In that same year, a black American was eight times more likely than a nonblack to commit homicide—and "nonblack" here includes Hispanics, not broken out separately in these figures. A racial-profiling ban, under which police officers are required to stop and question suspects in precise proportion to their demographic representation (in what? the precinct population? the state population? the national population?), would lead to *massive* inefficiencies in police work. Which is to say, massive declines in the apprehension of criminals.

The other problem is with the special status that Professor Kennedy accords to race. Kennedy: "Racial distinctions are and should be different from other lines of social stratification." Thus, if it can be shown, as it surely can, that state troopers stop young people more than old people, relative to young people's numerical representation on the road being patrolled, that is of no consequence. If they stop black people more than white people, on the same criterion, that is of large consequence. This, despite the fact that the categories "age" and "race" are both rather fuzzy (define "young" . . .) and are both useful predictors of criminality. Despite the fact, too, that the principle of equality before the law does not, and up to now has never been thought to, guarantee equal outcomes for any law-enforcement process, only that a citizen who has come under reasonable suspicion will be treated fairly.

It is on this special status accorded to race that, I believe, we have gone most seriously astray. I am willing, in fact, to say much more than this: In the matter of race, I think the Anglo-Saxon world has taken leave of its senses. The campaign to ban racial profiling is, as I see it, a part of that large, broad-fronted assault on common sense that our over-educated, over-lawyered society has been enduring for some forty years now, and whose roots are in a fanatical egalitarianism, a grim determination not to face up to the realities of group differences, a theological attachment to the doctrine that the sole and sufficient explanation for all such differences is "racism"—which is to say, the malice and cruelty of white people—and a nursed and petted guilt toward the behavior of our ancestors.

At present Americans are drifting away from the concept of belonging to a single nation. I do not think this drift will be arrested until we can shed the idea that deference to the sensitivities of racial minorities—however overwrought those sensitivities may be, however overstimulated by unscrupulous mountebanks, however disconnected from reality—trumps every other consideration, including even the maintenance of social order. To shed that idea, we must confront our national hysteria about race, which causes large numbers of otherwise-sane people to believe that the hearts of their fellow citizens are filled with malice toward them. So long as we continue to pander to that poisonous, preposterous belief, we shall only wander off deeper into a wilderness of division, mistrust, and institutionalized rancor—that wilderness, the most freshly painted signpost to which bears the legend RACIAL PROFILING.

The Solipsism of John Edgar Wideman

Taki's Magazine

OCTOBER 20, 2010

I HADN'T heard of John Edgar Wideman before reading his October 6 op-ed in the *New York Times*.* Googling around, I see that he is the author of many books, both fiction (twelve novels, six short-story collections) and nonfiction (memoirs, basketball, and social commentary). He is sixty-nine years old, rather handsome in appearance, African American of, I would guess from his pictures, about half white ancestry—a mulatto.

I'm not going to beat myself up for not having read any of Mr. Wideman's books. There are far too many books in the world and far too little time. In any case, his books seem to be about things that, with absolutely no offense to anyone at all, I'm just not interested in. Most seem to be about African Americans. In *Sent for You Yesterday* (1983), which got him a PEN/Faulkner award, he is "reimagining the black neighborhood of his youth." *Philadelphia Fire* (1990), which got him that same award over again—the only time that's been done, I think—is

---

*   John Edgar Wideman, "The Seat Not Taken," *New York Times*, October 6, 2010.

about "the 1985 police bombing of a West Philadelphia row house owned by the back-to-nature, Afrocentric cult known as 'Move.'"

Yeah, I remember Move, though they were not quite the guitar-strumming flower children suggested by "back-to-nature, Afrocentric cult." Move was in fact a white-hating revolutionary and criminal gang that robbed, murdered, and generally made a major social nuisance of itself. Seeking violence, they sure enough found it, with the police fire-bombing of their Philadelphia headquarters, the event that inspired Mr. Wideman's novel. Their most famous graduate is cop-killer Mumia Abu-Jamal, who in a just world would have died in the electric chair twenty-eight years ago for the horrible, pitiless crime he undoubtedly committed. I'm guessing this is somewhat at odds with John Edgar Wideman's point of view on the matter, but hey—po-tay-to, po-tah-to.

In any case, although I have not read any of Mr. Wideman's books, for the aforementioned reason, I did read that October 6 op-ed at the encouragement of a friend. My friend sent it to me with howls—I mean, e-howls—of disgust and exasperation. Sort of: "Read this piece of *scheissdreck* the Gray Ethnomasochist Lady has just puked out, then shoot yourself in despair." Something like that. So I read it. Plainly I have not yet shot myself; but I still might, after I'm through telling you about the piece and venting thereon. It will be a sacrifice on behalf of sanity, patriotism, and our children's future. You're welcome.

The gist of Mr. Wideman's piece is as follows. He lives in New York City. He teaches at Brown University in Providence, Rhode Island. He rides the Amtrak train between the two cities. He boards early and takes one half of a vacant double seat. En route the train fills up, but nobody sits next to him. *Because he's black!*

> I'm a man of color, one of the few on the train and often the only one in the quiet car, and I've concluded that color explains a lot about my experience.

Not that the situation doesn't have advantages, he allows. Unlike the fool crackers who are crushed and huddled together as far away from the black guy as they can get, he has an empty seat next to him where he can put his briefcase, papers, and snacks. Oh, *but . . .*

> But the very pleasing moment of anticipation casts a shadow, because I can't accept the bounty of an extra seat without remembering why it's empty . . .

It's empty because he's black! And white people hate, or fear, or hate'n'fear black people so much, they won't take a seat next to one!

Christ-like, though, Mr. Wideman shoulders his cross, with compassion for those who shun him:

> . . . without wondering if [the seat's] emptiness isn't something quite sad.

Then he remembers that Christ told us he came not to bring peace, but a sword. Just so with Mr. Wideman, who after all has fond feelings for the gunslinging rapists of Move. Time for a murmured threat, to keep Charley paying the Danegeld.

. . . And quite dangerous, also, if left unexamined.

The fire next time! There is, however, and alas, very little danger that Mr. Wideman's solitary train rides will go unexamined—they, or any other aspect of what I'd guess he would call "the black experience." After all, here he is examining them at six-hundred-word length on the op-ed page of the *New York Times*.

There is a large cohort of educated African Americans who seem to do little else. Mr. Wideman is billed in the byline of the *Times* piece as "a professor of Africana studies." He's examining his blackness all day long, and getting a handsome salary for it—and now a fee from the *Times*. Examining blackness in all its billionfold variety is Mr. Wideman's job, and the job of hundreds of other professors of Africana/Africano/Africani/Africanarum studies.

The unexamined life is, we are told, not worth living. If, like Mr. Wideman, you are one of the pampered pets of modern liberalism, with a plush affirmative-action sinecure teaching a made-up pseudo-discipline so that some university can darken up its brochures to the degree required by federal regs, the *over*-examined life is worth a neat two hundred grand a year, plus tenure.

Does John Edgar Wideman know anything about the world other than his own blackness? If I were to pick up one of his books and start in on it, would the words soon shift and blur in front of my eyes till they just read as *Black black black. Black black blackety black! BLACK! Blackblackblackblackblackblack* . . . , as happened with the last look-at-my-blackness* book I read? Does he have anything un-black to say to me, in all my shameful un-blackness? To me, as an American? To me, as

---

*   Namely, Barack Obama's *Dreams from My Father: A Story of Race and Inheritance* (2007).

a man and a brother? To me, his "poor, earth-born companion / An' fellow-mortal"?[52]

In one respect at least I am enlightened after reading Mr. Wideman's essay. I used to puzzle over the question: Is solipsism a viable point of view? Can one really be so firmly sealed in the prison of self that the color of one's skin is the primary datum of one's existence? Now I know the answers.

I'll tell a train story of my own; not because I nurse any hope of piercing the armor of Mr. Wideman's solipsism—by definition, nothing could do that—but because I have a hundred or so words to spare in my column allowance.

For seven years I commuted into New York City on the Long Island Railroad, an hour each way, Huntington to Penn Station. There were plenty of African American riders. I often had only two or three empty seats to choose from. There were seat partners I avoided: obese persons, obvious drunks, eaters of smelly foodstuffs, persons muttering to themselves, and in the last year or two (this was 1992–99), riders yapping into cell phones. It never crossed my mind though, not once in seven years, to include race as a selection factor. I was looking for *a seat on a train*, for crying out loud, not a best friend for life.

I don't of course expect you to believe that, Mr. Wideman. Your own blackness is so infinitely fascinating to you—heck, it's your living!—you can't conceive that it is uninteresting to me, or anyone. You imagine (because you can't imagine otherwise) that your companions in the Acela carriage are thinking about you and your blackness with malice in their hearts, all the way from Providence to Penn Station.

Sorry, pal: They're not even thinking about you with love and respect in their hearts, which I'm guessing would be your distant second preference. The dreadful, inconceivable truth—brace yourself, Mr. Wideman, please—oh, can you bear it?—the appalling truth is, they are not thinking about you at all.

The Talk: Nonblack Version

Taki's Magazine

APRIL 5, 2012

T HERE IS much talk about "the talk."*
   "Sean O'Reily was sixteen when his mother gave him the talk
   that most black parents give their teenage sons," Denisa R.
Superville of the Hackensack (NJ) *Record* tells us. Meanwhile, down in
Atlanta, "Her sons were 12 and 8 when Marlyn Tillman realized it was
time for her to have the talk," Gracie Bonds Staples writes in the *Fort
Worth Star-Telegram*.

Leonard Greene talks about the talk in the *New York Post*.[53] Someone bylined as KJ Dell'Antonia talks about the talk in the *New York
Times*.[54] Darryl Owens talks about the talk in the *Orlando Sentinel*.[55]

Yes, talk about the talk is all over.

There is a talk that nonblack Americans have with their kids, too.
My own kids, now nineteen and sixteen, have had it in bits and pieces

---

* "The talk" was a common trope during the first wave of Black Lives Matter framed as
a protective coming-of-age rite for black children to receive instruction on how to navi-
gate the dangers of systemic racism. Examples of "the talk" can be found in the end
notes. This talk about "the talk" ultimately led to Derbyshire's dismissal from
National Review.

as subtopics have arisen. If I were to assemble it into a single talk, it would look something like the following.

1. Among your fellow citizens are forty million who identify as black, and whom I shall refer to as black. The cumbersome (and MLK-noncompliant) term "African-American" seems to be in decline, thank goodness. "Colored" and "Negro" are archaisms. What you must call "the N-word" is used freely among blacks but is taboo to nonblacks.

2. American blacks are descended from West African populations, with some white and aboriginal-American admixture. The overall average of non-African admixture is twenty to twenty-five percent. The admixture distribution is nonlinear, though: "It seems that around ten percent of the African American population is more than half European in ancestry."[56]

3. Your own ancestry is mixed north-European and northeast-Asian, but blacks will take you to be white.

4. The default principle in everyday personal encounters is, that as a fellow citizen, with the same rights and obligations as yourself, any individual black is entitled to the same courtesies you would extend to a nonblack citizen. That is basic good manners and good citizenship. In some unusual circumstances, however—e.g., paragraph (10h) below—this default principle should be overridden by considerations of personal safety.

5. As with any population of such a size, there is great variation among blacks in every human trait (except, obviously, the trait of identifying oneself as black). They come fat, thin, tall, short, dumb, smart, introverted, extroverted, honest, crooked, athletic, sedentary, fastidious, sloppy, amiable, and obnoxious. There are black geniuses and black morons. There are black saints and black psychopaths. In a population of forty million, you will find almost any human type. Only at the far, far extremes of certain traits are there absences. There are, for example, no black Fields Medal winners. While this is civilizationally consequential, it will not likely ever be impor-

tant to you personally. Most people live and die without ever meeting (or wishing to meet) a Fields Medal winner.

6. As you go through life, however, you will experience an ever-larger number of encounters with black Americans. Assuming your encounters are random—for example, not restricted only to black convicted murderers or to black investment bankers—the Law of Large Numbers[57] will inevitably kick in. You will observe that the means—the averages—of many traits are very different for black and white Americans, as has been confirmed by methodical inquiries in the human sciences.

7. Of most importance to your personal safety are the very different means for antisocial behavior, which you will see reflected in, for instance, school disciplinary measures,[58] political corruption,[59] and criminal convictions.[60]

8. These differences are magnified by the hostility many blacks feel toward whites.[61] Thus, while black-on-black behavior is more antisocial in the average than is white-on-white behavior, average black-on-white behavior is a degree more antisocial yet.[62]

9. A small cohort of blacks—in my experience, around five percent—is ferociously hostile to whites and will go to great lengths to inconvenience or harm us. A much larger cohort of blacks—around half—will go along passively if the five percent take leadership in some event. They will do this out of racial solidarity, the natural willingness of most human beings to be led, and a vague feeling that whites have it coming.

10. Thus, while always attentive to the particular qualities of individuals, on the many occasions where you have nothing to guide you but knowledge of those mean differences, use statistical common sense:

    10a. Avoid concentrations of blacks not all known to you personally.

    10b. Stay out of heavily black neighborhoods.

10c. If planning a trip to a beach or amusement park at some date, find out whether it is likely to be swamped with blacks on that date (neglect of this one got me the closest I have ever gotten to death by gunshot[63]).

10d. Do not attend events likely to draw a lot of blacks.

10e. If you are at some public event at which the number of blacks suddenly swells, leave as quickly as possible.

10f. Do not settle in a district or municipality run by black politicians.

10g. Before voting for a black politician, scrutinize his/her character much more carefully than you would a white.

10h. Do not act the Good Samaritan to blacks in apparent distress, e.g., on the highway.

10i. If accosted by a strange black in the street, smile and say something polite but *keep moving*.

11. The mean intelligence of blacks is much lower than for whites.[64] The least intelligent ten percent of whites have IQs below 81; forty percent of blacks have IQs that low. Only one black in six is more intelligent than the average white; five whites out of six are more intelligent than the average black. These differences show in every test of general cognitive ability that anyone, of any race or nationality, has yet been able to devise. They are reflected in countless everyday situations. "Life is an IQ test."

12. There is a magnifying effect here, too, caused by affirmative action. In a pure meritocracy there would be very low proportions of blacks in cognitively demanding jobs. Because of affirmative action, the proportions are higher. In government work, they are very high. Thus, in those encounters with strangers that involve cognitive engagement, ceteris paribus the black stranger will be less intelligent than the white. In such encounters, therefore—for example, at a government

office—you will, on average, be dealt with more competently by a white than by a black. If that hostility-based magnifying effect (paragraph 8) is also in play, you will be dealt with more politely, too. "The DMV lady" is a statistical truth, not a myth.

13. In that pool of forty million, there are nonetheless many intelligent and well-socialized blacks. (I'll use IWSB as an ad hoc abbreviation.) You should consciously seek opportunities to make friends with IWSBs. In addition to the ordinary pleasures of friendship, you will gain an amulet against potentially career-destroying accusations of prejudice.

14. Be aware, however, that there is an issue of supply and demand here. Demand comes from organizations and businesses keen to display racial propriety by employing IWSBs, especially in positions at the interface with the general public—corporate sales reps, TV news presenters, press officers for government agencies, etc.—with corresponding depletion in less visible positions. There is also strong private demand from middle- and upper-class whites for personal bonds with IWSBs, for reasons given in the previous paragraph and also (next paragraph) as status markers.

15. Unfortunately the demand is greater than the supply, so IWSBs are something of a luxury good, like antique furniture or corporate jets: boasted of by upper-class whites and wealthy organizations, coveted by the less prosperous. To be an IWSB in present-day US society is a height of felicity rarely before attained by any group of human beings in history. Try to curb your envy: It will be taken as prejudice (see paragraph 13).

You don't have to follow my version of the talk point for point; but if you are white or Asian and have kids, you owe it to them to give them some version of the talk. It will save them a lot of time and trouble spent figuring things out for themselves. It may save their lives.

The Romance of American Blackness

Taki's Magazine

AUGUST 22, 2013

The following is a review of Lee Daniel's *The Butler* (2013).

I N LAST week's Radio Derb I uttered some unkind words about Oprah Winfrey. The week before that, in a *VDARE* column,[65] I had been uncharitable about the movie Ms. Winfrey has been so vigorously promoting recently and in which she takes a leading role. The movie's called *The Butler* and tells the story of a black man from humble origins who becomes a White House butler, serving presidents from Eisenhower to Reagan. In that *VDARE* piece I described the movie, on indirect evidence, as "black grievance porn."

It's not good journalistic integrity to insult a movie one hasn't actually seen; and besides, Ms. Winfrey has friends in high places. I therefore decided to go and see *The Butler* in hopes I might spare myself an IRS audit by finding something positive to say about the movie.

Not to keep you in suspense, gentle reader, but I couldn't. *The Butler* is dreck. It's dreck in a way that will bear a few hundred words of commentary, though, so here goes with a sort-of review.

Preparing this column in my mind before seeing the movie, I thought it would be neat to open by telling readers something about the demographics of the audience. Who goes to see black grievance porn? Just blacks? Aging white hippies? Young metrosexual products of college white-guilt indoctrination sessions?

Sorry, I still don't know. The showing I caught was at 1 p.m. on a weekday in my mostly white suburb. I counted thirty-six in the audience. There was just one twentysomething black couple; everyone else was white and old. Movie-schedule-wise, I guess I got the Early Bird Special.

The opening scene of *The Butler* shows the title character, Cecil Gaines, as a child in 1926 Georgia. He is picking cotton with his mom and dad and many other blacks. Young White Master swings by the field and with a sneer of cold command orders mom off to a nearby hut for a very audible quickie. Dad dare not object, but when Young White Master comes out adjusting his clothing, dad glares at him. For that, YWM shoots dad dead and suffers no penalty for the crime. "Any white man can kill any of us at any time," the child Gaines is told.

What nonsense! Even in slave times, a white man who killed a black slave in the South could expect some measure of justice. "Ten-year sentences were common, and occasionally the death penalty was invoked," says Eugene Genovese in *Roll, Jordan, Roll*.[66] Were matters actually worse in 1926? Could the producers of *The Butler* not afford a historical consultant—not even one who was, like Genovese when he wrote that book, a Marxist?

Well, well, I guess all is permitted in the promotion of black grievance culture. Stick around: another movie or two, and we shall see the white folks at dinner served up with a black baby that is roasted, basted, and stuffed.

The Butler goes downhill from there. Gaines ends up in the Eisenhower White House just as Ike is ordering federal troops into Little Rock. We are then taken on a plodding tour of the civil-rights battlefield: lunch counters, Freedom Riders, dogs'n'hoses, MLK, Selma, the Voting Rights Act, Malcolm X, the Panthers . . .

Speaking to *Parade* magazine about the movie, Ms. Winfrey opined that young people "don't know diddly-squat about the civil rights movement."[67] Speaking as the parent of two young Americans who, in their passage through public high schools, experienced twelve Black History Months apiece, I'll see Ms. Winfrey's diddly-squat and raise her a fiddledeedee.

The only non-civil-rights issue that passes before our eyes is the Vietnam War, in which Gaines loses a son. I braced myself for the old quip about Vietnam being the war in which black men were sent to kill yellow men on behalf of the country that white men stole from red men, but the producers unaccountably omitted it. (In fact: "Overall, blacks suffered 12.5 percent of the deaths in Vietnam when the percentage of blacks of military age was 13.5 percent of the population."[68])

Eisenhower, who did after all send those troops to Little Rock, is given a fair shake, and JFK is of course cool and sympathetic, but the other presidents are cartoon characters from the Cultural Marxist comic book: Nixon a creepy drunk, LBJ a crude boor (well . . .), Ford a cipher. It seems for a while, incredibly, that Reagan might get fair coverage, but then he vows to veto sanctions against South Africa. See?—just another white devil determined to keep the black man down.

The movie's nonpresidential whites are snarling, spitting bullies, except for a handful of nontalking parts: Pablo Casals, for example, is praised for his hostility to General Franco. That would be the General Franco who saved Spain from becoming Stalin's first European satellite.

The Butler is romantic in the precise sense given by Webster's *Third*: "marked by the imaginative or emotional appeal of the heroic, adventurous, remote, mysterious, or idealized characteristics of things, places, people."

Watching it and reading what Ms. Winfrey has said about it, you realize how deeply and narcissistically absorbed American blacks are in this romance—the romance of American blackness. Nothing else really exists for them. Ms. Winfrey has endorsed three politicians, to my knowledge: Barack Obama, Michael Tubbs, and Cory Booker. Notice anything?

If there are few likeable whites in *The Butler*, there are no unlikeable blacks at all. Everyone is well-spoken and well-behaved except when righteously angry. All are struggling to keep their honor and self-respect in a society whose every hand is against them. The proverbial visitor from Mars, given only this movie to work from, would be baffled why prejudice against blacks exists.

Where, you find yourself wondering, are the other blacks: the feral, criminal, ebonics-jabbering *lumpen-negrotariat* of the slums?[69] Where are their innumerable white victims? Wasn't there any room for these souls in Oprah Winfrey's movie? Not romantic enough, perhaps.

CHAPTER FOUR:

The Whites

White Like Me

National Review

JULY 10, 2003

"THAT'S WHITE of you, Derbyshire." I am just old enough to have had those words addressed to me in earnest, without, so far as I could discern, any facetious intent. The addresser was an Englishman I knew in my Hong Kong days thirty years ago. A middle-aged expatriate, he lived in the same seedy Kowloon rooming house from which I was just embarking on my lifelong vocation of impecunious idling. This Englishman had held some decent position in the Hong Kong civil service, but had been cashiered for taking advantage of Chinese boys. (Not an unusual case in the Hong Kong civil service. There was even an item of expat jargon identifying people of that kind: "rice queens.")

Having destroyed his career, and apparently not desiring to return to the mother country (a very common nondesire among white men in the Far East), this fellow had decided to drink himself to death, and was pretty far along with the project. I don't know whether his civil service pension had survived the cashiering, but he seemed to live mainly by sponging, at which he was skillful and persistent. After successfully sponging HK$20 from me one day, he said the thing I have just said he said: "That's white of you, Derbyshire." (Or it might have been: "You're a white man, Derbyshire," I can't recall the precise formula. At any rate, my whiteness was an essential component of his gratitude.)

Yes, it was pathetic, but he was a pathetic character, which is one reason I yielded to his sponging. Another reason was that, as an innocent young man just learning the ropes about life in distant places, I was susceptible to appeals based on racial solidarity—the beleaguered solidarity, I mean, of tiny numbers of Europeans scattered among native hordes, the solidarity you find echoed in Kipling and Sir Henry Newbolt, Somerset Maugham and Paul Scott. Being myself, so far as acquaintance with the natives was concerned, still at that early point where they seemed strange and forbidding, rather than just fellow human beings who happened to speak a different language, I was receptive to the idea that *we white men must stick together*.

I think that was the last time anyone made anything of my whiteness. Beyond that one brief *frisson* of racial solidarity thirty years ago, I can't say that being white has ever meant much to me. Imagine my surprise, therefore, to learn from the *Washington Post* that "whiteness studies" is now a respectable academic discipline, taught in at least thirty American universities, including Princeton, UCLA, and the University of Massachusetts.[70] The proponents of this new field of scholarly inquiry put out a great deal of blather about the "need to understand" this and that, but it is perfectly obvious from a scrutiny of the subject matter that the main purpose of "whiteness studies" is to make white students hate their ancestors, and preferably also themselves.

For example: One item that we have been told about is the "privilege walk." Students stand shoulder to shoulder in a line across the room. Then each student either takes a step back, or a step forward, or stays put, in response to sentences read out by the instructor. Here are the sentences. I have appended my own responses in brackets after each sentence: plus one for a step forward, minus one for a step backward, zero for staying put. I have also added any comments that occurred to me.

1. If your ancestors were forced to come to the United States not by choice, take one step back. (0. Those white Americans whose ancestors came over as indentured servants would be entitled to step back, I should think.)

2. If your primary ethnic identity is American, take one step forward. (0. This one doesn't make sense. "America," unlike, say, "Israel," or "Japan," or "Finland," is not the name of an ethno-state. There is a good case to be made that the founding fathers thought it should be; and I know some people in our

own time who wish it were; but as things have worked out, it just isn't.)

3. If you were ever called names because of your race, class, ethnicity, gender, or sexual orientation, take one step back. (-1. Are they kidding? As a columnist who regularly speaks his mind on matters of "race, class, ethnicity, gender, or sexual orientation," I can submit 100,000 reader emails in evidence.)

4. If there were people of color who worked in your household as servants, gardeners, etc., take one step forward. (0.)

5. If you were ever ashamed or embarrassed of your clothes, house, car, etc., take one step back. (-1. Again, are they kidding? What proportion of the population, of any color, would not step back here? I estimate five percent of men, some much smaller proportion of women.)

6. If your parents were professionals: doctors, lawyers, etc., take one step forward. (0.)

7. If you were raised in an area where there was prostitution, drug activity, etc., take one step back. (0. There was a time, reader—truly there was, and not so long ago—when poor people took pride in being honest, chaste, and respectable. They looked down with scorn on those who took poverty as an excuse for antisocial behavior. I am not making this up!)

8. If you ever tried to change your appearance, mannerisms, or behavior to avoid being judged or ridiculed, take one step back. (-1. See my note to sentence 5.)

9. If you studied the culture of your ancestors in elementary school, take one step forward. (+1. My own children, currently in US public schools, are not so privileged. Their history lessons thus far have featured mainly Sacajawea, Pocahontas, Frederick Douglass, and Harriet Tubman. I am sure those were all worthy people; but I suspect that my kids are acquiring the impression that there were no white folk at all in the United States until John F. Kennedy descended from the sky in a golden chariot.)

10.   If you went to school speaking a language other than English, take one step back. (0.)

11.   If there were more than fifty books in your house when you grew up, take one step forward. (+1. When I was a kid, poor people of an unsocial temperament either drank a lot or read a lot. Hardly ever both—it's difficult to read when you're pickled. My family were mostly readers.)

12.   If you ever had to skip a meal or were hungry because there was not enough money to buy food when you were growing up, take one step back. (0. Oh, for goodness sake! After forty years and several trillion dollars of spending on welfare, are there really any American college students who can step back here?)

13.   If you were taken to art galleries or plays by your parents, take one step forward. (0. Unless Christmas pantomime counts—everybody in England went to those.)

14.   If one of your parents was unemployed or laid off, not by choice, take one step back. (-1. If I got one step back for every time my Dad was laid off, I'd be in the next county. He was well-nigh unemployable. "A difficult man," was what everyone said. "He couldn't take orders," was my mother's explanation.)

15.   If you attended private school or summer camp, take one step forward. (0.)

16.   If your family ever had to move because they could not afford the rent, take one step back. (-1.)

17.   If you were told that you were beautiful, smart, and capable by your parents, take one step forward. (0. These blinkered idiots don't know jack about any culture outside late-twentieth-century middle-class America. My parents, or any other English parents, would no more have thought to say such things to me than they would have thought of embracing me and murmuring: "I love you, Johnnie." If they had done either, I would have called the police.)

18. If you were ever discouraged from academics or jobs because of race, class, ethnicity, gender, or sexual orientation, take one step back. (-1. Where I grew up, it was taken as a given that people of our background could not become judges, diplomats, surgeons, professors, senior civil servants, and a whole range of other things. Did some of us manage to do so anyway? Yes: but that's not the question. Discouraged? You bet.)

19. If you were encouraged to attend college by your parents, take one step forward. (0. I don't recall being positively *discouraged* on this. When the school sent home a letter saying that I could get a university place and should submit an application, my mother said: "That's nice." I can't remember Dad saying anything, though I feel sure he was pleased.)

20. If you were raised in a single-parent household, take one step back. (0. This wonderful modern regime of easy divorce and welfare-supported bastardy had not yet taken hold in my childhood. For which I thank God daily.)

21. If your family owned the house where you grew up, take one step forward. (0.)

22. If you saw members of your race, ethnic group, gender, or sexual orientation portrayed on television in degrading roles, take one step back. (-1. Yet again, I can't believe they are serious. My "gender" [by which I assume they mean my sex]? Degrading? Have these cretins ever watched any TV sitcom? Those shows, I mean, where the men are all dithering doofuses, being herded and corralled by sharp-witted women? My race, too: Starting with *Roots* twenty-five years ago, there has been a whole flourishing genre of TV dramas featuring cruel, evil white people doing beastly things to colored folk. For crying out loud: If a TV drama has a white person and a black person in it, which one is more likely to be the villain? Can I step back two here?)

23. If you were ever offered a good job because of your association with a friend or family member, take one step forward. (0.)

24. If you were ever denied employment because of your race, ethnicity, gender, or sexual orientation, take one step back. (-1. Yep. In my Hong Kong days again, I went to interview for a job I'd seen advertised in the newspaper. It was a Chinese firm. The lady took one look at me and told me rather sniffily that they did not employ expats. End of job interview.)

25. If you were paid less, treated unfairly because of race, ethnicity, gender, or sexual orientation, take one step back. (0.)

26. If you were ever accused of cheating or lying because of your race, ethnicity, gender, or sexual orientation, take one step back. (-1 . . . If having been English counts. It is an article of faith with the wilder sort of Irish Republican that all English people are liars and thieves, and I have had an earful of *that*. In any case, isn't this whole "whiteness studies" business premised on the axiom that being white, male, and heterosexual is ipso facto evidence of having cheated your way into high society?)

27. If you ever inherited money or property, take one step forward. (0. Though on a technicality. My mother saved a small amount from her pension, and bequeathed it to us. At the time of her death, though, the accumulated sum only amounted to just enough to cover funeral expenses, so I am not going to count it.)

28. If you had to rely primarily on public transportation, take one step back. (-1. Another dumb one. The entire population of New York City could step back on this.)

29. If you were ever stopped or questioned by the police because of your race, ethnicity, gender, or sexual orientation, take one step back. (0. This one's a fix. A crime is committed. Witnesses report that the perp is black. The cops go looking for a black person. Another crime is committed. Witnesses report that the perp is white. The cops go looking for a white person. So sometimes the cops are looking for a black person, sometimes for a white person. How often, in each case? That depends on the levels of criminality in the two

communities. Which are what, exactly? *That* you may not ask! What are you, some kind of racist?)

30. If you were ever afraid of violence because of your race, ethnicity, gender or sexual orientation, take one step back. (-1. Late one night in 1973, I was riding through the streets of Mount Vernon, New York, on a borrowed bicycle. A gang of black youths saw me, howled what the newspapers call "racial epithets," and started to chase me. Thank God it was a 10-speed bike. My leg muscles hurt for a week.)

31. If you were generally able to avoid places that were dangerous, take one step forward. (0.)

32. If you were ever uncomfortable about a joke related to your race, ethnicity, gender, or sexual orientation but felt unsafe to confront the situation, take one step back. (0. Occasionally, among Chinese people. Not really sure if this counts.)

33. If you were ever the victim of violence related to your race, ethnicity, gender, or sexual orientation, take one step back. (0. I can only record a couple of narrow escapes on this one—see sentence 30. I have never been the victim of any kind of violence. I have been in fights, but they were mostly, as most fights are, uncoordinated and inconclusive scuffles, stopped by bystanders after a few seconds.)

34. If your parents did not grow up in the United States, take one step back. (-1. But what does immigration have to do with whiteness? The idea here seems to be that immigrants of any origin are honorary blacks, rather as the Nazis considered Japanese to be honorary whites. Hey, I'll take what I can get.)

35. If your parents told you you could be anything you wanted to be, take one step forward. (0. See my response to sentence 17.)

As you can see, my own responses caused me to end up ten steps back—and that is after giving the benefit of any doubts to the questionnaire. May I have an affirmative action slot, please?

You might object that, as an older guy, I am not really part of the target population here. To the contrary, I would say that it's not me that is out of date, but the self-flagellating dipsnicks who thought up this "privilege walk." Just look at the assumptions underlying some of these sentences. Number 4, for instance. How many eighteen-year-old Americans grew up enjoying the attentions of "servants, gardeners, etc."? (And why, in any case, should we assume that such menials could not possibly have been white? New York City's first black mayor, David Dinkins, was fond of boasting that his mother had been in domestic service. Big deal: My mother's first job was in domestic service. Millions of white Americans must share this claim. I am told that domestic-service agencies in Manhattan have large numbers of Russians and East Europeans on their lists. There is nothing wrong with domestic service, anyway. Why is it less dignified to cook a millionaire's breakfast in a kitchen, than to cook his books in a business office? As a matter of fact, I have long nursed the sneaking desire to try work as a butler. I think I'd be rather good at it. *You rang, Sir?*)

Similarly with number 22. Good old Stepin Fetchit! He can be relied on for an example of the "degrading" roles black Americans were forced to play in the movies. Let it be noted, however, that the last movie of that kind was made half a century ago, and no TV channel would have dared to run it at any time since about 1970. And that even half a century ago, by far the dominant style of portrayal of black Americans in movies was the Noble Negro: *Lilies of the Field* came out in 1963, and was by no means the first of its kind. And number 22 actually deals with TV. When were black Americans portrayed in a degrading manner on TV? Not in my time; not in the time of any entering college freshmen.

Likewise with number 6. The United States, God bless her, now includes millions of middle-class black citizens holding down good jobs—yes, even as "doctors, lawyers, etc." Some of the most interesting recent sociological studies concern the plush suburbs where these citizens live—John Ogbu's recent *Black American Students in an Affluent Suburb* (2003), for example. Don't the kids of these well-heeled middle-class black people go to college?

The assumptions underlying the other sentences are equally anachronistic, or just plain silly. Number 14: White people never get laid off. This will be interesting news to several million victims of the recent recession. (As a matter of fact, since recessions hurt the private sector much more than the public, whereas black people are much better represented in public than in private employment, it seems probable to me that those laid off in a recession are disproportionally white.) Number

23: Patronage rackets are a white thing. Really? Let me introduce you to the New York City school system. Number 12: There are people in America so poor they go to bed hungry. No there aren't. *No there aren't.* There are, of course, people who go to bed hungry because they have a $200-a-day drug habit, but that is not the same thing.

One must always try to be charitable, in a proper Christian spirit. The . . . *persons* who thought up this "whiteness studies" fandango are at least trying to deal with a real issue: the still-awful condition of the disproportionately huge black-American underclass. Most of the rest of us just prefer not to think about this too much. True, the "whiteness studies" crowd are dealing with this issue in an exceptionally crass and lamebrained way; but that is because the kinds of people who rise to positions of authority in the nonscience departments of American universities are exceptionally crass and lamebrained people. *Let's see, what can we do to improve the condition of the black poor? I know—we'll work on raising the self-esteem of black kids! . . . [Thirty years later] . . . Hmmm. That didn't work too well. Those kids have terrific self-esteem now, but they are still stuck in the ghetto, or in jail, unable to read or do arithmetic. What else can we try? Got it!—Since raising the self-esteem of black kids wasn't much use, let's try lowering the self-esteem of white kids! Maybe that will help . . .*

It won't help, of course. Far, far more people will scoff at these courses than will attend them. But what *will* help? My impression is that nobody has a clue, and that most Americans have given up bothering about the issue. The black underclass? Throw them (or, more precisely, those politicians and middle-class black intellectuals who claim to speak for them) a bone now and then—affirmative action, a ban on "racial profiling," a couple of trillion more taxpayer dollars shoveled into the bank accounts of public-sector union bosses, "whiteness studies." Okay: That, together with a few more supersize jails, should keep 'em quiet for another twenty years. Let's get on with our lives.

Getting It White

The American Conservative

OCTOBER 20, 2008

The following is a review of Christian Lander's *Stuff White People Like: A Definitive Guide to the Unique Taste of Millions* (2008).

O UR BRAINS process information coming from our senses. Since we are social animals, a great deal of the processing concerns social information—data about the members of the various groups we belong to, and about our own place in those groups. There is no consensus among neuroscientists about the way this is done, but a number of distinct systems—"modules," in the jargon—seem to be involved. In *No Two Alike*, her 2006 book on "human nature and human individuality," Judith Rich Harris suggests a three-module schema, with a relationship module managing one-on-one attachments, a socialization module for group membership and awareness, and a status module to monitor who's up and who's down.

Whether this is a full and correct account of our social nature, I'm not qualified to judge; but that every human brain contains a status module like the one Ms. Harris describes can hardly be doubted. We all of us devote considerable mental energy to assessing where we stand in this group or that, calculating who's a rival and who an ally, trying to improve our own position, fretting over loss of status, and managing status-related emotions such as envy, contempt, triumph, embarrassment, ambition, and humiliation. Books and magazines offer a steady stream of advice, and advertisers tease and prod our status modules like the trainers of performing seals, trying to nudge us toward invidious consumption.

And then, once in a while, irony kicks in. We turn to look at our status striving, and mock ourselves. It's not that we have any intention of quitting the game. To the contrary, our self-mockery is at once incorporated into the status-computing algorithms, so that group members who are slow to get the joke lose status thereby. Probably that's the point. Wisdom is prized in every human group, and self-awareness is a species of wisdom, if only a minor one.

British author Stephen Potter pioneered this genre of what we might call "status irony" with his 1952 book *One-upmanship*. Now here comes Christian Lander with *Stuff White People Like*, a compilation of 150 one-page summaries of today's status markers, written in a tone of gentle derision. Lander tries for the status-irony equivalent of a somersault with tuck, encompassing irony itself in his performance: "Irony" is #50 on his list.

I can't be the first to note something wrong with the book's title. Status striving operates within some well-defined group. What's the group here? Certainly it is not white people at large. Most white people couldn't care less about natural medicine (#59), Tibet (#124), Noam Chomsky (#98), Rugby football (#93), or film festivals (#3) . . . while, come to think of it, there is at least a scattering of un-white people who could. I've been white for as long as I can remember, and I've never even heard of some of these items. Who or what is Mos Def (#69), LEED certification (#134), David Sedaris (#25)? Don't ask me. So who are these "white people"?

My first guess was that to the degree there is anything racially distinctive about the sensibility on display in Lander's book, it is Jewish: the reflexive leftism, the food faddishness, the moralizing, and yes, at #103, "Self-Deprecating Humor." Accompanying #64 ("Recycling") there is a picture of Lander wearing a Community Hebrew Academy of Toronto T-shirt. He tells us he's not Jewish, though, and that first name seems indubitably corroborative.

Stuff White People Like is Jewish only in the sense, described by Yuri Slezkine in *The Jewish Century* (2004), that we have all become a bit Jewish in the last fifty years. As Slezkine noted, quoting historian Joseph R. Levenson: "A Jewish style of life . . . may be more endangered when everyone eats bagels than when Jews eat hot cross buns." Lander's white people would, I am sure, want their bagels to be organically produced, but they wouldn't be seen dead eating a hot cross bun (#2, "Religions Their Parents Don't Belong To").

The white people here are in fact just thirtyish grad-school liberal-arts alumni, a young subset of the "bourgeois bohemians" whom David Brooks described in his 2000 pop-sociology book *Bobos in Paradise*. A pretty good way to get a fix on any group is to look at how its members make their livings. As part of #47, "Liberal Arts Degrees," Christian Landers lists eight careers: "Writer," "Artist/Photographer," "[movie] Director," "Organic Restaurant Owner," "Bike Mechanic," "Nonprofit CEO," "Professor," and "Brand/media consultant."

The common denominator is that these are all perfectly useless occupations, the career equivalents of conspicuous consumption. The white-people group apparently does not include civil engineers, software entrepreneurs, plumbers, farmers, the military, or the police. In fact, it hardly includes anyone without a liberal arts degree. From that same #47:

> But what about the white people who study Science, Engineering, and Business? Unless they become doctors, they essentially lose white-person status (which can be regained only by working at a nonprofit).

Lander himself was an English major at McGill who then studied communications at graduate school. Here, however, as with all the material in *Stuff White People Like*, you need to keep your irony detector switched on. There are hints throughout the book that those careers are not so much actual as oneiric, or at best aspirational. Most of the white people Lander is talking about are worker bees in corporate offices. From #143, "Bakeries":

> The bakery also inspires hope in white people. Many of them dream of quitting their 9 to 5 job and opening a small bakery . . .

Stuff White People Like is in fact a work of autobiography. Lander has done a clever thing: He has made a bundle of money by writing about his own tastes. The book's true title is: *Stuff Christian Lander Likes*. Our author has admitted as much in some of the innumerable interviews he's done. This from Alex Leavitt's website:

> Q: How much of [the StuffWhitePeopleLike.com website, from which the book is taken] describes the generic white person, and how much describes you yourself?

A: Almost all of the website describes me. It's hard to fix on how pretentious I really am . . .

The thing wouldn't work, of course, if there were not millions of people who like the same things Christian Lander likes and are willing to laugh at themselves. While laughing, they will quietly be checking their tastes against the zeitgeist, to update their inventory of bobo status markers. Behind the laughter, in other words, if you listen closely, will be the sound of garbage-can lids closing over Asics sneakers, Pitchfork CDs, bottles of Mateus wine or Evian water, baggy T-shirts, plastic shopping bags, and DVDs not from the Criterion Collection. If caught in possession of one of these sumptuary stinkers, a white person's only hope is to claim to be acting ironically, but this calls for expert-level status-management skills.

The original Stuff White People Like website has generated many spin-offs. Some quick googling turns up a feeble Stuff Black People Like (Their Momma, Big Butts, Being Good At Sports), a slightly better Stuff Educated Black People Like (Moving to Atlanta, Deck Shoes, Correcting Others), a far better Stuff Asian People Like (Cutting In Line, False Humility, Not Wearing Shoes Indoors), Christian Lander's declared favorite White Stuff People Like (flour, sugar, drywall), and a host of others of various quality and ironicity.

Given the audacity of this book's title, it's hard not to find oneself wondering if it is a harbinger of anything, a pointer to the future direction of racial attitudes in the United States. Objections to the *Stuff White People Like* concept as racist are hopelessly wide of the mark, as witness #7, "Diversity," #8, "Barack Obama," and #14, "Having Black Friends." Lander's white people are liberal to a fault (#118, "The ACLU"). None of them owns a copy of *Camp of the Saints* or a subscription to *American Renaissance*; probably none of them even knows what the Confederate flag looks like.

The up-front positioning of items #7, #8, and #14 suggests, however, that there is something perfunctory about the racial liberalism of Lander's white people. These gestures aside—and Obama is the grandest gesture of all—the impression one gets is that on the whole, Lander's white people are happy to live their lives as though black people—let alone Hispanics, whose lone representative in these pages is #113, "Che Guevara"—did not exist. From #7, "Diversity":

Many white people from Los Angeles, San Francisco, and New York will spend hours talking about how great it is that they can get sushi and tacos on the same street. But they will also send their kids to private school with other rich white kids so that they can avoid the "low test scores" that come with educational diversity. It's important to note that white people do not like to be called out on this fact. It will make them feel even more guilty than they already do.

Can such things be said out loud? Apparently now they can, so long as they are seasoned with enough self-mocking irony.

A more interesting question is: Are we looking here at the first stirrings of white tribalism? Social change often begins in the unlikeliest places. Perhaps *Stuff White People Like* is one more melancholy milestone on the downhill road from the hopes for integration and racial harmony that were nursed by the generation of Lander's parents to the cold racial realism of 2042, when, according to the most recent report from the Census Bureau, white people will become a minority in the United States—just about the time that Lander's children's generation take power.

Lander's white people are unhappily intermediate, raised among their parents' hopes, yet staring at a world in which those hopes have turned to dust. They can see the utter failure of racial integration—how could they not? Last week my son's football team played Commack; in two weeks' time they play Wyandanch. According to GreatSchools.net, the racial spread of Commack High School, in percentages white-Asian-Hispanic-black, is 86-9-4-1, while Wyandanch Memorial High School's is 0-0-18-82. Integration? Fuhgeddaboutit. The tension between dead hope and unwelcome reality is acute, resolvable only, as is always the case with such psychic stresses, by doublethink. Vote for Barack Obama (#8), but move to Portland, Oregon (#111), "Statistically . . . the whitest metropolis in the United States."

Stuff White People Like is a light and frivolous book, as of course it is intended to be. It gives the reader's status module a good workout. Meanwhile, however, our socialization modules ("Most of the work done by this system is not available to the conscious mind," writes Ms. Harris) continue their slow, world-changing transformation. Christian Lander's mild-mannered, trend-hugging, conflict-averse (#128, "Avoiding Confrontation"), ironic leftists will spawn a generation of frank white nationalists, and they will feel unironically terrible about having done so.

White People Are Pussies

Taki's Magazine

SEPTEMBER 6, 2012

O N A call-in radio program recently, we aired my infamous assertion in a *Taki's Magazine* column back in April* that white
people should avoid large concentrations of blacks as likely to
be dangerous.

A caller asked why I would not be similarly fearful of a large concentration of whites. I made the obvious reply—that the element of
racial animus, of black hatred of whites, would be missing. Then I
added, off the cuff: "Anyway, why would anyone be scared of a crowd
of whites? Whites aren't going to do anything to you. Let's face it, white
people are pussies."

The remark passed without comment, but I regretted it nonetheless.
It was, after all, an expression of ethnomasochism—of contempt for
one's own people. Having railed against ethnomasochism considerably
the past few years, on this and other websites, I really should be more
careful what I say about my own ethny.

---

* See above, "The Talk: Nonblack Version," page 106.

It's a thought that keeps coming up, though. It came up yesterday when I was reading a story about France's ban on Muslim women wearing the burqa (full-body with face veil) and niqab (shoulder-length face veil).[71]

Following the trashing of that Gypsy camp by French police the other day,[72] I'd been nursing hopes that the French at least were holding out against the tide of pussification. Alas, no—not in the matter of burqas and niqabs, anyway.

> Since the law went into effect, 425 women wearing full-face veils have been fined up to 150 euros ($188) each and 66 others have received warnings, said Pierre-Henry Brandet, spokesman for the Interior Ministry. *But even the police concede that they rarely enforce it, having no desire to further increase tensions* [italics added].[73]

Heaven forbid law enforcement officers should "increase tensions" by enforcing the law! And so the Muslims are free to continue insulting French culture and sapping away at French nationhood.

In Britain things are worse, as one of the Muslims in the *Times* story, a Monsieur M'hammed [*sic*] Henniche, tells us with satisfaction:

> But when he visits London, Mr. Henniche said, the first thing he notices is the number of women wearing the niqab walking freely on the streets. "I think, 'Whoa, it's an open country, English people are open,'" he said. "Such tolerance is a good thing."

Well, it sure is a good thing if you're an African or West Asian Muslim keen to escape the poverty, ignorance, intolerance, corruption, and backwardness that *your* ethny—assisted by your religion—has created in the land of your origin. That it's been a good thing for the native British, who would much prefer to have been left alone in their warm-ale-swilling, rhubarb-chomping, dentally-challenged, eccentrically-plumbed unique foggy culture, is hard to see.

But whose fault is it that the streets of London and Liverpool are now blighted with what expats living in Saudi Arabia refer to as "BMOs"—black moving objects?

Why, it's the fault of the British themselves for letting it happen. You get what you vote for. No native Briton should ever have cast a vote for any party whose platform did not include a clear ban on mass

Third World immigration. Why did the British yield on this? Because they're pussies.

The Scandinavians are even bigger pussies than the Brits. Read this,[74] for example, from Sweden.

> A Djiboutian who refused to be named in fear of reprisals from his fellow countrymen, said that he left Djibouti on May this year, and came to Sweden via France. There is no work in Djibouti, corruption is rampant, and it's hard to put food on the table there. Life in Sweden is very easy and getting papers is more easier, you don't even have to work to put food on the table, I advised all my friends and relatives to come here, most of them are on the way, five already arrived and sought asylum, two already managed to get Permanent residence permit.

Savor the lunacy there. Given the statistical profiles of sub-Saharan Africans—low averages for paternal investment and IQ, high ones for time preference and criminality—permitting settlement by thousands of Africans is a sensationally dumb idea. Africans from the Horn of Africa, though—Somalia, Ethiopia, Eritrea, Djibouti—are Africans *squared*, with societies even more dysfunctional than the African average, and sensational Total Fertility Rates: 6.26, 5.39, 4.37, 2.63 respectively.

(And yes, I did notice that Djibouti's 2.63 is way better than Somalia's 6.26; but the Djiboutians in that article I just quoted are entering Sweden under false pretenses, claiming to be Somalis,[75] *who are the people the Swedes REALLY want!* Lunacy upon lunacy.)

The Russians—who, after all, are just Scandinavians in fur hats—are not much better. They may have jailed the Pussy Rioters, but their pussyish response to the takeover of their capital city by an alien mob[76] the other day unmasks their true Scandinavian pussiness.

Of civilized peoples in general, I think it's only the whites that are pussies, and perhaps only white gentiles. I don't know enough about South Asians to give a ruling; but East Asians are not pussies.

To be sure, the Japanese are pussier than their ferocious ancestors, but they don't do collective guilt, and are adamant that the wretched of the earth should stay in their own wretched countries, and not infect Japan with their wretchedness by settling there *en* wretched *masse*.

China's an interesting case. I speak here from forty years' close acquaintance with that nation. What you mostly hear about in this context are the fierce nationalism and xenophobia of young Chinese men.

That is certainly a key feature of modern Chinese society, and the Chinese today are not pussies.

Among my Chinese acquaintances, though—especially the women—I think I detect the stirrings of some sympathetic guilt about the occupied territories of Tibet and Eastern Turkestan ("Xinjiang"), and about China's quasi-imperialist adventures in Africa. If this guilt were to seep outward into the society at large, aided perhaps by certain matriarchal tendencies in Chinese culture and history, the Chinese might conceivably join Western whites in pussitude.

And we white Americans? Are we the most pussified of all—the pussies of the world?

That's a thought I don't want to have. That way lies hard, irreversible ethnomasochism.

It's a thought that keeps bobbing up to the surface, though, prompted by some news item or image; or out of the blue, as on the radio that time, too publicly for me to disown it.

I must discipline my mind.

CHAPTER FIVE:

The Jews

The Jews and I

National Review

APRIL 10, 2001

S ATURDAY EVENING we went to a seder at the home of some friends. It was an easygoing affair: Our friends are not devout Jews. In fact the husband is not Jewish at all, and neither am I, and neither is my wife. Since we took our two kids, and our hosts' party consisted of only husband, wife, their one child and the wife's sister, Gentiles in fact outnumbered Jews five to three round the table (Elijah was a no-show).

Still it was a most enjoyable evening, and an occasion for thought. As a conservative, I approve of all customary and traditional observances, even when the religious content is minimal. I also appreciate the opportunity offered by Passover to take out my own thoughts and feelings about the Jews and examine them, an exercise I recommend to all Gentiles, though once a year is probably often enough.

I myself grew up among the traditional attitudes of the English lower classes. These were best expressed by the late Kingsley Amis, who was once asked by an interviewer whether he was anti-Semitic. "Very, very mildly," replied Amis. Pressed to elaborate, he offered this: "Well, when I'm watching the credits roll at the end of a TV program, I say to myself: 'Oh, there's another one.'"

That is about the temperature of anti-Semitism I knew as a child: barely detectable. (I have, of course, already outraged a number of

137

American readers, devotees of the proposition that anyone who makes the merest remark about the Jews that is not absolutely, irreproachably positive, is secretly plotting to massacre them. I acknowledge this with a resigned sigh. One thing you learn, writing for the public, is that *anything whatsoever* that you say about the Jews will be seen as virulently anti-Semitic by somebody, somewhere.) For a view of Anglo-Jewish life from the other side, I recommend the slow, quiet, modestly funny novels and stories of Chaim Bermant.

My father was a working man of little education, and his attitude in these matters was pretty much the same as Amis's. I never heard him say anything malicious—nor even, I think, derogatory—about the Jews, and I know from many conversations that he believed Hitler to have been a very wicked man. Dad's usual term for a Jew was "sheeny," which he deployed in utterances like: "You remember Marjorie Sykes. She married that sheeny bookkeeper from over Towcester way." Again, there was no malign intent that I could, or can, detect in this. It was just a way of speaking, very widespread in England thirty and forty years ago, and for all I know still so today.

The English have nothing to be ashamed of in this regard, having been exceptionally hospitable to the Jews since re-admitting them in Oliver Cromwell's time. (A marvelous story in itself, told in Part Four of Paul Johnson's *A History of the Jews* [1987].) English philosemitism has continued in a direct line of descent since then, enlisting such notable figures as Sir Walter Scott, Queen Victoria, Charles Dickens, George Meredith, David Lloyd George, and Margaret Thatcher.

Most Americans would consider it a wonderful and striking thing if a Jew were to be elected president of these United States. Pooh: We Brits had Benjamin Disraeli as prime minister 133 years ago. (Yes, I know, his father took the whole family to Christianity when Benjamin was thirteen. But Dizzy was *born* a Jew.)

I was a bit disconcerted some years ago, when some different Jewish friends took me along to a Kol Nidre service, and I discovered that the only reference to England in their prayer book was to the twelfth-century pogrom at York. Come on, guys: That was *eight hundred years* ago. Isn't there a statute of limitations on pogroms?

The sleepy English country town I grew up in had only a small contingent of Jews, who of course all knew each other. My first contact with this little world came through an elderly couple of Silesian Jews whose anonymity I shall preserve behind the name "Kellerman."

The Kellermans had fled Germany when Hitler came to power. After some unhappy years in Palestine, they had washed up in England, where

Martin Kellerman was export manager for a firm—Jewish-owned, of course—that manufactured greeting cards. Gussie Kellerman gave piano lessons, as a result of which those of the town's young people who had any aspirations to higher culture all knew her.

Martin used to conduct a sort of salon for us, in fact. Though close to sixty at that point, he was one of those people who genuinely like to be among intelligent youngsters. Half a dozen of us at a time would go over there to sit in his living room and talk about the events of the day, books we had read or plays we had attended, while Gussie fed us with wonderful little Middle-European snacks she made up herself, out of ingredients purchased at the county's lone delicatessen.

I still have a vivid memory of the Kellermans' house. They had brought with them into exile all the manners and attitudes of the old Central European Jewish bourgeoisie, one of the most civilized populations that ever existed. (It exists no more, of course, having been wiped out by Hitler and Stalin. Most of the Kellermans' childhood friends and relatives had perished in the camps.) They spoke German to each other, were intimidatingly well-read in that and a couple of other languages, and could identify any piece of classical music after a couple of bars.

On top of a fine, gracious old wooden bureau in their drawing room stood the most valuable object I had ever seen outside a museum: a Meissen vase, worth, according to Gussie, twenty thousand pounds—at least twice my father's entire lifetime earnings up to that point.

For a working-class boy from a family with very narrow horizons—I had never even *heard* the word "delicatessen" until I heard it from Gussie—this was heady stuff. Martin was a man of much learning and strong opinions. Some of his pronouncements were made with such force and conviction that I have not, even to this day, ventured to gainsay them.

When, one evening, someone asked him for an opinion on Proust, he shook his head and gave a firm "No!" Why? we asked. Replied Martin, in his heavy German accent salted with British slang: "Because I do not like *poofs*. Und I especially do not like *Chewish* poofs. It is against nature, und against my religion." I have never since felt the slightest urge to read Proust.

The Kellermans were not in fact very pious, and Martin could be rather scathing about this. The town's other Jews (he said) looked down on the Kellermans because, "They do not think we are religious enough."

They didn't even think of themselves as very Jewish. I remember once Gussie even corrected me, gently, when I referred to them as "a Jewish

couple." Said Gussie: "I would prefer you to say, 'A German couple.'"
For all the vile things the Nazis had done to them and theirs, and for all
that their hometown was now a part of Poland, they still thought of themselves as German. All the men of their parents' generation had fought—
for Germany, of course—in World War One, many with distinction.

I was very surprised, therefore, when I called on them one evening
by myself and found Martin seated in his customary armchair, but wearing a yarmulke and reading a black-bound book printed in Hebrew.
Here was his explanation.

> For some time I have been suffering from an embarrassing
> and very painful cyst. At one point, the pain was so intense
> that I made a vow to my Creator. I said if he would be so
> good as to relieve me of this pain, I would do my duty to him
> as a Jew, and attend shul for three months, and make proper
> observances. The pain went; and now, you see, I am fulfilling
> my side of the bargain.

(A true story, although now that I see it in readable form, it would
not be out of place in one of Chaim Bermant's books.)

I find myself now, in middle age, with complicated and sometimes
self-contradictory feelings about the Jews. Those early impressions—
culture, wit, intelligence, kindness, and hospitality—are still dominant,
and I have read enough to know what a stupendous debt our civilization
owes to the Jews.

At the same time, there are aspects of distinctly Jewish ways of
thinking that I dislike very much. The world-perfecting idealism, for
example, that is rooted in the most fundamental premises of Judaism,
has, it seems to me, done great harm in the modern age. That dreadful
speech Charlie Chaplin gives at the end of *The Great Dictator* made me
gag instinctively, even before I understood why.

I also find the theories of Kevin MacDonald (*The Culture of Critique*) about the partly malign influence of Jews on modern American
culture very persuasive—though this is not an endorsement of MacDonald's theory of "group evolutionary strategies," which I do not understand. And like (I suppose) every other Gentile, I have often been irri-
tated by Jewish sensibilities, and occasionally angered by them.

For an example of what I mean by that last, recall the *Spectator* incident of 1994.

In October of that year, the London *Spectator*—a literary and political magazine of impeccable gentility—published an article titled "Kings

of the Deal," analyzing, in a thoughtful and entirely unthreatening way, the dominance of Jews such as Steven Spielberg, David Geffen, and Jeffrey Katzenberg in Hollywood.

To the amazement of the *Spectator*'s editor (who was Dominic Lawson—a Jew!) this innocuous article caused a storm of outrage in the United States. The young author, William Cash, was denounced from the pulpits of political correctness—that is, from the op-ed pages of the *Los Angeles Times* and the *New York Times*. Prominent American Jews including Leon Wieseltier went into high-hysterical mode, denouncing Cash as the new Julius Streicher and so on.

The storm went on for weeks, led by a howling mob of buffoons—Barbra Streisand, for example—who had certainly never read, nor probably even heard of the *Spectator* up to that point. (I have been reading it for thirty years, and have also written for it.) It was a display of arrogance, cruelty, ignorance, stupidity, and sheer bad manners by rich and powerful people toward a harmless, helpless young writer, and the Jews who whipped up this preposterous storm[77] should all be thoroughly ashamed of themselves.

Taken all in all, though, I am proud to call myself a philosemite, and even at low points like the *Spectator* affair still, at the very least, an anti-anti-Semite. I recall the numberless kindnesses I have received at the hands of Jews, friendships I treasure, and lessons I have learnt. I cherish those recollections.

As a keen reader of history, I also stand in awe of the sheer staying power of the Jews. In Paul Johnson's words:

> When the historian visits Hebron today, he asks himself: where are all those peoples which once held the place? Where are the Canaanites? Where are the Edomites? Where are the ancient Hellenes and the Romans, the Byzantines, the Franks, the Mamluks and the Ottomans? They have vanished into time, irrevocably. But the Jews are still in Hebron.

These are not very happy days in Hebron. I have no doubt, though, that three thousand years from now the Jews will still be there, arguing, feasting, theorizing, charming, and vexing all who come to know them. What an astounding story theirs is!

"How odd of God / To choose the Jews." (To which one Jewish wag offered the response: "Not news, not odd: / We Jews chose God!") A peaceful, healthy, and happy Passover to each and every one of them. *L'chaim!*

The Marx of the Anti-Semites

The American Conservative

MARCH 10, 2003

The following is a review of Kevin MacDonald's The Culture of Critique: An Evolutionary Analysis of Jewish Involvement in Twentieth-Century Intellectual and Political Movements *(1998).*

O NE EVENING early on in my career as an opinion journalist in the United States, I found myself in a roomful of mainstream conservative types, standing around in groups and gossiping. Because I was new to the scene, a lot of the names they were tossing about were unknown to me, so I could not take much part in the conversation. Then I caught one name that I recognized. I had just recently read and admired a piece published in *Chronicles* under that name. I gathered from the conversation that the owner of the name had once been a regular contributor to much more widely read conservative publications, the kind that have salaried congressional correspondents and full-service LexisNexis accounts, but that he was welcome at those august portals no longer. In all innocence, I asked why this was so. "Oh," explained one of my companions, "he got the Jew thing." The others in our group all nodded their understanding. Apparently no further explanation was required. *The Jew thing.* It was said in the kind of tone you might use of an automobile with a cracked engine block, or a house with subsiding foundations. Nothing to be done with him, poor fellow. No use to anybody now. Got the Jew thing. They shoot horses, don't they?

Plainly, getting the Jew thing was a sort of occupational hazard of conservative journalism in the United States, an exceptionally lethal one, which the career-wise writer should strive to avoid. I resolved that I would do my best, so far as personal integrity allowed, not to get the Jew thing. I had better make it clear to the reader that at the time of writing, I have not yet got the Jew thing—that I am in fact a philosemite and a well-wisher of Israel, for reasons I have explained in various places, none of them difficult for the nimble web surfer to find.

If, however, you have got the Jew thing, or if, for reasons unfathomable to me, you would like to get it, Kevin MacDonald is your man. MacDonald is a tenured professor of psychology at California State University in Long Beach. He is best known for his three books about the Jews, developing the idea that Judaism has for 2,000 years or so been a "group evolutionary strategy." The subject of this review is a re-issue, in soft cover, of the third and most controversial of those books, *The Culture of Critique*, first published in 1998.[78] The re-issue differs from the original mainly by the addition of a sixty-six-page preface, which covers some more recent developments in the field, and offers responses to some of the criticisms that appeared when the book was first published. The number of footnotes has also been increased, from 135 to 181, and they have all been moved from the chapter-ends to the back of the book. A small amount of extra material has been added to the text. So far as I could tell from a cursory comparison of the two editions, nothing has been subtracted.

The main thrust of this book's argument is that Jewish or Jewish-dominated organizations and movements engaged in a deliberate campaign to delegitimize the Gentile culture of their host nations—most particularly the USA—through the twentieth century, and that this campaign is one aspect of a long-term survival strategy for the Jews as an ethny. In MacDonald's own words: "[T]he rise of Jewish power and the disestablishment of the specifically European nature of the US are the real topics of *CofC*." He illustrates his thesis by a close analysis of six distinct intellectual and political phenomena: the anti-Darwinian movement in the social sciences (most particularly the no-such-thing-as-race school of anthropology associated with Franz Boas), the prominence of Jews in left-wing politics, the psychoanalytic movement, the Frankfurt School of social science (which sought to explain social problems in terms of individual psychopathology), the "New York intellectuals" centered on *Partisan Review* during the 1940s and 1950s, and Jewish involvement in shaping US immigration policy.

MacDonald writes from the point of view of evolutionary psychology—a term that many writers would put in quotes, as the epistemological status of this field is still a subject of debate. I have a few doubts of my own on this score, and sometimes wonder whether evolutionary psychology may eventually turn out to be one of those odd fads that the human sciences, especially in the United States, are susceptible to. The twentieth century saw quite a menagerie of these fads: Behaviorism, Sheldonian personality-typing by body shape (ectomorph, mesomorph, endomorph), the parapsychological research of Dr. J. B. Rhine, the sexology of Alfred Kinsey, and so on. I think that the evolutionary psychologists are probably on to something, but some of their more extreme claims seem to me to be improbable and unpleasantly nihilistic. Here, for example, is Kevin MacDonald in a previous book: "The human mind was not designed to seek truth but rather to attain evolutionary goals." This trembles on the edge of deconstructionist words-have-no-meaning relativism, of the kind that philosopher David Stove called "puppetry theory," and that MacDonald himself debunks very forcefully in chapter 5 of *The Culture of Critique*. After all, if it is so, should we not suppose that evolutionary psychologists are pursuing their own "group evolutionary strategy"? And that, in criticizing them, I am pursuing mine? And that there is, therefore, no point at all in my writing, or your reading, any further?

To be fair to Kevin MacDonald, not all of his writing is as silly as that. *The Culture of Critique* includes many good things. There is a spirited defense of scientific method, for example. One of the sub-themes of the book is that Jews are awfully good at creating pseudosciences—elaborate, plausible, and intellectually very challenging systems that do not, in fact, have any truth content—and that this peculiar talent must be connected somehow with the custom, persisted in through long pre-Enlightenment centuries, of immersing young men in the study of a vast body of argumentative writing, with status in the community—and marriage options, and breeding opportunities—awarded to those who have best mastered this mass of meaningless esoterica. (This is not an original observation, and the author does not claim it as such. In fact he quotes historian Paul Johnson to the same effect, and earlier comments along these lines were made by Arthur Koestler and Karl Popper.) MacDonald is very scathing about these circular and self-referential thought-systems, especially in the case of psychoanalysis and the "pathologization of Gentile culture" promoted by the Frankfurt School. Here he was precisely on my wavelength, and I found myself cheering him on. Whatever you may think of MacDonald and his theories, there is no doubt he believes himself to be doing careful objective science. The same could, of course, be said of Sheldon, Rhine, Kinsey, et al.

It is good to be reminded, too, with forceful supporting data, that the 1924 restrictions on immigration to the United States were not driven by any belief on the part of the restrictionists in their own racial superiority, but by a desire to stabilize the nation's ethnic balance, which is by no means the same thing. (In fact, as MacDonald points out, one of the worries of the restrictionists was that more clever and energetic races such as the Japanese would, if allowed to enter, have negative effects on social harmony.) MacDonald's chapter on "Jewish involvement in shaping US immigration policy" is a detailed survey of a topic I have not seen discussed elsewhere. If the Jews learned anything from the twentieth century, it was surely the peril inherent in being the only identifiable minority in a society that is otherwise ethnically homogeneous. That thoughtful Jewish-Americans should seek to avoid this fate is understandable. That their agitation was the main determinant of postwar US immigration policy seems to me more doubtful. And if it is true, we must believe that ninety-seven percent of the US population ended up dancing to the tune of the other three percent. If *that* is true, the only thing to say is the one Shakespeare's Bianca would have said: "The more fool they."

Similarly with MacDonald's discussion of Jewish involvement in the Bolshevik takeover of the Russian Empire and the many horrors that ensued. This was until recently another taboo topic, though the aged Aleksandr Solzhenitsyn, presumably feeling he has nothing much to lose, has recently taken a crack at it.[79] I believe MacDonald was driven by necessity here. Having posited that Jews are out to "destroy" (this is his own word) Gentile society, he was open to the riposte that if, after two thousand years of trying, the Jews had failed to accomplish this objective in even one instance, Gentiles don't actually have much to worry about. So: The Jews destroyed Russia. Though MacDonald's discussion of this topic is interesting and illuminating, it left me unconvinced. As he says: "The issue of the Jewish identification of Bolsheviks who were Jews by birth is complex." Paul Johnson gives only fifteen to twenty percent of the delegates at early Party congresses as Jewish. If the other eighty to eighty-five percent were permitting themselves to be manipulated by such a small minority, then we are back with Bianca.

Since the notion of "group evolutionary strategy" is central to MacDonald's case, I wish he had been better able to convince me of its validity. For instance: I happen to be fairly well acquainted with the culture and history of China, a nation that, like the diaspora Jews, awarded high social status and enhanced mating opportunities to young men who had shown mastery of great masses of content-free written material. Anyone who has read stories from the pre-modern period of China's history knows that the guy who gets the girl—who ends up, in fact, with a bevy of "secondary wives" who are thereby denied to less intellectual males—is the one who has aced the Imperial examinations and been rewarded with a District Magistrate position. This went on for two thousand years. Today's Chinese even, like Ashkenazi Jews, display an average intelligence higher by several points than the white-Gentile mean. So: Was Confucianism a "group evolutionary strategy"? If so, then plainly the Chinese of China were, in MacDonald's jargon, the "ingroup." But then . . . what was the "outgroup"?

The more I think about the term "group evolutionary strategy," in fact, the more I wonder if it is not complete nonsense. From an evolutionary point of view, would not the optimum strategy for almost any European Jew at almost any point from AD 79 to AD 1800 or so have been conversion to Christianity? Rather than learning to argue fine points of theology, wouldn't a better strategy have been to learn, say, fencing, or Latin? Sure, the Jews held together as a group across two thousand years. The gypsies held together pretty well, too, across many centuries; yet their "group evolutionary strategy" was the opposite of the Jews' at almost every point. And the Jewish over-representation in important power centers of Gentile host societies became possible only after Jewish emancipation—which, like abolition of the slave trade, was an entirely white-Gentile project! Did the genes of twelfth-century Jews "know" emancipation was going to happen seven hundred years on? How? If they didn't, what was the point of their "evolutionary strategy"? There is a whiff of teleology about this whole business.

Kevin MacDonald is working in an important field. There is no disputing the fact that we need to understand much more than we currently do about how common-ancestry groups react with each other. Group conflicts are a key problem for multiracial and multicultural societies. Up till about 1960, the United States coped with these problems by a frank assertion of white-Gentile ethnic dominance, very much as Israel copes with them today by asserting Jewish ethnic dominance. This proved to be quite a stable arrangement, as social arrangements go. It was obviously objectionable to some American Jews, and it is not surprising that they played an enthusiastic part in undermining it; but they were not the sole, nor even the prime,[80] movers in its downfall. It was replaced, from the 1960s on, by a different arrangement, characterized by racial guilt, shame, apology, and recompense, accompanied by heroic efforts at social engineering ("affirmative action"). This system, I think it is becoming clear, has proved less stable than what went before, and has probably now reached the point where it cannot be sustained much longer. What will replace it? What will the new arrangement be?

At times of flux like this, there are naturally people whose preference is for a return to the older dispensation. It is obvious that Kevin Mac-Donald is one of these people. If this is not so, he has some heavy explaining to do about phrases such as "the ethnic interests of white Americans to develop an ethnically and culturally homogeneous society." Personally, I think he's dreaming. The older dispensation wasn't as bad as liberal commentators and storytellers would have us believe, but it is gone forever, and will not return. For America, the toothpaste is out of the tube.

And on the point of Israel having something very much like the old American dispensation, I am unimpressed by MacDonald's oft-repeated argument—it is a favorite with both Israelophobes and anti-Semites—that it is hypocritical for Jews to promote multiculturalism in the United States while wishing to maintain Jewish ethnic dominance in Israel. Unless you think that ethnic dominance, under appropriate restraining laws, is immoral *per se*—and I don't, and Kevin MacDonald plainly doesn't, either—it can be the foundation of a stable and successful nation. A nation that can establish it and maintain it would be wise to do so. The United States was not able to maintain it, because too many Americans—far more than three percent—came to think it violated Constitutional principles. Israel, however, was founded on different principles, and there seems to be no large popular feeling in that country for dismantling Jewish-ethnic dominance, as there was in Lyndon Johnson's America for dismantling European dominance. The Israelis, most of them, are happy with Jewish-ethnic dominance, and intend to keep it going. Good luck to them.

The aspect of MacDonald's thesis that I find least digestible is his underlying assumption that group conflict is a zero-sum game, rooted in an evolutionary tussle over finite resources. This is not even true on an international scale, as the growing wealth of the whole world during these past few decades has shown. On the scale of a single nation, it is absurd. These Jewish-inspired pseudoscientific phenomena that *The Culture of Critique* is concerned with—Boasian anthropology, psychoanalysis, the Frankfurt School, and so on—were they a net negative for America? Yes, I agree with MacDonald, they were. Now conduct the following thought experiment. Suppose the great post-1881 immigration of Ashkenazi Jews had never occurred. Suppose the Jewish population of the United States in 2003 were not the two to four percent (depending on your definitions) that it is, but the 0.3 percent it was at the start of the Civil War. Would anything have been lost? Would America be richer, or poorer? Would our cultural and intellectual life be busier, or duller?

It seems incontrovertible to me that a great deal would have been lost: entrepreneurs, jurists, philanthropists, entertainers, publishers, and legions upon legions of scholars; not mere psychoanalysts and "critical theorists," but physicists, mathematicians, medical researchers, historians, economists—even, as MacDonald notes honestly in his new preface, evolutionary psychologists! The first American song whose words I knew was "White Christmas," written by a first-generation Ashkenazi Jewish immigrant. The first boss I ever had in this country was a Jew who had served honorably in the US Marine Corps. Perhaps it is true, as MacDonald claims, that "most of those prosecuted for spying for the Soviet Union [i.e., in the 1940s and 1950s] were Jews." It is also true, however, that much of the secret research they betrayed to their country's enemies was the work of Jewish scientists. The Rosenbergs sold the Bomb to the Soviets; but without Jewish physicists, there would have been no Bomb to sell. Last spring I attended a conference of mathematicians attempting to crack a particularly intractable problem in analytic number theory. A high proportion of the two-hundred-odd attendees were Jews, including at least two from Israel. Sowers of discord there have certainly been, but on balance, I cannot see how anyone could deny that this country is enormously better off for the contributions of Jews. Similarly for every other nation that has liberated the energies and intelligence of Jewish citizens. Was Hungary better off, or worse off, after the 1867 *Ausgleich*? Was Spain better off, or worse off, before the 1492 expulsions? "To ask the question is to answer it."

Now, Kevin MacDonald might argue that he, as a social scientist, is not obliged to provide any such balance in his works, any more than a clinical pathologist writing about disease should be expected to include an acknowledgment that most of his readers will be healthy for most of their lives. I agree. A scientist, even a social scientist, need not present any facts other than those he has uncovered by diligent inquiry in his particular narrow field. He is under no obligation, as a scientist, to soothe the feelings of those whose sensibilities might be offended by his discoveries. Given the highly combustible nature of MacDonald's material, however, it wouldn't have hurt to point out the huge, indisputably net-positive, contributions of Jews to America, right at the beginning of his book, and again at the end. MacDonald has in any case been fairly free in *CofC* with his own opinions on such matters as US support for Israel, immigration policy, and so on. He is entitled to those opinions: but having included them in this book, his claim to dwell only in the aery realm of cold scientific objectivity does not sound very convincing.

This is, after all, in the dictionary definition of the term, an anti-Semitic book. Its entire argument is that the Jews, collectively, are up to no good. This may of course be true, and MacDonald is entitled to say that the issue of whether his results are anti-Semitic is nugatory, from a social-science point of view, by comparison with the issue of their truth content. I agree with that, too: but given the well-known history of this topic, it seems singularly obtuse of MacDonald not to keep a jar of oil close at hand to spread on the troubled waters his work is bound to stir up. From my own indirect, and rather scanty, knowledge of the man, I would put this down to a personality combination of prickliness and unworldliness, but I am not sure I could persuade less charitable souls that my interpretation is the correct one, and that there is not malice lurking behind MacDonald's elaborate sociological jargon.

Be Nice or We'll Crush You

Jewcy

FEBRUARY 28, 2007

The following is part of an extended email exchange with Joey Kurtzman, editor of the Jewish periodical *Jewcy*.

FROM: John Derbyshire

TO: Joey Kurtzman

SUBJECT: The flame of thoughtful conservatism burns low

All right, Joey, I will indulge your curiosity.

If tomorrow I submitted a piece to *National Review* saying, "Kevin MacDonald is really onto something. He's doing great work and I think everyone should read him," the editors would reject the piece, and they would be right to do so. I don't think I would be canned for submitting such an article, but if it happened, I would not be much surprised.

You forget how lonely conservatives are. The flame of thoughtful, responsible American conservatism burns low, and needs constant careful attention. In the folk mythology of present-day America, conservatism is associated with Jim Crow and the persecution of racial minorities. I have not the slightest doubt that many millions, probably tens of millions, of Americans believe that, say, Pat Buchanan is a secret member of the Ku Klux Klan.

I live in an ordinary middle-middle-class New York suburban neighborhood. My neighbors all know I am a conservative commentator. A couple of them will not speak to me on that account. The others just think I am mildly nuts—a thing associated in their minds, somehow, with my being British-born. They regard me with a sort of amused sympathy. The nearest conservative I know lives about eight miles away.

Anyone running a mainstream conservative magazine has to constantly demonstrate ideological purity in matters of race. They have to show repeatedly, by indirect means of course (I mean, it would be no use to just stamp *"This is not an anti-Semitic magazine! We do not favor the return of Jim Crow Laws!"* in Day-Glo letters on the cover) that they are ideologically pure in this zone. Otherwise, they won't be taken seriously by the cultural establishment.

And that matters. In America, persons who have, or are suspected to have, incorrect opinions on race, are low status. Human beings are primarily social animals, and we are intensely conscious of status rankings within the groups we belong to.

The best guide here is novelist Tom Wolfe. Recall that passage in *The Bonfire of the Vanities* (1988)—I don't have the book on hand so I'm working from memory here—where the young New York district attorney and his wife have hired a British nanny to look after their baby. This makes for an uncomfortable situation at first, because British people get status points in urban US society just on account of being British. (Yes, of course it's absurd, but I assure you it is the case.)

So this struggling, ill-paid young DA and his wife, both from modest backgrounds, have an employee with more status points than a domestic servant ought to have. The status structure of their household is out of joint. Then one day the nanny makes some mildly un-PC remark about black people, and the DA and his wife fairly weep with relief. The nanny is low status after all! Nothing to worry about!

So if *National Review* were to print unqualified praise (or even praise not severely qualified) of a guy who argues that Jews have a "group evolutionary strategy" that involves the transformation—I think in *The Culture of Critique* MacDonald actually says "destruction"—of Gentile society, they would have done what that nanny did: dumped several status points down the toilet.

A conservative magazine simply can't afford to do that. Its hold on the attention of the US public is too precarious. A conservative magazine can't afford to let a writer say anything nice about MacDonald without putting it under some such title as "The Marx of the Anti-Semites."

There isn't any kind of chicanery or dishonesty there. That's just how the world is, how America is, under what Bill Buckley calls "the prevailing structure of taboos," and the prevailing system of status perception, both of individual human beings and of easily anthropomorphizable entities like opinion magazines.

National Review wants to get certain ideas out to the US public—ideas about economics, politics, law, religion, science, history, the arts, and more. To do that, the magazine needs standing in our broad cultural milieu. It needs status. That's hard at the best of times for a conservative publication. To lose status points—to lose standing—just in order to draw readers' attention to some rather abstruse socio-historical theories cooked up by a cranky small-college faculty member, would be dumb. Ergo, as I said, *National Review* would reject a piece of the kind you suggested, and they would be correct to do so. *I* would do so if I were editor of *National Review*.

To your next point (I am working from the bottom up again) that my professed fear of ticking off Jews is some kind of affectation or pose, I can only assure you that this is not so. Almost the first thing you hear from old hands when you go into opinion journalism in the United States is, to put it in the precise form I first heard it: "Don't f*ck with the Jews." (Though I had better add here that I was mixing mainly with British expats at that point, and the comment came from one of them. More on this in a moment.)

Joe Sobran expressed it with his usual hyperbole: "You must only ever write of us as a passive, powerless, historically oppressed minority, struggling to maintain our ancient identity in a world where all the odds are against us, poor helpless us, poor persecuted and beleaguered us! Otherwise we will smash you to pieces."

Though if you look up the William Cash affair* I mentioned in my last post, Sobran's quip is really not all that hyperbolic. When the *Los Angeles Times*, the *New York Times*, the CEO of United International Pictures, Barbra Streisand, assorted other media bigshots, and of course the ever-vigilant Mr. Leon Wieseltier, all denounce you in public, you are in pretty serious trouble.

---

*   For more information on the William Cash affair, see page 141.

This may be characteristic only of conservative journalism—I don't know, never having done the other kind. A person doing liberal-oriented opinion journalism surely needs no such cautions, having completely internalized all the "blank slate," egalitarian, and victimological tenets of the majority culture, and the status-ordering precepts I sketched above. (And this is even leaving aside the high probability that a liberal commentator is anyway Jewish himself!)

The place of Jews in modern American conservatism is a deep and fascinating story, with of course the conversion of the neocons at its center. You have to bear in mind the overwhelming dominance of Jews in every kind of leftist movement in the United States until about thirty years ago. Yuri Slezkine has the astonishing numbers. (Did you know that of the four student protesters shot by National Guardsmen at Kent State in 1970, three were Jewish? So says Slezkine, anyway. If you take four people at random from the US population, the chance that three or more of them will be Jewish, given the most generous estimate of the proportion of Jews in the population, is worse than one in four thousand.)

In any case, it was a great achievement, and a great boost, for American conservatism to have peeled off a platoon of articulate, energetic intellectual heavyweights from the great socialistic mass of American Jewry.

Generally speaking—and I certainly include myself here—American conservatism is proud of its Jews, and glad to have them on board. Not that there aren't some frictions, particularly on mass immigration, the mere contemplation of which just seems to make Jews swoon with ecstasy (American Jews, at any rate. Israeli Jews have a different opinion . . .). MacDonald gives over a whole chapter of *The Culture of Critique* to the Jewish-American passion for mass immigration.

There is also some odd kind of bonding going on between Jewish conservatives and evangelical Christians. I say "odd" because of how, I imagine, this bonding would have looked to the grandparents of today's Jews. The explanation I have most commonly heard is that Jewish conservatives want to be accommodating toward evangelicals because the latter are friendly to Israel. Hence you get prominent Jewish intellectuals saying nice things about nutty evangelical preoccupations like intelligent design.

The Israel explanation doesn't seem particularly convincing to me. Don't evangelicals want all the Jews to return to Israel so that the End Times can commence, in the course of which the Jews will be annihilated? Nevertheless, once or twice a week I read something that leaves me thinking that in the mind of this or that Jewish conservative intellectual, evangelical Christianity is "good for the Jews."

At any rate, these minor frictions and divisions are inevitable in a movement as broadly defined as conservatism. Jews are welcome in the American conservative movement. The great energy and intelligence of Jews, and their strong sense of group identity, do, though, sometimes lead to the same kinds of pathologies in the conservative movement as Kevin MacDonald logged in the Jews' self-created movements (such as Freudianism, Boasian anthropology, and the New York intellectuals).

In particular, they are under the same temptation to defer to charismatic intellectual "rabbis," and to enforce rigid standards of orthodoxy, with vituperation and expulsion for dissidents. I'd emphasize that these are occasional tendencies, and I believe they are much less marked among Jewish conservatives than among, say, Freudians (or for that matter among Jewish liberals). They are there, though; and if you get on the wrong side of them, you are in deep doo-doo.

And in the larger culture, a Gentile conservative who riles up Jewish liberals is really asking for trouble. You could ask William Cash.

Let me deal with your point about the British, and the larger point about group identification.

On the Brits: You are certainly right that the correct approach here is anthropological; though I don't think your insufferable tone of sneering moral superiority would be tolerated in professional anthropological circles today.

So far as I understand modern theories of the mind, a great deal of our brainpower is given over to processing social information. The theory that seems to me most plausible involves three different modules in the brain: a relationship module, a social module, and a status module.

The relationship module manages our one-on-one relationships with other human beings. It includes a sort of lexicon of all the persons we know, tagged by their attributes as we see them. (Not just common attributes like "fat" or "red-haired," but me-centric attributes like "enemy" or "borrowed my copy of *The Culture of Critique* and never returned it.")

A second, the social module, manages our behavior in our group, and our attitudes to our group and to outside groups. Group stereotypes, for example, that perform very valuable social-psychological functions, dwell in this module.

A third, the status module, computes our status within our group, either by objective criteria, or by attempting to "read" the entries about us in other people's relationship-module lexicons, via those people's external behavior. This status module has algorithms for computing status. The code of the algorithms, and the data we input to them, differs from one society to another, and from one group to another in a given society. (We all belong to several groups, of course.)

Among the Masais, a male's status in his village is measured by the number of cattle he owns. An American academic who belongs to the groups "mathematicians," "dedicated amateur hang-gliders," and "opera lovers" will measure his status in the first group by how many papers he has published, his status in the second by how long he has managed to stay aloft, and his status in the third by how many donations he has given to his local opera company.

Now, in the broad and general group "respectable middle-class Americans," one's attitudes toward other races are very, very important criteria in determining one's status. A person like the nanny in that Tom Wolfe novel, who reveals incorrect attitudes on race, suffers massive loss of status thereby.

As criteria for status-in-group evaluation, these attitudes are less important in Britain. In many subsets of modern middle-class British society, mildly negative remarks about black people, like those uttered by the nanny, would not lose you any status points at all.

This does not mean that Americans are morally superior to Britons; still less does it mean that Britons are more sophisticated, more worldly-wise, than Americans. All it means is that for historical reasons—mainly because the United States once had legal race slavery, while the British Isles (as opposed to the British territories overseas) never did—British people compute status-in-group slightly differently from the way Americans compute it. The nanny's error was to assume that her employers' status modules were running the same code as British people's. Coming from Britain to the United States, I made many such errors myself, and still occasionally do.

So far as it is possible to make generalizations about such things, British behavior in this regard is closer to the norm for modern humans than is American behavior. The critical importance of racial attitudes in middle-class American status rankings is extraordinary. This has been the case for decades. Agatha Christie's 1939 novel *Ten Little Niggers* was deemed unpublishable under that title by US publishers even then; they changed the title for US audiences. Yet the play version was being performed in provincial British theaters, under Christie's original title, well into the late 1960s.

As I said, this is not a question of moral superiority on the part of Americans, nor of superior worldliness on the part of Brits; it's just that our thinking is slightly different, probably as a result of different national-historical experiences. (Though as always nowadays, group genetic peculiarities cannot be ruled out. Recent studies indicate that the population of the British Isles has been very little disturbed for tens of thousands of years. The successive invasions of Celts, Romans, Teutons, and Normans only slightly altered a common Paleolithic genome, likely derived from a small, and therefore distinctive, founder group.)

The exquisite sensitivity of Americans in these matters causes no end of misunderstanding and bad feelings, as the William Cash episode shows. I am sorry to say that it often makes Americans look like hypocrites to foreigners, making rather a mockery of all our pretensions to moral superiority. House hunting in the New York suburbs in 1992, my (Chinese-born) wife and I were once sitting in the office of a realtor, an American lady, trying to spell out just what we were looking for. We had no kids at the time, but were moving to the burbs precisely to raise a family. Well, chatting with the realtor, I said that of course we wanted to be in a good school system, one with not too many black kids. The realtor's reaction was similar to the one described by P. G. Wodehouse when he wrote: "Ice formed on the butler's upper slopes."

You don't say things like that. You just do them: Practically no white Americans, looking for a place where they can settle down and raise a family, will seek a school district that is majority black. In fact, that realtor, when she had thawed some, carried out what I am sure is her normal procedure of steering us well away from heavily black school districts. Patterns of housing segregation in the United States speak for themselves, very eloquently. This is, however, the only way in which honest speech about race in America is allowed. (I believe, in fact, that if the realtor had said: "Don't worry, I won't waste your time and mine by showing you properties in heavily black neighborhoods," she would have been breaking the law. Her behavior, however, was indistinguishable from what it would have been if she had said that, and meant it.)

And if you are not raised in the United States, you are sometimes totally nonplussed by the stuff native-born Americans come out with in this area. For example, I stared hard at the following paragraph of yours, struggling to get some sense out of it:

> Like *Irishman* and other antiquated coinages, it suggests that ethnicity is a fundamental feature of a person's identity. . . . American Jews, like other Americans, dislike that implication, and we once dealt with it by insisting on wacky constructions such as "Americans of the Hebrew faith."

"Irishman" is an "antiquated coinage"? This is news to me. What, then, am I supposed to say this week? "Person of Irishness"? And does calling someone an Irishman really "suggest that ethnicity is a fundamental feature of a person's identity"? All it suggests to me is that the guy comes from Ireland.

And if American Jews "dislike" the notion that "ethnicity is a fundamental feature of a person's identity," then why are we having these exchanges? And why is "Americans of the Hebrew faith" any more risible than "persons of the Hibernian ethnicity," or whatever damn fool thing it is you want me to say instead of "Irishman"?

I once wrote a novel about Chinese people. My first-person narrator, a Chinese immigrant in America, refers to himself once or twice as "an Oriental." The book reviewer for *USA Today* took me to task for that. "Oriental," she told me sternly, was a word that could only be used for carpets and furniture. For people, the correct term was "Asian American."

So I guess Confucius, Li Po, and Mao Tse-tung were all "Asian Americans." And then, of course, there was that wonderful moment in the 2002 Winter Olympics when a black American woman won a gold medal, thereby becoming the first black woman from any country to win a winter gold. The announcer for the NBC network could not bring himself to say it as I just said it, though. God forbid anyone should think he had noticed the lady's blackness! The only way he could bring himself to say it was: "She's the first African-American woman from any country to win a winter gold medal." I'm sorry, but this stuff just makes me fall around laughing.

Now to the very interesting question of whether or not ethnicity *is* "a fundamental feature of a person's identity." I think the only honest answer is that for some people, including some Jews, it surely is, at least some of the time, and for others, not.

Look: My ethnicity (white English) is part of what I am. It is one of the groups I identify with. This is not deplorable, or wicked, or exclusivist of me; it is just human, dammit. We are social animals who organize ourselves into groups. An individual in a complex modern society identifies with several groups. These identifications have different weights in his mind; in fact, they have different weights (the term of art is "salience") in different circumstances.

I had occasion to remark recently, in a discussion elsewhere about whether or not I am a racist, that I would feel much more at ease in a room full of black African mathematicians than I would in a room full of white English soccer hooligans. In the first group my salient identification would be "mathematician," and I would be a mathematician at ease among mathematicians.

My identification with the group "white English" would not be very salient in that group—definitely not as salient as it would be if I wandered into a bar on 125th Street in Manhattan. In the second group I would be very uncomfortably aware of my membership in the group "bookish types who dislike physical violence and have little interest in sport." That would be my salient group identification in that milieu; and as the only person in the room nursing that group identification, I would be exceedingly ill at ease.

Membership in the group "Jewish people" must be something every Jew is aware of at least some of the time, even if it is only rarely his salient group identification. Jewishness is, after all, as group identifications go—compared with "white English," for example—exceptionally well defined and historically rooted.

To draw from Slezkine's fine book again, those Russian Jews who consciously de-Judaized themselves in the late-nineteenth and early twentieth centuries, and moved from the Pale into metropolitan Russia, and became such an important part of the Bolshevik revolution and the Soviet state suddenly found their Jewishness—which they thought they had shucked off, left behind in the shtetl!—very, very salient when Hitler's Panzers rolled across the border. It's situational, see.

The idea you seem to be retailing—that these group identifications, with all their inner complexities of status, and all their situational vagaries of salience is all some airy figment of our imaginations, or some relic of a barbarous era we (or at any rate, the most morally advanced of us) have left behind—strikes me as bizarre and preposterous to the furthest degree. Do you really believe that? Good grief!

The beginning of wisdom is to look at humanity as it is, with its arms and legs, its eyes and tongues, its livers and kidneys, and its brains organized into modules, in some way like I sketched above, those modules busily processing information—information about light and temperature, visual and aural information, and above all (for we are social animals) social information.

I may choose, freely choose, to treat my fellow human beings well or badly; but my interactions with them are governed by my brain, which has evolved with the ability to do some things but not others. Utter indifference to group identity is a thing the brain cannot do. The denial of human nature gets us nowhere.

Whatever we think of Kevin MacDonald and his theories about Jews and their "group evolutionary strategy," he is at least talking about a real human personality, one that I recognize when I look at myself and other people. It's a personality that is aware of belonging to groups, that vies for status in those groups and that nurses negative feelings of various degrees to at least some other groups. Even when it wishes no harm to any other group, if given the choice between advancing the interests of a group it belongs to, versus advancing the interests of a group it does not belong to, the human personality will choose the former action nine times out of ten.

That is humanity as I know it, and as the great novelists and dramatists have portrayed it, and as the human sciences are beginning to uncover it in fine detail through such disciplines as evolutionary history. The bloodless, deracinated, group-indifferent, "blank slate," omnisympathetic creature promoted by the merchants of political correctness is one I do not recognize as human. Those merchants are human, though, for all they seek to deny it. Their lofty pretensions to have risen high above us grubby group-identifying lesser beings strike me as just another form, a particularly obnoxious form, of in-group status-striving.

Best,
JD

Are There Enough Jews on the Supreme Court?

Secular Right

MAY 16, 2010

THERE HAS been some muted comment about the religious composition of the US Supreme Court after a Kagan approval: six Catholics, three Jews.

Is this enough Jews, though? Let's crunch numbers.

First permit me to switch from religion to self-identifying ethnicity, which is closer to how this stuff actually works. Less than two percent of non-Hispanic white Americans are religious Jews, but around five percent have Jewish ancestry and consider themselves to some degree Jewish. Let me just take, as round numbers, 220 million non-Hispanic white Americans, ten million of them self-identifying (to some degree) Jewish. You can of course rework the following with different numbers if you like.

There are nine seats on the US Supreme Court. By general agreement (it seems to me) there is one quota-seat for an African American, one for a Hispanic. That leaves seven seats available for non-Hispanic white justices. How many of those seven would we expect to go to Jewish nominees?

Leaving aside the obvious temptation to carry out a five-thousand-word analysis on that word "expect," let's *drastically* simplify: Let's pick 'em by IQ. Supposing non-Hispanic white Gentiles to have mean IQ 100 and Jews mean IQ 112 (the figure usually cited, though again you can re-crunch with a different number if you like), with standard deviation 15 in both cases, here's what I get for various cutoff minimum IQs:

MIN IQ	GENTILES	JEWS	SEATS
110	53,023,433	5,530,351	0.66
115	33,317,603	4,207,403	0.78
120	19,154,356	2,969,014	0.94
125	10,035,974	1,930,623	1.13
130	4,777,528	1,150,697	1.36
135	2,061,219	625,969	1.63
140	804,380	309,741	1.95
145	283,479	139,034	2.30
150	90,103	56,492	2.70
155	25,802	20,741	3.12
160	6,651	6,871	3.56
165	1,542	2,052	4.00
170	321	552	4.42
175	60	133	4.82
180	10	29	5.19
185	2	6	5.51
190	0	1	5.80

You get three Jewish seats round about cutoff IQ 153, which is pretty darn smart—only 43,000 non-Hispanic white Gentile Americans are that smart. At cutoff 165 you'd expect four Jewish seats; at around 178 you'd expect five.

That's all highly abstract, of course. It assumes up front that anyone actually *wants* justices as smart as possible, when what presidents usually want is justices that (a) are on their side, lib-con-wise, and (b) are sufficiently bland and unimaginative never to have said or written anything that will raise an eyebrow from the drones on the confirmation committee.

It also assumes that a 180-IQ nominee would be better at judging cases than a 140-IQ-er. That's not obvious to me. I favor the "sweet spot" notion of IQ, where cognitive ability + sense/wisdom max out around 125–135, the sense/wisdom component then dropping off steeply in higher IQ numbers. If that's right, we may have one Jewish justice too many!

CHAPTER SIX:

The Asians

Importing Sino-Fascism

VDARE

SEPTEMBER 13, 2000

I HAVE proposed before on *VDARE* that immigrants from different cultures—even, as David Hackett Fischer showed in *Albion's Seed* (1989), from different regions of England—bring quite different notions of governance, nationhood, and citizenship with them. These attitudes can be very persistent, surviving long after actual memories of the "old country" are forgotten.

The first part of this proposition has been brought home to me with great force recently. A few months ago, I signed up for an email list run by and for Chinese software engineers in the United States. A Chinese friend told me it was a good place to pick up software tips, a matter of professional interest to me. He also said that I, as the author of a novel about Chinese people in America (*Seeing Calvin Coolidge in a Dream*) might find interesting some of the occasional opinion pieces posted on the list.

The list turned out to be of little use. Notices of volleyball games, advertisements for rooms to rent, and advice on immigration issues were the main topics. Software tips were few and far between, and a query of my own went unanswered. The few opinion pieces were mostly vaudeville head-whacking exchanges between proponents of Taiwan independence and the Mainland One-China crowd.

I did notice that the Mainlander sides of these exchanges were expressed with extraordinary vehemence. A typical line of argument was that the Taiwanese had been psychologically deformed by the Japanese occupation (which ended fifty-five years ago!) and yearned to abandon their Chineseness and become slaves of the Japanese. A fiercer element thought that China should use her nuclear weapons against Taiwan, to "teach them a lesson." (On historical and oratorical evidence, China must be the odds-on favorite for the title "First Nation to Nuke Its Own People." As far back as the Korean War, Madame Chiang Kai-shek asked the United States to use atomic weapons against her countrymen.) The Taiwaners mainly responded with patient explanations that they didn't want to fall into the hands of the Chinese Communist Party, and that, given the CCP's historical record, nobody could blame them.

Eventually I decided to put my two cents in. The topic of Taiwan seemed a bit inflammatory, so I offered some fairly commonplace remarks about whether a democratized China would be able to hold on to the western territories of Tibet and East Turkestan. The base populations of those territories are non-Chinese and do not want to be ruled by China, and presumably would say so at the ballot box. If China was to have democracy (I said), this conundrum would have to be faced.

I signed myself off with my Chinese name—not out of any real intent to deceive, only because this was a Chinese e-list and I thought they might throw me off if they knew I was a round-eye. At this point I was still hoping the list might be useful.

The response to my mild, questioning remarks was astonishing. What kind of Chinese was I, that wanted to dismember the Motherland? Didn't I know that those territories had been Chinese since the beginning of time? That their inhabitants were sunk in slavery and oppression under wicked priests and landlords until rescued by Chinese occupation? (Yes, these two assertions were often made by the same person.) That all the countries of the world recognized Chinese sovereignty over them? That China's right of possession had been acknowledged by the Nationalist governments of the 1930s and 1940s, even before Mao came along? The range of tones was from baffled to furious. How could a Chinese person cast doubt on the integrity of the national borders?

We went back and forth a few times, until someone noticed that my sign-off Chinese name, "Yuehan," was the common Chinese transcription of "John." Was I really Chinese? I confessed frankly that I am not; that I am an Englishman living in America, with a Mainland-Chinese wife and two half-Chinese children.

Now the floodgates of race-hatred opened. One of the subsequent emails addressed me as: "England Big Nose." Another offered, as part of a long, labored attempt at sarcasm, to "kiss my hairy hand." Yet a third laid out a very complicated psychological theory trying to demonstrate (if I have understood it correctly) that for a white man to wish to marry a Chinese woman was a form of mental illness, dooming both partners to misery and their offspring to madness. Hardly any of these charming epistles failed to remind me that the British were notorious imperialists, of infamous rapacity and cruelty, whose dream of everlasting world domination now lay in ashes. There was a general opinion that we British must be fuming with rage at the impudence of our once-subject peoples in throwing us out, and that this impotent fury was what accounted for our willingness to say such incomprehensibly shocking things as that Tibetans might prefer to be ruled by other Tibetans rather than by Chinese.

Bear in mind, please, that the writers of these emails are the intellectual cream of Mainland China, now immigrants to the United States. Few do not have master's degrees; many have PhDs. The average age is around thirty, I suppose. Their academic and professional qualifications, and their command of English, are sufficient to have impressed an American consul into awarding them a visa—no easy matter, allegedly. Yet for all this, their notions about national sovereignty were essentially those of the Ming dynasty mandarinate, and their knowledge of history a collection of false and preposterous clichés.

Underneath all this were some even more disturbing currents: a deep, atavistic hatred of the West and all its works; a profound scorn for Western "civilization" and "democracy"—the quotation marks seem to be obligatory. Also, a rooted conviction that China had never done anything wrong, and never could. Here are the words (I have polished the grammar a little) from a correspondent who has a master's in sociology from Peking University, a very prestigious institution:

> Every time I read recent Chinese history, I can't help crying. What did we do in the past to make this nation, this race suffer so much? Nothing we did! It was those "honorable," "democratic," and "noble" Western "civilized" people and culture! . . . I suffer as my nation suffers, I cry as my people cry.

Now the greatest catastrophes to afflict the Chinese people this past fifty years have been:

- the post-Revolution "land reform" (1949–52)
- the Anti-Rightist campaigns (1957–58)
- the "Great Leap Forward" famine (1959–61)
- the Cultural Revolution (1966–76)

Total deaths: about sixty-five million. Total foreign involvement: zero.

If you go further back, to earlier horrors such as the Boxer uprising (1900) and the Taiping rebellion (1852–64), the West does indeed share some small part of the responsibility. Yet even here, the overwhelming majority of Chinese dead (twelve to fifteen million in the Taiping) were killed by other Chinese, acting on Chinese orders.

"Nothing we did!" All the fault of the foreign devils!

That writer is by no means a lone eccentric. This is the voice of the new generation of Mainland Chinese, born in the 1970s and 1980s: puffed up with self-pity and self-righteousness, all their rage and frustration directed against the outside world, utterly ignorant of the modern history of their country. A well-adjusted Chinese citizen is expected to have "moved on" from the horrors of the Mao period (1949–76), yet to be seething with indignation about the Opium Wars (1839–42).

This mindset has been fostered by the Communist educational system. As Steven W. Mosher has documented in his new book *Hegemon: The Chinese Plan to Dominate Asia and the World* (2000), the Communists have been at pains to replace the discredited Marxist-Leninist rationale for their rule with nationalism of the grossest and coarsest type. Chinese school history textbooks make no mention of the 1959–61 famine—in terms of the number dead, a greater human calamity than World War Two—but dwell bitterly on the tale about a sign saying NO DOGS OR CHINESE at the entrance to a Shanghai park in the 1920s. (Does anybody know if this story is true?) This hypernationalism is not limited to the schools, either; it is carried over to movies, TV shows, popular magazines, and even roadside billboards.

> *Cherish the Motherland, which never has done, and never could do, any wrong. Hate the foreign devils, who have inflicted untold miseries on our people, and who never cease plotting to weaken and dismember our country. The borders of the People's Republic [which are actually those of the Manchu empire, minus Outer Mongolia] are sacred and inviolable, and must not be questioned.*

This is the worldview with which Chinese people emerge from their schools and universities. "England Big Nose" and "hairy hand" are the terms in which China's MAs and PhDs address foreigners who question these dogmas. What thoughts swirl in the minds of less well-educated, less-privileged young Mainlanders, one can only wonder.

Now, an American—especially, perhaps, an American who has logged on to *VDARE*—might say: "Good luck to them! I only wish our people would be that fierce in their nationalism." He might also point out that I could have got some similar responses from an e-group of Irish software engineers.

Both reactions miss the point. Modern Western nationalisms such as the American and Irish are tied up with a longing for freedom from oppression, and have been tempered and civilized by Enlightenment rationalism. The emotions let loose in my little encounter were premodern, primitive; uninformed by anything from the Enlightenment, or even from the Reformation or the Renaissance for that matter, and unconnected to—in fact, rabidly hostile to—any concept of liberty, self-determination, or government by consent.

I have sat with Irishmen for long evenings, discussing their history and their nationhood as topics on which different points of view might be exchanged, different opinions passionately, yet reasonably, held. No such discussion is possible with these younger Mainland Chinese. When you raise their "national question," they just lose their temper and ask how you dare be so impudent as to offer an opinion on something that only concerns Chinese people. If you ask them whether they would prefer a free, democratic China *without* the "three Ts" (Tibet, Turkestan, and Taiwan) or the present corrupt despotism *with* them, they unhesitatingly go for the latter.

Moreover, this Chinese group feeling is consciously racial and explicitly anti-white. Irish immigrants do not have this reflex working to alienate them from their new countrymen.

The United States now has several million Chinese immigrants and soon-to-be citizens who are at least susceptible to these prehistoric attitudes. Across the Pacific, there are a billion more—armed with nuclear weapons.

Be afraid; be very afraid.

An Arctic Alliance?

New English Review

OCTOBER 2007

A CHINESE (Chinese-born, Chinese-educated, came to the West as an adult) friend of mine made a remark to me a few months ago that has been bobbing up to the surface of my mind at intervals ever since.

I should preface my retailing of it by noting that the Chinese are considerably more outspoken on issues of human biodiversity than is considered polite in the West. This should not be taken as crude or insensitive. It is only that China is an overwhelmingly monoracial country. Away from a few expatriate communities in major cities such as Shanghai, and small non-Chinese minorities on the fringes of the empire, well-nigh everybody you meet in China is Chinese: black straight hair, dark eyes with epicanthic folds, yellowish glabrous skin, small hands and feet, and—according to the late Carleton S. Coon (*The Living Races of Man* [1965]), crumbly earwax. Only rarely, if ever, meeting people of other human stocks, Chinese people have had no need to develop much in the way of racial etiquette.

Well, my friend and I were talking about demographics. It's a popular topic of conversation nowadays, as it has hooks into so many of our contemporary concerns: the Islamization of Europe, our own ructions over illegal immigration, the future funding of our welfare systems, and so on.

We shared the opinion—it is pretty much a commonplace among educated Chinese people—that China's demographic future will follow the example already set by Japan and South Korea, both of which nations have rates of fertility that are sensationally low, and still falling. (Total fertility rates for Japan, South Korea, and China are 1.23, 1.28, and 1.75, respectively. The United States is at 2.09.)

My friend repeated the observation, which I have heard many times from Chinese acquaintances, that so far as urban young women are concerned, the One Child Policy is nugatory. These yuppie gals are far too busy building careers and sampling the newfound delights of consumerism to bother with breeding. If not for parental pressure and the remnants of Confucian filial piety, they would forgo even the one child.

"Ah," sighed my friend, "I am afraid that the civilized races—yours and mine, the white and the yellow—are finished. We will die out. The browns and the blacks will inherit the earth."

Please do not be shocked, gentle reader. As I said, there is a different standard of outspokenness at work there. And if you drop the offensive word "civilized"—I am not here going to argue the relative merits of Chartres, the Taj Mahal, the Temple of Heaven, Great Zimbabwe, Angkor Wat, and Tenochtitlan's Great Temple—my friend may very well be right. From a UN press release:

> Because of its low and declining rate of population growth, the population of developed countries as a whole is expected to remain virtually unchanged between 2005 and 2050. . . . Very rapid population growth is expected to prevail in a number of developing countries, the majority of which are least developed. . . . The population of 51 countries or areas, including Germany, Italy, Japan, and most of the successor States of the former USSR, is expected to be lower in 2050 than in 2005. . . . During 2005–2050, eight countries are expected to account for half of the world's projected population increase: India, Pakistan, Nigeria, the Democratic Republic of the Congo, Bangladesh, Uganda, the United States of America, Ethiopia, and China, listed according to the size of their contribution to population growth . . .[81]

The actual *numbers* for the projected increases in those eight named countries, in tens of millions, are: 58, 14, 17, 13, 11, 6, 10, 12, and 8. The figure of 10 (that is, a hundred million) for the United States is, as that last link points out, about thirty percent due to projected immigration, with much of the rest due to the high birthrates of recent youthful immigrant cohorts. Practically all of it will be minorities.

Still leaving aside the implied slur in "civilized" (not going there, just *not*), let's contemplate the question: Can we all get along?

A striking thing about the great existential military conflicts of the industrial age, from Napoleon's wars to the Cold War, is that the principal nations involved were European or East Asian. Let's take a hint from my friend and consider these nations all together: the EuroSinoNippons, or (very loosely speaking) the Arctics.

From the perspective of 2007, the intra-Arctic nature of all nineteenth- and twentieth-century major conflict really is striking. I recently went to look something up in Niall Ferguson's fine book about World War One, *The Pity of War* (1999). I got to browsing in it, and found myself reflecting on how unthinkable such a clash of nations would be today, if the nations were all Europeans. You can even throw Vladimir Putin's glowering Russia into the mix: A great existential war between Europeans is simply not going to happen again. Who thinks it is? Who even talks about it?

Can the same be said more broadly of the Arctics? People *do* talk about, and I suppose even worry about, a war between China and the United States. I am not one of those people. There is simply no sufficient *casus belli*. A Chinese blockade of Taiwan, or even an attempted invasion, would outrage Americans, but I very much doubt there would be any real support for going to war. China is not—trust me—going to make a grab for Alaska or Hawaii.

Other possibilities—a Russo-Chinese war for resources in Siberia, a Sino-Japanese war over . . . what?—seems to me equally remote. The inclination of the modern Chinese is to buy what they need, with at worst some diplomatic browbeating of competitors, and covert support to willing but undemocratic supplier regimes. To the degree that the United States remains an Arctic nation, I see no prospect of future intra-Arctic conflict.

The Temperates and the Tropicals are a different matter. Taking the Temperates to be the swathe of peoples from North Africa, through the Middle East, across Pakistan, north India, and Bangladesh, we are already in a state of conflict or serious tension with several nations, on account of the fact that this is the primary zone of Islam. Whether the current conflict is an existential one is a matter of opinion. Norman Podhoretz thinks it is,[82] but many of us disagree with him.

Islam is a factor in the Tropicals, too—the nations of sub-Saharan Africa and Southeast Asia—but not such an essential one, even in

Indonesia. (I am assuming throughout that the Latin Americans will continue to vegetate in inconsequentiality as they did through the last century.)

The determinants of geopolitics over the next few decades will be:

- The degree of intra-Arctic solidarity, our nations united in a common concern about demographic collapse, and in common anxieties about threats from Temperates.
- The degree to which Europe, the United States, and the old British dominions (Canada, Australia, New Zealand) can maintain their identity as Arctics while their populations of immigrant Temperates and Tropicals swell.
- The ability of Arctic nations to maintain their edge over Temperates and Tropicals in intelligence and creativity. (Lynn and Vanhanen's comprehensive studies suggest a gross mean IQ of over 100 for the Arctics, about 90 for the Temperates, less than 80 for the Tropicals.[83])

Perhaps it is time that we Arctics resolved to sink our minor differences and address our common problems, beginning with those demographic ones.

The Ice People Club

Secular Right

OCTOBER 11, 2009

I S THERE, as some commentators have claimed, affirmative action at work in the awarding of Nobel Prizes?

If there is, it has been almost entirely restricted to the Peace Prize in recent years. The Nobel Committee publishes a year-by-year list of winners, with photographs and clues to nationality. Scanning back through the last ten years, I get the following head counts.

I have used the Ice People/Sun People schema of *We Are Doomed*,[84] with Europeans and East Asians as Ice People, Africans and Amerindians as Sun People. Subcontinental Asians I have cut crudely, with Muslims as honorary Sun People and non-Muslims as honorary Ice People. It's a fair balance, I think, and doesn't actually make much difference to the numbers.

Here we go. For each year I list the six Nobel categories in order: Physics, Chemistry, Medicine, Literature, Peace, and Economics. The score in each box is Ice People/Sun People, so "2–0" means two Ice People and no Sun People.

That gives us totals of 28–0 for Physics, 25–0 for Chemistry, 27–0 for Medicine, 10–0 for Literature, 4–6 for Peace, 19–0 for Economics.

There are some gray patches. The guy from Mauritius may be a Muslim,[85] for all I know—one-sixth of Mauritians are. It doesn't make

YEAR	PHYSICS	CHEMISTRY	MEDICINE	LITERATURE	PEACE	ECONOMICS
2009	3-0	3-0	3-0	1-0	0-1	2-0
2008	3-0	3-0	3-0	1-0	1-0	1-0
2007	2-0	1-0	3-0	1-0	1-0	3-0
2006	2-0	1-0	2-0	1-0	0-1	1-0
2005	3-0	3-0	3-0	1-0	0-1	2-0
2004	3-0	3-0	2-0	1-0	0-1	2-0
2003	3-0	2-0	2-0	1-0	0-1	2-0
2002	3-0	3-0	3-0	1-0	1-0	1-0
2001	3-0	3-0	3-0	1-0	0-1	3-0
2000	3-0	3-0	3-0	1-0	1-0	2-0

much difference. The Nobel Prize looks awfully like an Ice People club, and those earnest Scandinavians feel terrible about it.

Maternity and Tyranny

National Review

FEBRUARY 7, 2011

A MY CHUA, who is a law professor at Yale University, has a new book out: *Battle Hymn of the Tiger Mother* (2011). The book describes the parenting methods Professor Chua employed when raising her two daughters, now aged eighteen and fourteen. An extract published in the January 8 *Wall Street Journal* caused a small sensation.[86] Within a week, the online version of the extract had generated more than six thousand comments and was the talk of the nation.

Professor Chua's prescriptions are, to put it very mildly indeed, at odds with current American notions of wise parenting. Determined "not to raise a soft, entitled child," she makes her daughters' childhood sound like Marine Corps boot camp minus the rest breaks. This, she argues, with some supporting statistics, is the Chinese way. (Professor Chua is of Chinese ancestry.) "Western parents are concerned about their children's psyches. Chinese parents aren't. They assume strength, not fragility, and as a result they behave very differently."

Professor Chua relentlessly harassed, bullied, and insulted her daughters to do the best they could do in schoolwork and music practice. They were forbidden all "frivolous" activities, with the word "frivolous" encompassing well-nigh anything nonacademic, including most forms of peer-group socialization. Her daughters, she tells us, were never allowed to have sleepovers, or to be in a school play, or to watch TV, or to get any grade less than an A, or to "not be the No. 1 student in every subject except gym and drama," or to play any instrument other than the piano or violin. When the younger daughter, then seven, was unable to master a difficult piano piece, Tiger Mom took the girl's treasured dollhouse to the car with a threat to donate it to the Salvation Army. Then she kept the child at the piano "through dinner into the night," even refusing to let her go to the bathroom.

Professor Chua's article was a bracing rebuttal to the sappy-clappy "we're all special" sentimentality that is too prevalent in American child-raising. Her methods worked, too, at least in meeting her own goals: Her daughters are straight-A students, and one has played piano at Carnegie Hall. Probably we American parents *should* practice more tough love with our kids and fuss less about their self-esteem. Few of us would disagree with observations such as, "Nothing is fun until you're good at it. To get good at anything you have to work, and children on their own never want to work." And assuming "strength, not fragility" concurs with current scientific understanding of the child's psyche. They are indeed tough little critters.

There are, however, things to be noted. One is that the Chua kids are very smart, as the offspring of two Ivy League professors are likely to be. (Professor Chua's husband, Jed Rubenfeld, is also a Yale law professor. Her father was a professor of computer science at Berkeley.) Most features of personality, including intelligence and conscientiousness, are considerably heritable. They appear very early in life and are stable thereafter.

Some of these traits occur at different frequencies in different ethnic populations. Daniel Freedman, a developmental psychologist, conducted a study in the 1970s of the behavior of newborns in San Francisco, working with his wife, Nina Chinn, who is Chinese. They found significant differences between Chinese and Caucasian babies: "Caucasian babies cried more easily, and once started, they were harder to console. Chinese babies adapted to almost any position in which they were placed," etc., etc. The babies were less than forty-eight hours old.

It is also worth noting that there are severe logical problems inherent in the idea of a school full of children whose tiger moms demand they be the No. 1 student in all academic subjects, and that the intense parental investment displayed by Professor Chua is problematic in families larger than hers—begs, in fact, for a "one-child policy." Even the most determined tiger mom might find her zeal flagging at child number three or number four.

Furthermore, most people are not very academically inclined. If a child's natural bent is toward some other kind of excellence—social, mechanical, athletic, creative—Chua-style parenting will only misdirect him. Children need some nagging and supervision, but they also need freedom to explore, to discover their own interests and aptitudes. We may, in our current child-raising practices, have overemphasized self-esteem and self-discovery, but that does not make these notions nuga-tory. Children are entitled to a *childhood*, with frequent spells of play, idleness, and freedom from hovering adults.

That is certainly the case made by the classic Anglo-American liter-ary classics on boyhood: *The Adventures of Tom Sawyer* (1876) and *The Adventures of Huckleberry Finn* (1884), Booth Tarkington's *Penrod* (1914), and Richmal Crompton's *Just William* books (1922–70). All emphasize liberty, mischief, adventure, and disdain for adult authority. Reading Professor Chua's extract, I found myself thinking: "No boy of spirit would put up with that." Was Professor Chua's task made easier by the fact of her children being female? Perhaps not: In a follow-up interview with the *New York Times* she tells us that her younger daugh-ter staged bitter rebellions: "Lulu, then 13, begins smashing glasses in a Moscow restaurant and yelling at her mother, 'I HATE my life, I HATE you.'"[87]

There is too the matter of national culture and our ideas about what kind of fellow-citizens we wish to live among. The United States is not a bookish nation. Milton Friedman's great essay "The Role of Govern-ment in Education" (1955) barely mentions academic excellence. Its focus is on liberty. If parents want their kids to study basket-weaving or social dancing, let them exercise their free choice, says Friedman. "That is their business."[88] The bookish grind is not a hero to Americans, unless he is a successful entrepreneur. Bill Gates dropped out of Harvard. Robert Weissberg, in his recent book *Bad Students, Not Bad Schools* (2010), notes the president of an American college who declared his ambition to be that his school develop an academic program the football team could be proud of. That's the American way.

We might also, with no particular offense intended toward Professor Chua's ancestors, ask what China has reaped from the methods of tiger moms. The social order in imperial China was encapsulated in the phrase *shi nong gong shang*. At the top were the *shi*, the scholar-bureau-crats who had passed the imperial examinations, thereby acquiring a ticket to government employment. Then came *nong*, the farmers, then *gong*, the craftsmen. Last of all were the *shang*, the despised merchants.

American society has never been like that. The history of imperial China suggests that this is something we should be grateful for. Nor does modern China, with its vast inequality, its endemic corruption, and its thuggish, lawless government, offer an attractive advertisement for Chinese mommery.

We are not, at least not yet, a nation of arrogant credentialed mandarins tax-farming a cowed, sullen peasantry. We are a commercial republic of free citizens under impartial laws: a nation of tinkerers and inventors, of entrepreneurs and prospectors, pioneers and adventurers, barn-raisers and welcome wagons, dreamers and debaters, preachers and politicians. Our kids should be raised appropriately, free to seek out and build upon their own enthusiasms, which will not often include Advanced Placement calculus or classical piano.

A Study of Unchanged National Character

VDARE

FEBRUARY 18, 2018

The following is a review of Paul Midler's *What's Wrong with China* (2017).

T HE CHINESE sure can be exasperating. Paul Midler writes in his new book *What's Wrong with China*:

> No one is sure when it began, but the phrase "I'm having a bad China day" has become synonymous with the expatriate experience. . . . Those who become testy in this country are not limited to the cholerically predisposed. China has a way of also taking easygoing milquetoasts and turning them into hotheads. The phenomenon is so common that long-term expatriates have coined various terms: *The Laowai Wigout*, *The Expat Snap*, and *Angry Foreigner Syndrome* are three such expressions floating around the bigger metropolitan areas.

(*Laowai* is the common—informal, nonhostile—Chinese term for a foreigner, equivalent to Japanese *gaijin*. During my own China days in the early 1980s the usual expat term for the syndrome under discussion here was "China Fatigue." I, a representative of the easygoing milquetoast community, recall experiencing one or two episodes.)

Paul Midler is an Old China Hand. He has lived and worked in China for more than twenty years, mainly as a business consultant helping foreign firms in their dealings with Chinese manufacturers. His wife is Chinese. His 2009 book *Poorly Made in China* (reviewed by me on NRO[89]) is wonderfully informative on the Chinese way of doing business.

These two books of his are in a fine old tradition, to which Midler pays homage in the very title of this latter one.

I encountered that tradition myself when studying Chinese in London thirty-eight years ago. I had a reader's ticket to the magnificent library of SOAS, the School of Oriental and African Studies, and spent whole days there, in the stacks of the China section.

I can read Chinese only with difficulty, though; so after two or three hours of intense cognitive effort I would, for relaxation, drift over to the shelves of English-language books about China.

The items that most got my interest there were the memoirs and diaries of foreigners living in China during the nineteenth and early twentieth centuries—the late-imperial and republican periods.

The SOAS library has a great collection of these, almost all by authors whose names have sunk into oblivion: missionaries, merchants, diplomats, adventurers, and oddities such as the botanist Robert Fortune (who was one of the most upbeat: "In no country in the world is there less real misery and want than in China."[90] That was written in the mid-1840s.)

One particularly striking book in that genre is Rodney Gilbert's *What's Wrong with China*, first published in 1926. I was so taken with this book, I acquired a copy of my own from the secondhand shelves at Probsthain's oriental bookstore, around the corner from SOAS.

I still have that copy: So there are now two books on my own shelves with exactly the same title but by different authors, published ninety-two years apart.

Rodney Gilbert wrote with a frankness about race that would make his book utterly unpublishable nowadays, and he sometimes slipped into the supercilious diction of a Victorian lady complaining about the servants. At one point he actually *does* complain about his servants.

Also, Gilbert's partiality for his own race occasionally led him into error. He recounts, for instance, the episode from the Battle of Maldon in AD 991 when the Anglo-Saxon leader allowed his Viking enemies to ford a waterway and form up for battle before he attacked them. No Chinese leader, said Gilbert, would ever show such chivalry.

Wrong! In fact there is a closely parallel incident in Chinese history from the Battle of Hongshui (638 BC), the source of a well-known remark of Mao Tse-tung's.[91]

If you can get past all that, though, Rodney Gilbert, writing a long lifetime ago, had some penetrating insights into China's history, culture, and national character.

Most of those insights are of a negative kind. For a person so intimately acquainted with the Chinese people, he seems not to have liked them much. His keynote, which he returns to again and again, is:

> In China the psychic flame burns low, for want of fuel.

Gilbert is not uniformly negative, though. He gives credit where he thinks it's due.

> Like all Orientals, [the Chinese] have a strong dramatic sense, and a professional storyteller, speaking his primitive and undeveloped language [by comparison with the classical style of the scholarly literati, Gilbert means], can rise to heights in characterization, description, narrative and metaphor to which not one Occidental in ten thousand could aspire in his own tongue. An infallible sense of rhythm and cadence is born in the great majority of Chinese. In ordinary speech, they divide their sentences up into euphoniously balanced periods . . . [92]

Paul Midler quotes Rodney Gilbert numerous times in this new book for which he has borrowed Gilbert's title. He also quotes many other foreign commentators from that late-imperial, early republican period. I get the impression Midler had the same experience I had when studying Chinese. But for a few years' difference in the dates of our studies, we might unknowingly have bumped into each other among the stacks in SOAS library.

Much water has of course flowed under the bridge since those earlier observers wrote. Midler, however, does not think the quality of observation has improved.

> It is curious that books written on China in the 1960s— Dennis Bloodworth's *The Chinese Looking-Glass* (1967) is

> an example—should read finer than most of what is pro-
> duced these days, and that even these books pale in compar-
> ison to the works of the previous generation. The trend
> appears to go back quite some time. In the 1930s, Ralph
> Townsend was convinced that his contemporaries wrote
> nothing as accurate as that which was produced by Arthur
> Smith [1890s][93] and Abbé Huc [1840s][94] . . . Economic and
> technological progress alone ought to have made it easier to
> watch China; but modernity, as it turns out, had actually a
> negative influence. . . . You will find more insights in a book
> written one hundred years ago than in something written
> last month.

I think that's right as a generalization. Reading it, in fact, brought to
mind something I have found myself thinking rather often in recent
years: The much-discussed Flynn Effect notwithstanding, we are in some
important, unquantified way stupider than our forebears of a hundred
years ago. Paul Midler is, however, an exception to that generalization.
His observations, based on those twenty years of wrangling with Chinese exporters, take us right back to the unsparing, unillusioned cri-
tiques of those *old* Old China Hands.

Like them, he is eloquent on the ferociously optimizing skills in
negotiation that Chinese people bring to commercial transactions.

> Chinese factory owners hate to see their customers happy,
> because it means that money has been left on the table.

Similarly with Chinese customers. A Chinese friend of mine, once
established in America, decided to buy a car. He picked the model he
wanted, went to a showroom, and began haggling. So persistent was
he—"Oh come on, you can give me another fifty dollars on that!"—they
threw him out, almost literally. Two of the salesmen pushed him into the
street, one at each elbow.

"That," he exulted, telling me the story, "was when I knew I'd
found their price!"

The downside of this high level of commercial acumen is long-term
commercial failure. Chinese merchants can't resist the temptation to kill
the golden goose for the sake of a couple more cents on the dollar.

Midler tells the story of tea, which I think is quite well-known.
Given that tea is native to China, not (except very marginally) to India,
why did the West end up drinking Indian tea, not Chinese tea? Midler:

The tea industry collapsed in part because growers were sending leaves to market without drying them. This was not a time-saving maneuver. It was done because wet leaves weigh more, and the additional weight brought in more revenue. The problem with moisture is that it leads to mold, which affects taste.

Some similar style of cheating may have affected the opium trade, with dire consequences.

In the grand scale of psychoactive substances, opium as smoked in China from the seventeenth century onward is not exceptionally harmful. A wealthy Chinese opium smoker " 'does not seem much the worse' for his habit," noted an 1890s observer (quoted by Midler).

So why was opium smoking so devastating among China's poor? Adulteration, says Midler. In the extreme, a cheap variety named Hankow Cake contained no opium at all, only sesame seeds. Midler:

> Historians are so hell-bent on blaming the West for everything that went wrong with China in the nineteenth century that they have no room for an investigation into the serious possibility that the nation may have actually poisoned itself.

I would like to see some rigorous historical research on that, but it's not implausible, and fits very well with the tiresome Chinese bellyaching about the wrongs done to them by foreigners.

Chinese people acknowledge that an individual fellow-countryman may be wicked, but China *as a nation* can do no wrong.

National self-esteem is of course not an exclusively Chinese phenomenon. We Americans—well, some of us—treasure our "exceptionalism." Chinese propagandists take it to the extreme, though.

Midler calls it "collective narcissism" and quotes Lucian Pye, writing fifty years ago:

> Nothing can be wrong with the Chinese spirit and their inward identity. All problems must lie outside and therefore be the work of "foreigners."

The most wince-inducing aspect of this national trait is the frequent announcements out of Peking that some action by some foreign government—holding a meeting with the Dalai Lama, for example—has "hurt the feelings of the Chinese people." Poor things!

Midler shows that there is nothing communist, or at all modern, about this ploy. He tracks it back to a 1901 article written by Wu Ting-fang, an official in the imperial government, who implored foreign critics to "respect the feelings of the Chinese." Our author really has read everything.

That point, and many others Midler has drawn from his reading and his commercial dealings, reinforces the grand theme of foreign commentary on China down through the ages: continuity.

The great event in China's twentieth-century history was Mao Tse-tung's revolution. Mao boasted that he would remake China into a socialist utopia.

No such thing happened. In fact nothing much happened. There was a spell of turmoil, to be sure; but when the dust settled, all was as before under Heaven.

> The supreme ruler possesses the same attributes and discharges the same functions; the governing classes are chosen in the same manner; the people are bound in the same state of servitude, and enjoy the same practical liberty; all is now as it was.[95]

Leszek Kolakowski in *Main Currents of Marxism* (1976) described Mao Tse-tung's thought as "a naïve repetition of a few commonplaces of Leninist-Stalinist Marxism." He allows, however, that Mao was "one of the greatest, if not the very greatest, manipulator of large masses of human beings in the twentieth century."

So Maoism was a cheap Chinese knock-off of Marxism-Leninism. Once Mao's extraordinary personality ceased to drive events, the political system quickly reverted to the imperial norm.

The continuity of national character comes out clearly in Midler's use of older commentators. Mao's revolution, for all its upheavals and horrors, had very little effect on the national psyche, perhaps none at all.

To speak of a "national psyche" nowadays, however, is to trespass into the minefield of Political Incorrectness. The Scots are mean, we used to say blithely; the French are arrogant; the Germans are orderly; the Italians, excitable; the Russians, gloomy; the Irish, pugnacious; and so on.

Saying such things aloud in 2018 will get you horsewhipped on the steps of your club; but common observation suggests that there is some underlying reality to these unmentionable old perceptions, as is usually the case with stereotypes.

(In the current enstupidated condition of our public discourse about human nature, the weary commentator is obliged to add that these are statistical generalities. *Of course* there exist generous Scots, humble Frenchmen, disorganized Germans, placid Italians, and cheerful Russians. There may even be placatory Irishmen: I don't know, I couldn't say.)

The Chinese in this schema are characterized by love of money and addiction to gambling. Midler:

> Whenever you read about a stampede in India, you can rest assured that it has taken place during a religious festival. In Europe, stampedes that result in death usually happen at sporting events. In China, the mad rush of a crowd almost always has something to do with economics. A sales promotion on cooking oil and rumors of a rice shortage have both sent Chinese into frenzied action.

What, then, *is* wrong with China? Paul Midler offers many suggestions. He tells us for example that the Chinese, their colossal national self-regard notwithstanding, have no faith in the permanence of their political arrangements. All Chinese people, including the rulers, have internalized the dynastic cycle. Every Chinese person knows the opening words of a classic novel written seven hundred years ago:

> What was long divided must unite,
> What was long united must divide.[96]

Much, says Midler, flows from this; the passion to get while the getting is good, the gambling instinct, the leaders' determination to put off the inevitable day of dissolution as long as possible by fierce repression, and so on.

The Chinese also nurse ambivalence about their relation to the other peoples of the world. For long millennia the situation was clear to them: They were a civilized enclave surrounded by barbarians.

The nineteenth-century encounter with Europeans woke China from this particular opium dream, but they have not yet found an alternative equilibrium point on which to rest their identity.

Rodney Gilbert thought the Chinese of ninety years ago yearned to be isolated once again. If he was right, Mao Tse-tung fulfilled that yearning, isolating China for thirty years. The results were not altogether satisfactory, and now China poses as a nation among other nations.

The pronouncements of China's leaders, though, suggest that their hearts aren't really in it. Chinese nationalism is something other than Westphalian; Chinese globalism, as currently manifested in the Belt and

Road initiative, has a clumsy, out-of-tune quality to it, so that it inspires not admiration and respect, only suspicion and fear.[97]

China's internal governance, too, is chronically unstable. Midler:

> China is a vase teetering on its edge, and maintaining balance has been a goal throughout its history.

He goes on to give an account of post-1949 China's lurching from centralization to decentralization and back.

None of this should be taken as a slander on the Chinese, although of course it *will* be so taken. They, like the rest of us, have emerged as they are, in all their distinctness, from the long slow churnings of history, geography, and population genetics.

And, as Midler writes:

> Much of what's wrong with China is actually something wrong within us. We are too fond of this country. We are too forgiving. We willingly have amnesia on the basis that we care.

He is writing there about the remarkably unadvertised fact that the Chinese have conducted many massacres of foreigners.

Why *are* so many of us so forgivingly fond of this exasperating, paradoxical, unstable place? Paul Midler quotes from the answer given by Progressive sociologist Edward Alsworth Ross in 1911.

> Chinese are extremely likable and those who have known them longest like them best. Almost invariably those who harshly disparage them are people who are coarse or narrow or bigoted. They are not a sour or sullen folk. Smile at them and back comes a look that puts you on a footing of mutual understanding. Their lively sense of humor is a bond that unites them to the foreigner.

Ross (1866–1951) is an odd person for Midler to quote in this context. He would himself be denounced as the worst kind of bigot today. He was a race realist, nativist, and eugenicist who strongly objected to race mixing—so strongly, he was fired from his professorship at Stanford in 1900 for his views.

Much as he liked the Chinese, Ross did not want them settling in the United States. This is a perfectly tenable position, although intolerably shocking to present-day orthodoxies.

Ross got the likability right, though, and "those who have known them longest like them best." (Rodney Gilbert may have been an exception.)

And to the further collective credit of the Chinese must be added this: Unlike the nations of the West today, they have no intention of opening up the borders of their nation to tens of millions of foreigners. Stupidity on that scale is peculiarly Western.

What's wrong with *us*?

The Arctic Alliance Revisited

VDARE

MAY 19, 2019

Originally a speech delivered to the American Renaissance conference and published on *VDARE* shortly afterward.

G REETINGS, FELLOW heretics! Permit me to introduce myself. My name is John Derbyshire. I was born and raised in England, but have spent most of my life—at this point, actually fifty-one percent—in the United States.

I am a freelance writer. When I tell someone that, a frequent response is: "That's nice. But what do you do for a *living*?" Well, that's my living, and has been for eighteen years. I haven't gotten rich, but I haven't gone hungry, either.

Not that the writing business has worked out as I intended. I started with the aim to be a novelist, using persons and situations from out of my own imagination and experience to make penetrating observations about human nature and the human condition.

As it turned out, far and away my best-selling book has been a non-fiction work about mathematics.[98]

Sixteen years after its publication, I still get a nice royalty check from it twice a year. That's not bad in the book business. Still, like the slapstick comedian who yearns to play Hamlet, I would rather have been a novelist.

These are the vicissitudes of fate.

MY 2007 COLUMN "AN ARCTIC ALLIANCE"

ACROSS THE YEARS I have also produced a vast mass of fugitive journalism for various outlets—book reviews and opinion pieces. The great majority of that mass has sunk without trace, no doubt deservedly, although I have tried to be diligent about archiving it at my personal website www.johnderbyshire.com.

There have, however, been a handful of pieces that caught the attention of many readers in such a way that I still get asked about them years later. One of those was a column I wrote in October 2007 for *New English Review*, a web magazine that is the brainchild of a charming and energetic lady here in Tennessee. The title of the piece was "An Arctic Alliance?"

This was a throwaway opinion piece that I wrote to meet a deadline. It is not closely argued and contains no very deep analysis. It does, however, offer an idea that I believe is worth airing, and which I have not seen discussed elsewhere. That idea is contained in the title, which I shall now unpack.

First, the word "Arctic." I divide the human race into Arctics and non-Arctics on paleoanthropological grounds. So Arctics are those present-day races whose remote ancestors inhabited the forests and tundra of northern Eurasia—the whites and the yellows, to a first approximation. In my book *We Are Doomed* (2009) I used the synonym "Ice People."

In the world today, the Arctics exhibit two characteristics that separate them quite clearly from non-Arctics, or "Sun People."

- ◆ High intelligence. The world average IQ is somewhere in the 80s—82 is the latest estimate I have seen.[99] Among Arctics the average is much higher, probably over 100, with the mean for East Asians slightly higher than the one for whites.
- ◆ Low fertility. For stable population size you need a mean TFR of 2.1 children per woman. Hardly any Arctic nations have TFR that high.[100] Some are sensationally low (Taiwan 1.13). Practically all nations with higher TFR are non-Arctic. Many are sensationally high (Niger 6.35).

It thus seems that Arctics face a demographic threat, and humanity at large a longer-term dysgenic threat.

My 2007 article suggested that we Arctics—whites and yellows—put our clever heads together and come up with a common strategy against those threats. Hence the word "Alliance" in my title.

COMMON OBJECTIONS

ACROSS THE YEARS I have met with many objections to the idea of an Arctic Alliance. In the rest of this talk I shall cover the commonest of those objections.

Objection #1: "Arctics" is absurd.

Singapore is majority East Asian [i.e., what I call "Arctic"] but it's only one degree north of the equator!

And what about Native Americans, whose deep ancestry is Siberian?

So weren't the Aztecs, Mayans, and Incas all "Arctics"? And therefore likewise their present-day descendants, the Indios and mestizos of Latin America?

My Reply

The underlying question here is: Why did some Arctic peoples of the remote past evolve into modern races with high mean IQ and low mean fertility, even while (much) later spreading into the Tropical zone, while others evolved differently?

Answer: I don't know. I have, however, read enough about human origins, history, and population genetics to be unsurprised at this outcome. It is not absurd: Genetic change of the required magnitude in isolated populations is certainly a possibility across ten thousand years. So is stasis.

But I concede that my usage of "Arctics" is short for "Arctics who have remained stubbornly 'Arctic.'"

Objection #2: Alliance or Union?

Are you suggesting that we subsume our nationhood in some kind of EU-style union with Russians and East Asians?

My Reply

I am a strong nationalist. The sovereign nation-state, with a settled, ethnically stable population, minding its own affairs under its own historically evolved folkways, is my preferred form of highest-level political organization.

I hope only for common awareness *among* Ice People nations of the impending threat, and some common strategy in dealing with it without compromising our national sovereignties in any supranational union.

Objection #3: Projection

Some unkind people have scoffed that I was merely projecting my own domestic circumstances onto the world at large. (I am married to a Chinese lady.)

My Reply

Possibly I was, but the Arctic Alliance may nonetheless be worth considering.

Stopped clocks occasionally show the right time. George Orwell remarked that some things are true *even though* the Party says they are true. Similarly, some ideas are worth considering *even though* the person who offers them for consideration is working from personal motives.

Tell me why there are *no* such threats as I have described, and why the Arctic Alliance is *not* worth considering on its own merits.

Objection #4: The Long Twentieth Century

My column noted that all the great existential military conflicts of the industrial age, from Napoleon's wars to the Cold War, were fought between Arctic nations.

I seemed to assume that that era is over; that a new age has dawned in which an Arctic Alliance is possible.

Yet in fact the national passions and rivalries that generated those wars are very much alive. Ask a Chinese person for an opinion of Japan. Ask a Russian for an opinion of America (or an American neocon about Russia). Ask a North Korean . . . anything.

The age of intra-Arctic conflict has not ended. We are still, as it were, in the twentieth century, just as people in the years 1900–1914 were still in the nineteenth century—as historians say, "the long nineteenth century."[101]

My Reply

See my reply to the next item. Closely related to that point are a group of criticisms I put under the heading:

Objection #5: The Narcissism of Minor Differences

Similarity on genetic or paleoanthropological grounds is no guarantee of harmony, nor even of the ability to work together for common goals.

If you had lived in Belfast in 1972, you would have noticed that the white Irish Protestants and white Irish Catholics of that city had *much* stronger group feelings directed against each other than either had toward blacks or Muslims.

Charles Darwin in *On the Origin of Species*, chapter IV:

> [I]t is the most closely-allied forms,—varieties of the same species, and species of the same genus or of related genera, —which, from having nearly the same structure, constitution, and habits, generally come into the severest competition with each other; consequently, each new variety or species, during the progress of its formation, will generally press hardest on its nearest kindred, and tend to exterminate them.

Sigmund Freud remarked on a similar phenomenon in *Civilization and Its Discontents*. He called it "the narcissism of minor differences."

I have enlisted this principle in my own writings about America's current ideological conflict, calling that conflict "the Cold Civil War"— two big groups of white people who can't stand the sight of each other, with other races sometimes pulled in as auxiliaries to feed the horses and dig field latrines.

If you engage in today's ideological conflict you quickly notice that American whites care passionately what other whites think and say; but no white person cares what blacks, Indios, or Asians think. They are *hors de combat*.

So why should not intra-Arctic tensions and animosities prove stronger than common interests in defending against Sun People?

My Reply

They might. History suggests that uniting against a common peril does not come easily to human beings. It is most likely to come when the peril is obvious, urgent, and existential.

OK; but if boatloads of black Africans in the Mediterranean and "caravans" of Indios swarming our southern border don't rouse Arctics to thoughts of common defense, what might?

Well, even bigger numbers—*much* bigger numbers—might. Those numbers are coming.

Or disease might. Back in January 2018, after President Trump was revealed to have used a low scatological expression when referring privately to certain countries, I did some research on sanitary conditions worldwide, and reported on those researches in my *VDARE*.com weekly podcast.

At a listener's suggestion, I then read Rose George's recent book *The Big Necessity: The Unmentionable World of Human Waste and Why It Matters* (2008).

Suffice it to say that I hope I never have to go to India for any reason.

Compounding the issue is the fact that in Sun People countries that are *not* desperately poor—India again leads the way here—overuse of strong antibiotics is rampant. This of course accelerates the evolution of antibiotic-resistant pathogens.

So a sudden, major, unifying threat from Sun People nations may be not demographic but epidemiological.

Objection #6: The Polar Alliance

I have had emails from, and two or three personal encounters with, persons from the Antipodes saying, "What about *us*?"

Should not Australia, New Zealand, and the white countries of the southern South American "cone"—Argentina, Chile, and Uruguay—be included in the Alliance? They face the same issues as ourselves, notably the threat of mass Sun People immigration.

My Reply

Paleoanthropologically speaking, these southern hemisphere peoples are still Arctics, not Antarctics. However, for public relations purposes, I might consider soothing their feelings by renaming my concept to "the Polar Alliance."

(My first thought was "the Bipolar Alliance." Then I realized what unpleasantly clinical connotations that has . . .)

(And the list of our southern-hemisphere brethren should of course include white South Africans, at least for a while longer.)

Objection #7: The White Race Is Too Far Gone in Ethnomasochism

While East Asians (China, Japan, Korea, Mongolia) have remained demographically conservative, *white* Arctics have sold the demographic pass, recklessly importing great masses of Sun People into their homelands.

This process has gone too far now to be reversible.

Why should East Asians yoke themselves in an alliance with whites, who are clearly a loser race with a collective death wish?

My Reply

Why indeed? But this is a counsel of despair. Movements like ours exist in the hope of reversing the ethnomasochistic trend. *Dum spiramus, speramus.**

And while that point is a depressing one, it is not the *most* depressing response I have received. Here is the real wrist-slitter:

Objection #8: Ethnomasochism Is an Inevitable Development in ANY Post-Industrial Society

There is nothing exclusively white about ethnomasochism. East Asians just aren't there yet. We Arctics are *all* headed into multiculturalism.

My Reply

Yes, there are periodic news stories about Japan loosening up on immigration. On the other hand, the rules remain strict and selective.

On the other *other* hand, there are now more than two hundred mosques in Japan, up from just two in 1970.

And there is a big colony of black Africans in Guangzhou, South China's megacity. Their numbers have been declining the past five years, it's true; but the decline has been driven more by economic and public-health issues than by Chinese ethnocentrism. Most of the Africans are merchants whose fortunes depend on movements in the commodities markets, and recent movements have been all against them. Further, the SARS epidemic of the early 2000s badly spooked the Chinese government, so that when Ebola hit the international headlines in 2014, they clamped down hard on African immigration.

So: Are these things—loosening of Japanese immigration, African settlement in China—minor circumstantial aberrations, or straws in the multicultural wind?

I don't know. East Asian ethnocentrism looks pretty robust to me; but then, I am old enough to remember when British ethnocentrism looked robust.

Could East Asians succumb to multiculturalism? I wouldn't say it's impossible. *Will* they? I don't know.

---

* "While we breathe, we hope."

CHAPTER SEVEN:

Religion

The Uses of Quietism

The New Criterion

APRIL 2002

The following is a review of Laozi's *Dao De Jing: The Book of the Way*, translated and with commentary by Moss Roberts (1997).*

T HE CONNECTION between simple-life quietism and the political Left has often been noted. Orwell, in his diatribes against the armchair progressives he so despised, never failed to include, along with Trotskyite poets, pamphleteering pacifists, and "pink" sodomites, the legions of sandal-wearing, vegetarian, teetotaling tree-huggers he knew so well from Independent Labour Party summer schools. Among my own acquaintances are two dear old friends in England, a married couple, who are Left as Left can be: keen readers of the *Guardian* (Britain's furthest-left broadsheet newspaper), hostile to nuclear weapons and nuclear power, anti-American and, while the USSR existed, pro-Soviet, convinced that the troubles of the Middle East all result from the machinations of the oil companies, and so on. The wife was in fact a red-diaper baby: Her parents were principals in the post-war Austrian Communist Party. They are both simple-lifers, who owned

---

* Note: Professor Roberts has used the most popular current method for transliterating Chinese, in which an unapostrophized "t" becomes a "d" and an unapostrophized "ch" often becomes a "j."

no television or car until well into their forties; he briefly ran a self-sufficient craft commune in rural Lincolnshire.

Homemade furniture and worship of state power; nutburgers and anti-Americanism; why this persistent connection? I think we all have a sketchy idea of how it hangs together. For deeper understanding, though, you could do worse than pick up the *Tao Tê Ching*. A new annotated translation of this classic text of ancient Chinese quietism has just been produced by Moss Roberts, professor of Chinese at New York University. Roberts's version of the *Tao Tê Ching* (from which I have taken all quotes below, except where I have clearly indicated a different translator) raises the political issue with unusual clarity. Why this is so, and where, if anywhere, the trail leads, are matters I shall return to presently. First, some background on the *Tao Tê Ching*.

– ♦ ♦ ♦ –

I IMAGINE THE one thing that everyone knows about the *Tao Tê Ching* is that it was written by a sage named Lao Tzŭ. This is, in point of fact, the thing least worth knowing. Lao Tzŭ may or may not have existed; and, supposing he existed, he may or may not have written the *Tao Tê Ching*. We simply have no idea, nor any way to pursue the matter. We have no accounts of Lao Tzŭ by people who knew him, nor any knowledge of his relationships with other writers of his time (most likely the later fifth or early fourth century BC, if he existed). There are some stories about him, but they all have an apocryphal quality to them. There is even a thumbnail biography by the historian Sima Qian, "the Chinese Herodotus," but it was written at least two centuries, and a huge national convulsion, after the latest date at which Lao Tzŭ could have lived, if he lived, and is not supported by any other evidence. Lao Tzŭ is a blank, a mystery.

Which is entirely fitting, because the *Tao Tê Ching* is fundamentally a work of mysticism. Organized as eighty-one stanzas of mixed verse and prose, it includes material on several different topics: self-cultivation, statecraft, military science, health. All this, however, is set in a metaphysical framework, and the metaphysics is of the mystical type, with principal elements that accord with the mystical truths revealed in other times and places, and that will be familiar to anyone who has looked into mysticism of any school. We are given to understand that there is an all-embracing law or spirit called the Tao (that is, the Way), which is supreme in the universe and governs the workings of nature. There is a corresponding spirit moving human beings, named Tê (that is, Virtue—this word is pronounced "duh"). Tao and Tê work together in one of those dualities the ancient Chinese thinkers were so fond of, like Heaven and Earth, *yin* and *yang*, gods and demons, *ren* (benevolence) and *yi* (righteousness), or the prince and the minister—those last two dualities much worked over by Confucius. The interaction of these dualities generates all the phenomena of the so-called "real world." Both Tao and Tê are essentially ineffable, but by certain spiritual exercises we can attain enough acquaintance with them to improve our lives, our government, our military prowess, and even apparently our health. These exercises center on the cultivation of something called *wu-wei*, which translators have variously rendered as "nonaction," "unattached action," "Non-Ado," "not-doing," and so on. Here are the first lines of stanza 48 in Moss Roberts's translation:

> To pursue learning, learn more day by day;
> To pursue the Way, unlearn it day by day:
> Unlearn and then unlearn again
> Until there is nothing to pursue;
> No end pursued, no end ungained.

These precepts are explicitly enjoined upon the rulers of states, who are assured that if they practice *wu-wei* on their subjects' behalf, then tranquility, harmony, and sufficiency will result. Doctor Johnson said that George the First "knew nothing, and desired to know nothing; did nothing, and desired to do nothing." This, apparently, would be the ideal Taoist ruler.

The political "tendency" of the *Tao Tê Ching* at first looks to be reactionary in the extreme. Boats, carriages, and mechanical contrivances of all kinds are condemned as deplorably newfangled, hindrances to the peace of mind of the common people. Even writing is objected to:

> Guide them back to early times,
> When knotted chords served for signs. (stanza 80)
> The people are, in fact, to be kept as ignorant as possible:
> Thus under a wise man's rule
> Blank are their minds
> But full their bellies. (stanza 3)

Talk about the simple life! These lines are uncharacteristically explicit, though. Most of the *Tao Tê Ching* is written in an enigmatic style that occasionally defies translation altogether, even by experts. "There is no consensus on the first two lines of this stanza," Roberts admits in his annotation of stanza 10. For another instance, consider the famous couplet that opens stanza 38. In Chinese: *Shang de bu de, Shi-yi you de*—literally "Upper virtue not virtue, Therefore has virtue." Say what? (Roberts: "High virtue by obliging not / Acquires moral force.")

Part of the problem is in the nature of the classical Chinese language. In its earliest form—the form employed in *Tao Tê Ching*, and by all the other great philosophers—written Chinese was extremely abbreviated in its syntax. Even modern Chinese people cannot read the language of the classics easily without special training. The purpose of early written Chinese was really mnemonic—to help one recall matter acquired by oral transmission, not to tell you something you didn't know before. This makes for an extremely short-winded form of presentation. In book 1, chapter 9 of the *Analects* of Confucius, for example, we read the four-character injunction: *Shen zhong zhui yuan* (慎終追遠). James Legge translates this as: "Let there be a careful attention to perform the funeral rites to parents, and let them be followed when long gone with the ceremonies of sacrifice"—a syllable-to-syllable ratio of very nearly one to ten. (It would be about one to six in modern colloquial Chinese.) Burton Watson, in the introduction to his invaluable handbook *Early Chinese Literature* (1962), emits the following sigh of exasperation: "Is it too much to ask that the writer indicate at least the subject of the sentence? . . . In the case of classical Chinese the answer is usually, yes."

- ◆ ◆ ◆ -

ONE CONSEQUENCE OF all this minimalism is that translators can "color" their work in many different ways. Dr. Ching-Hsiung Wu, for example, who was a Catholic,* produced a version of *Tao Tê Ching* in 1961 that has been very popular with Christians:

> . . . only he who is willing to give his body for the sake of the world is fit to be entrusted with the world.
> Only he who can do it with love is worthy of being the steward of the world. (stanza 13)

---

* Among other notable accomplishments, Ching-Hsiung Wu (1899–1986) served as Minister Plenipotentiary to the Holy See under Chiang Kai-shek's government on Taiwan.

Similarly, Witter Bynner's *The Way of Life According to Laotzu* (1944) reflects his own pacifism, the more strongly felt because his country was at war: "[T]he way for a vital man to go is not the way of a soldier" (stanza 31).

Moss Roberts's view is that the book should be taken mainly as a treatise on statecraft. Thus where, in the first line of stanza 41, other translators render *shang shi* as "scholars of the highest class" (Legge), "men of stamina" (Bynner), "a wise scholar" (Wu), or "superior students" (Charles Muller), Roberts says: "men of service." Similarly with the passage: "Block all exchanges, shut all doors," in stanza 52. Other translators take this as a command to withdraw from social intercourse, the better to cultivate oneself, but Roberts sees it as in line with other instructions to the ruler to keep his people ignorant.

This business of keeping the people ignorant has now turned up twice in these notes and is critical to an understanding of Taoism's political consequences. At first sight it is difficult to fathom how a doctrine so mystical, quietist, and extremely reactionary could have any political consequences at all. In ancient China, though, well-nigh the only available employment for men of letters was as advisers to the princes who ruled the petty kingdoms of that time, and who were engaged in a constant and unblinking struggle for mastery over each other. A philosopher who had nothing to say about statecraft could get no hearing, and so all the schools had political consequences. Those that flowed from the *Tao Tê Ching* were of particular importance, and the most important of them all was the development of Legalism.

Legalism is traditionally supposed to have been thought up by a gentleman with the title Lord of Shang, who lived 390–338 BC and served as an adviser to Count Xiao, ruler of the state of Qin in northwest China. To place the origins of Legalism with this person, though, is certainly an oversimplification, and the so-called *Book of Lord Shang* (there is an English translation by J. J. L. Duyvendak) is for the most part a later forgery. There are, however, good reasons to think that it offers a fairly true picture of the means by which Lord Shang reformed Qin and set it on the path which led its rulers to the conquest of all China, the last of those rulers styling himself "First Emperor" in 221 BC. The *Book of Lord Shang* preaches totalitarianism with breathtaking frankness. One of its sections has the title: "Weakening the People." In another place it lists ten evils the wise ruler should shun: They include virtue, integrity, and music. It was, beyond any doubt, by dint of these odious doctrines that China was first united on roughly the scale that is familiar to us today.

And yet, if you read the *Book of Lord Shang*, you see showing clearly through its harsh precepts the quietism and restraint of the *Tao Tê Ching*. "Weakening the People," for example, sounds dreadful to modern man—to "we, the people"—but is a fair extension of the meaning of *rou*, one of the key terms in *Tao Tê Ching*, which can mean "meek," "gentle," or "restrained" as well as "weak." It is as if, starting from the proposition that "the meek shall inherit the earth," one were to argue that a state under a strong central leader, whose people were kept meek and submissive, could conquer a mighty empire. Which, in fact, is what the *Book of Lord Shang* does argue, and what in fact happened! And how are the people to be kept in that meek, submissive state? By an inflexible system of rewards and punishments, explicitly endorsed in stanza 74 of *Tao Tê Ching*:

> If they are in constant fear of death
> And we seize and put to death
> Committers of crimes, then who would dare?

The horrid doctrines of Legalism attained their finished form in the teaching of Han Fei Tzŭ (280–233 BC). In opposition to Confucius's yearning for traditional hierarchies and to the more meritocratic schemes of post-Confucian thinkers such as Mo Tzŭ, Han Fei Tzŭ proposed a state organized around a system of laws so all-embracing and correct that it required no elites at all to administer, nor even a very active monarch—*wu-wei* enthroned; or, to recast it in terms of a somewhat later thinker, the state withered away. Henri Maspero, in his survey of the period titled *China in Antiquity* (1927), discusses Legalism in a chapter headed "Schools Derived from Taoism," and concludes his account of Han Fei Tzŭ as follows:

> The doctrine of Han Fei, and that of the Legalists in general, tended to lower still further the position of the individual life, so little developed in ancient China and so constantly sacrificed to the life of society. . . . The theories of the Legalists, applied by the [Qin] dynasty to the government of the empire, had a great influence . . . upon the formation of the modern Chinese mind.

- ◆ ◆ ◆ -

THE TAO TÊ *Ching* has been a great favorite with translators. Witter Bynner, living in a provincial Mexican town during World War Two, seems to have had no difficulty acquiring fourteen different English translations, to which he then added his own version. Fourteen, though of course a different fourteen, was also the count on the shelves at my local Barnes & Noble, a perfectly humdrum suburban chain bookstore, last weekend. The only attempt at a methodical tally of English translations that I have been able to locate is one performed in the early 1980s by Clark Melling, a scholar at the University of New Mexico. He listed forty-two, but I feel sure that was an undercount. In any case, there are certainly many more than that now. A quick trawl through book sites on the Internet suggests sixty as a lower bound, but more diligent inquiry might come up with a larger number. Some of these are high-sellers, if not bestsellers: My copy of the aforementioned Dr. Wu's translation is in the tenth printing by its second publisher; the version put out by its first publisher went to at least eighteen printings. That internet search also revealed a wide variety of "spin-off" books, applying themes from the *Tao Tê Ching* to subjects as disparate as child-raising, cooking, drumming, sex, and nuclear physics. Plainly there is a huge market for Taoism among Americans of our time.

The reason for this probably lies in the obscurity of the language, which allows *Tao Tê Ching* to serve its readers as a "mirror" text—one into which they can project their own hopes and fears, rather like a newspaper horoscope. The psychological processes involved here were drawn very well by Tom Wolfe in his 1998 novel *A Man in Full*. One of Wolfe's characters is Conrad Hensley, a thoughtful but ill-educated and unformed young man who by chance encounters the works of Epictetus and soon becomes a proselytizing Stoic. In an age like ours, when many people—probably most people—reach adulthood without ever having passed through any strict moral education deeper than the vapidities of "political correctness," there is bound to be a demand for such products. Given that demand, it is not very surprising that few of those who have been visited by the temptation to make a translation of *Tao Tê Ching* seem to have been able to restrain themselves, to practice *wu-wei*. The nature of the book itself strengthens the temptation. For one thing, it is not very long—only five thousand characters. Suppose you didn't know any Chinese, but knew how to use a Chinese dictionary (an impossible state of affairs, as it happens . . . but let's suppose); if you spent five minutes looking up and figuring out the syntactical significance of every single character, you could get the whole job done in three months of forty-hour weeks. Bynner, who could not read Chinese at all, in fact took an even more audacious approach, simply "distilling" the essence of as many other translations as he could find. If you do actually know Chinese, translating the *Tao Tê Ching* is a fairly minor undertaking. Moss Roberts has previously published a translation of the fourteenth-century novel *Three Kingdoms*, at 650,000 characters, a task 130 times more daunting.

The pity of all these translations is, of course, that none of them can convey the poetry of *Tao Tê Ching*. There is no way that I can do this, either. I can only suggest that you find a Chinese speaker with a good stage voice and have him or her declaim one of the more sonorous passages to give you some flavor of the book as it has appealed to a hundred generations of Chinese enthusiasts. The tremendous, high-soaring and deep-diving stanza 21 would be a good choice:

> Boundless virtue all-accepting
> Attends the Way, the Way alone.
> Assuming form, the Way reveals
> Shapes half-seen and then half-hid.
> In dark half-hid, a likening;
> In light half-dark, forms visible . . .

It is melancholy, and slightly disturbing, to realize that these passive, mystical doctrines, expressed with such beauty and vigor, helped set in motion a system of despotism that lasted almost unchanged for two thousand years, and which the Chinese people have not been able to rid themselves of to this day. Yet after all, is it not in the Great Harmony, the universal City of the Sun, the Dictatorship of the Proletariat, where all are uniform and all submissive, where all votes are unanimous and all controversy stilled, that "nonaction" finds its truest fulfillment? Strange are the uses of quietism.

The Ancient Enemy

National Review

MAY 19, 2004

> What is civilisation? I don't know. I can't define it in abstract
> terms—yet. But I think I can recognise it when I see it . . .
> —Kenneth Clark, *Civilisation* (1969)

TWO THOUSAND one hundred and seventy years ago, in the reign
of the emperor Wen of the Han dynasty, northern barbarians,
possibly ancestors of the Huns who assaulted Europe six centuries later, broke through the Great Wall and raided the frontier provinces of China. They burned cities and massacred or enslaved the inhabitants. One Chinese survivor, asked to describe the savage horde, said:
"They have no faces . . . only eyes."

These horrors followed several decades of attempts on the part of
the Chinese emperors to appease these barbarians, sending them
extravagant gifts—including even an imperial princess. Emperor
Wen—"Wen the Filial," the chronicler calls him: He reigned from 179
to 157 BC—seems to have lived in hope that he could subdue the Huns
by giving them an example of wise and virtuous rule, and thereby attain
peace and stand down his armies. Twelve years previously he had agonized over this, stating: "I have been unable to extend the practice of
virtue to different regions, and I brood with anxiety upon the miscon-

duct of foreign peoples. Therefore I am not yet able to dispense with defense measures . . . "

They have no faces. That phrase came to mind when I saw the photographs of those masked terrorists about to kill Nick Berg. So did the misfortunes of the Emperor Wen. (Which were reversed by his successor's successor, the martial Emperor Wu, who sent great armies out into the steppe to punish the Huns. The Emperor led one of these armies in person. The Huns were, says the chronicler, "breathless with fear.")

In our war against Islamic terrorists we are replaying this ancient drama, so familiar to all the great civilizations of antiquity. It was not only the ancient Chinese who faced this menace—the menace of barbarism—but the Romans, too, and the Persians, the Egyptians, the Greeks of the Hellenic Age, and of course medieval Christendom.

What happened on September 11, 2001, was a kind of barbarian raid. It is true that it was not driven by the desire for plunder, but by the desire for destruction and glory, yet it was a barbarian raid for all that. In style and perhaps also in its deep motivation, it was the old spectacle of the wild herders from steppe and desert irrupting into the settled, orderly, civilized places that they simultaneously hated and envied. It was a raid across the Great Wall.

In our own age there is of course no Great Wall to mark the line between civilization and barbarism. In this world of easy travel and globalized commerce, it is not easy even to tell where the one thing ends and the other starts. "Civilization" is in fact a very slippery concept. As Kenneth Clark said in my opening quote, it is one of those things, like romantic love, that you are confident you can recognize when it shows up, but find it difficult to pin down with words.

It is not even clear to what kind of nouns the adjective "civilized" can properly be applied. If, for example, you say in print that such-and-such is a barbarous society, you will be sure to get an email from some person born and raised in that society, now a middle-class American with a PhD in microbiology and four published novels to his credit, taking great umbrage and asking indignantly: "Who are you calling a barbarian?"

I would like to lay down the rule that "civilized" and "barbarous" can only be used in reference to entire nations or societies, and are not meaningful when applied to individuals. "You're a better man than I am, Gunga Din . . . but the form of society to which you give your allegiance is a barbarous shambles."

I can't quite make this work, however. Noting the recent death of the Duke of Devonshire in the May 8 *Spectator*, Peter Oborne describes the late Duke as: "this modest, wise, tolerant and civilised man." Of course we know what he means. I spent the other evening at the Park Avenue apartment of a well-off American couple. The husband's father was there: a man I would judge to be in his late seventies, with a distinguished record of legal service both with the US government and in private practice. He had the exquisite manners that Americans of that age and background always have. Another civilized man, though this one with the American spelling. (A lady I know had a husband of that same generation, who died a few years ago. Toward the end of his life his mind became feeble and he rambled in speech: but, says the lady with great pride, "He kept his manners to the very end!")

As well as being of uncertain denotation, "civilization" is also, historically speaking, a moving target. Nobody much is going to argue if you say that the city-states of Golden Age Greece were civilized, yet they exposed unwanted infants, kept women out of public life, and practiced chattel slavery. Was Tudor Britain civilized? It followed a sophisticated religion, about which learned people—including two of the monarchs—wrote profound books. It had a high level (for the time) of personal liberty and judicial fairness. It gave us Shakespeare and Spenser, Compton Wynyates and Hampton Court, Holbein and Hilliard. Yet it also practiced public torture, spectacles of gross cruelty to which the populace thronged for entertainment. There were political prisoners, aggressive wars, the glorification of piracy, and a brutal colonial policy in Ireland. Civilized? Well . . .

I think most people would agree that no society practicing slavery in this modern world could be called civilized; but what about 150 years ago? Was the Old South civilized? Hmm . . . And what about democracy? I have presented ancient China as standing for civilization against the barbarians of the steppe. Yet ancient China had no conception of human liberty or consensual government. It was a despotism, with savage punishments for those who dissented from state dogmas or offended the sovereign. Why, then, do I think it was a civilization, a great civilization (which I certainly do)? And since standards are clearly higher nowadays, with consensual, constitutional government a precondition for a society to be called civilized, is modern China civilized? Er . . .

Not even manners are an infallible guide. Barbarians can be very well-mannered, in their own style. "An armed society is a polite society," after all, and in a barbarian society everyone is armed to the teeth, because violence settles everything. Proper manners can be a matter of life and death among barbarians, as you may recall if you saw the movie

Lawrence of Arabia (1962). Not even the inhabitants of Park Avenue take manners *that* seriously.

The transformation from one state of society to the other can also be surprisingly swift. There is nothing intrinsic or genetic about being a barbarian. The savage Magyar horde—barbarians if ever there were such—became the Christian Kingdom of Hungary in almost a single generation. Contrariwise, the Germany of Wilhelm II had a fair claim to being the most civilized nation of Europe in 1900; forty years later, it was the most barbarous.

Other conundrums show up, too, once you start contemplating these terms "civilization" and "barbarism." For example, every time you think you have identified a society that embodies the one, if you look closely, you see pockets of the other imbedded in it. I would say that Tudor Britain *was* civilized; yet the Anglo-Scottish border of that time can fairly be said to have been in a condition of gross barbarism, with the Scottish reivers—the "steel bonnets" of George MacDonald Fraser's book—raiding and plundering at will. (The "Scotch-Irish" of the American backcountry are descended from border people. As historian David Hackett Fischer points out, the trailer parks of "Scotch-Irish" America today embody the folk memory of the Borders, where there was little point going to the trouble of erecting a well-built, permanent house, as it would only be burned down in the next raid.)

Early medieval Ireland exhibits the contrary thing: pockets of civilization—the monasteries, where ancient learning was kept alive through the Dark Ages—imbedded in a civil society that was lawless and barbarous, illiterate Gaelic warlords roaming the country looking for plunder, sacks full of human heads hanging from their saddles.

Even the Great Wall was not always such a clear marker as I have implied. The gradient from civilization to barbarism as you crossed the Wall was not always very steep. The Manchus of the seventeenth century who came through the Wall and seized the Empire had been aping Chinese manners and social institutions for decades, were already half-sinified in fact. After taking the Empire, they quickly produced a succession of clever, literate, and successful rulers. Barbarians? Um . . . Likewise, though the fifth-century Huns were undoubtedly barbarous, while the later Roman Empire was surely still civilized, there was considerable mingling, and some odd preferences[102] on the part of Romans for the former over the latter.

One response to the difficulty of pinning down where civilization ends and barbarism begins has simply been to deny the difference altogether, or even to elevate the barbarian (spontaneous! spiritual! in touch with nature!) over the civilized person (repressed! materialistic! heartless!). This has been a typically modern project, launched by the odious Jean-Jacques Rousseau 250 years ago. Rousseau's "noble savage" concept is now an ineradicable part of our culture and forms one of the underpinnings of the modern cult of political correctness.

(Similar modern projects have attempted to deny the existence of other key polarities in human nature and society. The difference between the sane and the mad, for example, was flatly denied by Scottish psychologist R. D. Laing, who argued that it was in fact schizophrenics who had the more correct view of the world, while the rest of us are demented. Relativistic morality and "root causes" sociology have tried the same trick with the difference between the criminal and the law-abiding. The Unholy Trinity of enemies of normal human life—barbarism, madness, and crime—have thus been "normalized," at any rate to the satisfaction of key cliques of influential thinkers.)

There is, in fact, a sort of sneaking admiration for the barbarian life among some civilized folk. Vice versa, too, of course. Seeing Osama bin Laden, with his expensive digital watch, talking into a video camcorder, you could not help reflecting that the barbarous order of society this man represents could never produce such artifacts, much less the mathematics and science that inspired their invention and manufacture.

For all the conundrums and contradictions, though, the opposition between civilization and barbarism remains perfectly clear to anyone with moral good sense. A few weeks ago I published a piece in which I described Israel as being on the front lines of civilization. This roused the legions of Israel-haters and paleocons, who took a break from cataloging their collections of Third Reich memorabilia and sticking pins in their Abraham Lincoln dolls to email in and tell me of all the horrid things that Mossad and the IDF are guilty of.

Well, yes, to be sure, civilization has its dirty work to do. "He [Kipling] sees clearly that men can only be highly civilized while other men, inevitably less civilized, are there to guard and feed them"— George Orwell.[103] (Who knew what he was talking about, having once worked as a policeman.) Still, it is an extreme kind of moral obtuseness that refuses to notice the difference between a people who strive to minimize noncombatant casualties and a people who do their best to *maximize* them. I note also that when Arabs are injured in an Arab terrorist attack against Jews, they are cared for in Israeli hospitals, to which they have been transported by Israeli ambulances. Imagine the converse, if it were possible: Jewish inhabitants of an Arab country, injured in a Jewish-terrorist attack on Arabs. They would be torn to pieces by ululating mobs of Arabs, and the pieces would be paraded triumphantly through streets crowded with laughing revelers, the whole thing broadcast on Al-Jazeera to general rejoicing around the Arab world.

There you have the difference between civilization and barbarism. If you can't see it, I can't help you: You are morally blind. The wars we are fighting now—the war against Islamic terrorism, and also the war against the desperate, degraded, dangerous state of Middle Eastern political culture at large—are wars of civilization against barbarism. There is no guarantee of victory, and it is possible that our people's will might waver and fail; but these are not contrived or unnecessary wars against equal cultures—this is no "clash of civilizations." The enemy we face today is the same that Emperor Wen faced, and Aetius, and the monks of Lindisfarne, and Otto the First. We are not fighting against Islam, or against Arabs, or against Iraqis. We are fighting barbarism, the ancient enemy, the most ancient enemy of all.

The Church
of Somewhere

The American Spectator

MARCH 2013

The following is a review of Roger Scruton's *Our Church: A Personal History of the Church of England* (2012).

> "When I mention religion, I mean the Christian religion; and not only the Christian religion, but the Protestant religion; and not only the Protestant religion, but the Church of England."

THUS REVEREND Thwackum, the schoolmaster in *Tom Jones* (1749). That was the 1730s, or about halfway through Roger Scruton's *Our Church*. The Rev. Thwackum is drawn satirically, but his smugness was well justified.

The religious passions of the previous century had subsided or been pushed off to inconsequential border territories in Ireland and the North American colonies. The Church of England had been incorporated into England's unwritten constitution. Her—the gender of that pronoun is explained by Scruton—bishops sat in Parliament. Her clergy, typically younger sons of aristocrats or landed gentry, were comfortably knitted into the English class system. ("The Church or the Army" was the rule for those drawing short straws in the primogeniture lottery.)

The Church's core documents, the *King James Bible* and the *Book of Common Prayer*, were known at least in part to all educated Englishmen and had lent innumerable phrases to the common language. She coexisted peacefully with numerous Nonconformist sects and with remnant patches of Roman Catholicism. (That "Roman" prefix is necessary in this context: Reciting the Nicene Creed in their Eucharist service, Anglicans declare their belief in "one holy catholic and apostolic Church.")

Roger Scruton's book sufficiently covers the previous two hundred years of the Church's history to Reverend Thwackum, and the following 280. *Our Church* is not really a history, though. Scruton keeps to a chronological sequence, but takes off on long diversions into theology, literature, hymnology, architecture, and entirely personal reflections. The book is, as Scruton says of the Church herself, "a creative muddle." Possibly some readers will dislike it on that account. For myself, I found it charming, very English.

The Church of England is easy to mock. The English themselves have never taken her very seriously, as that *Tom Jones* quote illustrates. The silly Vicar has been a stock character in English comedy and satire through Jane Austen and Trollope to P. G. Wodehouse, Benny Hill, and *Beyond the Fringe*. ("Life is rather like opening a tin of sardines. We're all of us looking for the key . . .") Not just silly either, but also sexually eccentric: Choirboy jokes were a staple of playground humor in my own English schooldays.

Not all the mockery is well-founded. Roman Catholics jeer that the Church only exists because Henry VIII wanted a divorce. There is much more to be said than that. Henry's father had become king after decades of strife over who should succeed to the throne. Henry wanted to ensure a clear succession, for the peace of the nation, but his wife was barren. Scruton: "The refusal of the Pope to grant an annulment of Henry's first marriage was experienced by the King as a threat to his sovereignty." Henry was driven by rational statecraft, not—or not only—by sexual boredom.

Henry's break with the papacy was, in any case, only the last act in a centuries-long record of restlessness against Roman authority among England's political elites. The English barons, pushing back after King John's groveling to Innocent III in 1213, made John sign the Magna Carta, in which the Church is referred to as *Ecclesia Anglicana*. A half-century before that there had occurred the colorful dispute between Henry II and Thomas à Becket, his Archbishop of Canterbury, centering on clerical immunity to the King's laws. (Having mentioned Becket, I want to thank Scruton for including the "à," which is nowadays usually dropped for reasons of footling pedantry.)

Henry's reforms did not go unchallenged. Among the common people of England there was still much devotion to the Roman religion, which they perceived in terms of relics, images, pilgrimages, fasts, and the doctrine of Purgatory. Eamon Duffy's *The Stripping of the Altars* (1992) describes all this in superb detail. It also, however, supports Scruton's point that "the parish priest, rather than the wealthy bishop" was seen as the true representative of the church. "Heaven is high, the Emperor far away," murmured the Chinese of old; sixteenth-century Englishmen seem to have felt the same about the pope. Given the great piety of the medieval English, noted by many foreign visitors, the surprising thing is how *little* resistance Henry met. This was, remember, a regime with no standing army or police.

A key point of difference at the intellectual level was the doctrine of transubstantiation, which asserts that the Communion bread and wine actually become the body and blood of Christ. Anglican authorities were still thundering against this in Queen Anne's time (early eighteenth century). Scruton makes much of the dispute, stating:

> The revulsion that the doctrine aroused among the Elizabethan divines derived not from any rejection of sacraments but, on the contrary, from a desire to retain them—to establish a sacramental church that honestly explained itself to its members. This, in a nutshell, was the Anglican mission, and it began with Wyclif [an Oxford theologian, late fourteenth century], long before the Reformation had turned the order of Christendom upside down.

I am not sure why transubstantiation is less "honest" or harder to explain than its Anglican competitor, the "real presence" doctrine. As with those centuries of aristocratic restlessness, though, it is useful to be reminded that revolutions, including religious revolutions, are usually culminations of a long process, not thunderbolts from blue sky.

And when Scruton returns to his point about a sacramental church, as he does several times, he clarifies it with each returning. Thus eighty pages later we read of Scruton in the organ loft of the fifteenth-century English country church whose instrument (it "has one manual, three stops, and no pedals") he plays. He is musing on the institution for which he is "pumping out" hymns.

> The Anglican communion is a form of sacramental religion . . . in which anathemas and excommunications long ago ceased to have a point. And I rejoice that the Church to which I belong offers an antidote to every kind of utopian thinking. The Church of England is the Church of *somewhere*. It does not invoke some paradisal nowhere; nor does it summon the apocalyptic destruction of everywhere in the manner of the seventeenth-century Puritans.

That is all very well; but does the *somewhere* that the Church of England is the Church of, still exist? It is poignant to read Scruton, early in his book—he is writing about the Norman and Plantagenet kings—say this: "Our common law is inimical to laws made outside the kingdom." Not anymore it isn't, pal. England is currently bracing itself for a flood of immigrants from Romania and Bulgaria, who from January 1, 2014, under EU rules, cannot be denied entry, common law be damned.

The Church herself has been losing market share for decades. Entire large districts of English cities and towns are under occupation by foreign immigrants who give not a fig for the Church, nor indeed for Christianity. News stories about the installation of the new Archbishop of Canterbury are decorated with gloomy asides about dwindling church membership.

Part of the problem, Scruton notes, has been the Empire, which diffused the Church over vast territories whose English inhabitants later melted away, taking their Englishness with them; or in the case of the North American colonies, rebelled . . . but American Episcopalianism was birthed in Scotland, not England—an offshoot of an offshoot. The Church of Somewhere became the Church of Everywhere, and therefore of course of Nowhere. As Scruton writes glumly:

> Its most important controversies today—those over women priests and homosexuality—are being fought out between American liberals and African conservatives, with the old English establishment looking on in mild astonishment at the fuss.

Our Church is full of good things. Scruton writes fluently, with many memorable touches. I especially liked his recollection of his teenage self at Communion, listening to the organist's improvised sequences: "It was as though the Holy Ghost himself were present, humming quietly to himself in an English accent." He has provocative insights, too, as when he writes of "the pagan heart of the Roman

Catholic liturgy." He is only occasionally tedious, mostly when writing about theology, a subject in which I, along with most Anglicans (admittedly lapsed, in my case) have zero interest.

I liked this book. However, I was raised, like Scruton, in mid-twentieth century England, in a culture now as comprehensively extinct as that of the Moabites. Whether *Our Church* will find favor with, or even be comprehensible to, readers of different nativity, I would not venture to speculate.

CHAPTER EIGHT:

Math
and Science

So, You Want to Write a Pop-Math Book?

FOCUS

MARCH 2004

IN APRIL 2003 I published a book named *Prime Obsession*, an account of the Riemann Hypothesis for not-very-mathematical readers. My book has been more successful than a book of that kind has any right to be, for which I am of course very grateful. One of the editors of this magazine asked me to write down some notes about the making and selling of the book, and about the matter of pop-math books in general.

First I should explain how I came to write a book of this kind. I am not a professional mathematician, nor even a teacher of mathematics (though I once, briefly, was that). I am a freelance writer, journalist, and web journalist. Before that, I was a computer programmer in the financial services industry. I had started out in life with the intention of becoming a mathematician, though, and attended University College, London, for three years, graduating with a bachelor's degree in math. At that time in England, at any rate at that college, there was no nonsense about majors and minors; we just did three straight years of unadulterated math. This got us to a pretty high level—much higher than that reached by a first-degree course in a present-day American (or, probably, British) university.

In the course of rising to those rarefied mathematical altitudes I gained an item of what, according to the Ancient Greeks, is the most precious type of knowledge: self-knowledge. I discovered that I was not very good at math. I discovered this by the oft-repeated experience of watching more gifted classmates "see through" a problem in five minutes of reflection, while I myself had to spend a weekend sweating over the same problem to get the same result. There were also some areas, particularly in algebra, where I simply "hit the wall"—where I found that, with the most diligent application I was capable of, I could not understand the material.

With this precious item of self-knowledge in hand, following graduation I did the sensible thing and took up a nonmathematical career. I never lost my affection for math, though, nor my belief that it is the highest form of intellectual endeavor. My own love for the subject was unrequited—I loved math, but math didn't love me—yet it is a well-known peculiarity of human nature, illustrated for example by the career of the poet W. B. Yeats, that unrequited love can sometimes be the most enduring and inspiring kind. I continued to love math, to read math books and magazines, occasionally to work my way through a textbook, patiently completing all the exercises. (A math textbook, to my way of thinking, is useless if it doesn't have lots of exercises.) Since living in the United States, I have kept up membership in both the Mathematical Association of America (MAA) and the American Mathematical Society (AMS), and sit at the breakfast table chuckling over math periodicals, to the bafflement of my wife, who is deeply un-mathematical.

And so, in the summer of 2000, I happened to be reading Abe Shenitzer's excellent translation of the late Detlef Laugwitz's book on Bernhard Riemann.[104] Just at this time, my literary agent was trying, without any success, to place a novel I had written. I like my agent, and wanted him to go on being my agent, so I thought I had better have a book proposal ready for him, for that inevitable day when he declared that he had done all he could do with the novel. It occurred to me that there was a book to be written about the Riemann Hypothesis, in which the math of the topic could be agreeably mixed with historical and biographical background material. I did some further reading, carried out some explorations on the internet, and had dinner with Andrew Odlyzko, whose name had kept turning up in my internet browsing.

Andrew is now at the University of Minnesota, but at that time he was still working for Bell Labs in New Jersey. I drove over there from my home on Long Island, and we had dinner at an Italian restaurant near the labs. Andrew was a key player in some of the events related to the Riemann Hypothesis in the 1970s and 1980s, and maintains a keen interest in the topic. That's why I had kept seeing his name on the internet. He is also, I should add, something of a character. When you mention his name, people start to tell amusing, affectionate Odlyzko stories, along the lines of the apocrypha that often develop around colorful mathematical personalities—Paul Erdős and David Hilbert come to mind. I may at some future date make a collection of these stories and present it to Andrew. At any rate, he was extremely patient and kind in the face of my, at that point, not-very-well-informed inquiries. It was that dinner with Andrew that really got my book project off the ground. I went home with a sheaf of notes and, in less than a week, had a twenty-page proposal ready.

My literary agent was at first skeptical. I introduced him to the idea over lunch in Manhattan one day.

"Howard," I announced, "I'd like to write a book about a great unsolved mathematical problem. You know, like Simon Singh's book, *Fermat's Last Theorem* [1997]." (Singh's book was, as everyone in the book business knows, phenomenally successful.)

He perked up. "Oh? What is this problem?"

"Well," I said, "it is the Riemann Hypothesis."

"I see. And what does it say, this Riemann Hypothesis?"

"It asserts that all the nontrivial zeros of the Zeta function have real part one-half."

My agent looked at me in silence for a minute or two. Then he looked at his food. Then he looked at me again, and said: "You know, John, there are some doors Man was never meant to open."

Despite this discouraging start, I eventually sold him on the idea. It remained for him to sell it to some publisher. This did not go very well. Months passed, and all we were getting was rejections. I was busy changing careers, and the Riemann project slipped from my mind.

In the summer of 2001, I took my family to China for a few weeks to visit with my wife's family and allow my children to get to know something about the country of half their ancestors. A few days after arriving, I thought I had better check my email, so I logged in at one of the internet cafés that can be found everywhere in China (where they are actually called "internet bars"). The very first email message I opened was from my agent: "I have placed the Riemann book!" The proposal I had made up was now so far in the past, and I had been so preoccupied with moving my family around China, it was a moment or two before I understood what was meant. Riemann book? What Riemann book? Once I did understand, there was very little I could do, other than authorize the agent to negotiate the best deal he could get, which I would sign off on when I came home in the fall.

I duly came home and signed the agreement, which was for a healthy advance from a respectable publisher, with the manuscript to be delivered in January 2003. That gave me fifteen months to write the book, which was not as long as I would have liked, but manageable.

At that point the Fickle Finger of Fate decided to point my way. The publisher had assigned an editor to me, and this editor went off on a tour of some European countries. One of his duties now was to sell translation rights to my book in those countries. Attempting to do so, he discovered an unhappy fact: Two other authors were already at work on Riemann Hypothesis books, one of them with over a year's lead time on us. This kind of thing often happens in book publishing. A certain idea is "in the air," and two or more authors will decide to tackle it. This may not necessarily be bad news. Depending on the timing, one book, if successful, might awaken enough interest to make the others successful too. However, my publisher took the view that we needed to speed up my particular project dramatically. At their insistence, though with some concessions on my advance to soften the blow, we had to renegotiate the contract. Delivery of the manuscript was now set for June 30, 2002—a mere eight months ahead. This was a horribly tight schedule.

I dropped everything but some casual web journalism and threw myself into the project, reading everything I could find. Fortunately I live in an area well-supplied with first-class university math libraries, none of which raised any objection to my walking in and browsing their stacks. I read Euler in Latin and half a dozen authors in German—languages I had learned at school but had mostly forgotten. I badgered Andrew Odlyzko, and any other mathematicians willing to be badgered. (And one or two who were not at first very willing . . . But all were extraordinarily generous with their time and trouble, and I finished the project with a warm regard for mathematicians in general.) I spent hours fiddling with Mathematica, a tool I had hardly used before. I attended a scholarly conference on the Hypothesis, much of which went right over my head.

At last, somehow, it all got done. The book came out, and I started consuming my way through the publisher's marketing budget. Though not large, the budget covered several trips to "events" at bookstores and radio stations around the country. I quickly learned some necessary precautions for getting through these events. For example, I learned to make it clear at the very beginning of the proceedings that I am not a mathematician, only a writer who likes math. This allowed me to shrug off with proper insouciance questions like "Don't you think that Connes' noncommutative formulation of Poincaré duality in K-homologies offers a promising approach?" I developed a set of stock responses to commonly asked questions, especially: "What use is the Riemann Hypothesis?" I accumulated a repertoire of small jokes and minor theatrical stunts to enliven my talks. I began, in fact, to enjoy myself . . . just as the marketing budget ran out.

The relative success of *Prime Obsession*—by the end of 2003 we had sold somewhat over 25,000 hardcover copies, whereas the "expected" hardback sales for a book of that type would be in the range from five to ten thousand—caused me much reflection. The book has, after all, a lot of heavy math in it. I had decided from the start that there is no point in writing a book about the Riemann Hypothesis if you don't tell your readers what the Hypothesis is and why mathematicians want to resolve it. To do that, I needed to give my readers a lot of math, so I buckled down to it and gave them that math, making it as palatable as I could, and scattering it among the historical and biographical material as thinly as possible. *Prime Obsession* is still, though, I think, a hard book for anyone who left math behind in high school, and I am not at all sure I understand why so many people have bought it.

Interest in mathematical topics among nonmathematical but well-educated readers is not entirely a new thing. Edward Kasner and James Newman's *Mathematics and the Imagination*, first published in 1940, was a great success. (And was an inspiration to me in my teen years.) There are certainly more pop-math books around today than there have ever been, though. In part I think that this is a consequence of the spread of personal computers. Not that there is much of a direct connection between using a computer and doing math; but widespread acquaintance with, for example, spreadsheet programs, has helped break down the wall of anxiety that left a lot of people repelled by anything to do with math. The rise of experimental math, and the availability of picturesque pop-math artifacts such as the Mandelbrot set, are also part of this phenomenon.

There is also, I think, a deeper issue, to do with the yearning for certainty in a society of relativistic morality, declining religious faith, economic insecurity, and fast-changing technology. College-educated people of all disciplines have internalized Aristotle's observation that only mathematical knowledge is certain, all other kinds being merely probable. (Whether this is true or not is beside the point; I am only saying that most educated Americans are nowadays acquainted with the notion.) Thoughtful people would like to know more about this realm of absolute certainty, as in the world around them they see standards blurring, old verities questioned, new job classifications coming up as long-established old ones fall into oblivion. It is possible that the public appetite for math books is related in some distant sense to the forces that, in less happy lands, drive intelligent young people into religious fundamentalism.

I cherish the private fancy that in the particular case of *Prime Obsession*, part of the reason for the book's success has been Bernhard Riemann himself. Every book worth reading cloaks a human personality, if only the author's. I was drawn to my topic at first by the personality of Riemann, by the curious contrast between his outer and inner lives: between the shy, timid, sickly, unsocial, poverty-stricken body, and the blazing fire of imaginative genius within. I had all that in mind from the beginning; I dedicated my book, in my prologue, to Riemann's memory; and I like to think that if he is anywhere right now, he is smiling down fondly on my brief, hurried efforts.

The Starry Messenger

The New Criterion

JANUARY 2011

The following is a review of David Wootton's *Galileo: Watcher of the Skies* (2010) and J. L Heilbron's *Galileo* (2010).

I DIDN'T make it to the First Annual Catholic Conference on Geocentrism, held in South Bend, Indiana, on the November 6 weekend. I was interested, and badgered some editors to expense the trip, but no one thought it worth their funds. Nor have I read the 1,048-page, two-volume book *Galileo Was Wrong: The Church Was Right* by R. A. Sungenis and R. J. Bennett, published in 2007. ("Your world will be rocked," promises the promotional material, somewhat missing the point of geocentrism.)

If you do any science writing you get on the mailing lists for this kind of thing. It's amazing how many people see it as their life's mission to disabuse us of some scientific theory or other. Creationists, who dispute the foundations of modern biology, are only the best-known of these dissenters. Publish a science book or write a few articles and you will soon find your mailbox clogged with letters and pamphlets clamoring to set you straight on the real truth about the natural world and the sinister conspiracies that seek to keep us deluded.

Though neither a geocentrist nor a creationist, I confess to a sneaking sympathy for these contrarians. I fancy that in some small way they help to keep science honest. What, after all, do we know? Outside the narrow realm of what the philosopher J. L. Austin called "medium-sized dry goods"—the kinds of phenomena whose size and duration are on the scales our senses evolved to cope with—we are in a counterintuitive wonderland of curved spacetime and wave-particle duality. Real knowledge of that wonderland is awfully hard to extract. Copernicus's book *De revolutionibus*, which argued for a moving Earth and a stationary Sun, was published in 1543, yet the strongest objection to his system—the absence of stellar parallax—was not resolved until 1838. That's nearly three hundred years to clear up one key point in a theory.

The most famous of early Copernicans, after Copernicus himself of course, is Galileo Galilei. His book *Sidereus nuncius* ("The Starry Messenger"), the first to describe systematic observations of the heavens by telescope, was published in 1610. By way of marking the quatercentenary of this event, the university presses of both Oxford and Yale have brought out new biographies of the astronomer by two distinguished historians of science. Curiously, the OUP's author is an American while Yale's is an Englishman. Both, however, are diligent scholars and credentialed experts in their field, fully acquainted with the source materials for Galileo's life and work. Even though neither book, nor indeed both put together, matches the length of *Galileo Was Wrong*, they offer masses of well-informed detail about their subject and his works.

That subject is a difficult one. As well as being a person and a scientist, Galileo has also been a token in the conflict between science and religion. The key event here is his formal abjuration of Copernicanism in June of 1633 under pressure from the Inquisition. Partisans of the Catholic Church, along with some philosophical relativists such as Paul Feyerabend, have portrayed Galileo as a testy crank dogmatically committed to an unproven theory. Their case is not without merit: Galileo *did* have a cross-grained personality, and Copernicanism *was* short on supporting evidence. Galileo's attempt in his 1632 book *Dialogue on the Two Main World Systems* to supply the missing evidence with his preposterous explanation of the tides—he attributed them to a kind of rhythmic sloshing caused by the earth's movement—fortifies the anti-Galileo case.

The more common point of view tells the Galileo story as one skirmish in a Manichean conflict between Renaissance and Counter-Reformation, a war in which brave free-thinking empiricists struggled to escape a decaying, suffocating mass of religious dogmatism and obscurantism. There is something here, too. The Roman Church was a power center: a locus of order in a very disorderly world, but all too prone to the arrogance, corruption, and ideological rigidity attendant on political power every-where.

Both these authors go much deeper than these partisan caricatures. The intellectual landscape of early seventeenth-century Italy was, they show, exceedingly complex. Church intellectuals of Galileo's time were conducting an orderly retreat from the astronomy of Ptolemy and Aris-totle, with Tycho Brahe's quasi-heliocentric system as a popular fallback position. (It had the earth stationary and all other planets revolving round the sun, which revolved round the earth. This, by the way, is the system favored by today's geocentrists.)

Astronomical systems of all sorts were in any case seen by the Church as mathematical, not physical; as handy algorithms for comput-ing the positions of objects in the sky, not as descriptions or explana-tions of observed reality. It was made clear to Galileo that if he clove to this "save the appearances" approach, his Copernicanism would be acceptable. He could not do so, though, being too convinced of helio-centrism as physical fact.

Both these books are professorial, in the sense of assuming more familiarity with the subject matter than a nonspecialist reader is likely to have. Heilbron redeems himself somewhat with a useful glossary of names and a Galilei family tree. His book has some very fine color plates, too. (Though both books should have included a simple map of northern Italy. If you don't have the relevant locations and distances clear in your mind, you'll want an atlas handy.) Heilbron's book is also the more straightforward narrative, proceeding directly from birth to death with a few supplementary pages on the fortunes of Galileo's reputation.

David Wootton's book is comparatively meditative and moves around more freely in time. It is structured on a four-part framework: each section devoted to a particular part of Galileo's life and afterlife—i.e., his reputation—but with many forward and backward references. Its defects, for me, were a whiff of cod Freudianism ("Galileo's internal conflict over the nature of knowledge is best understood as an ever deferred settling of accounts with his father") and poor math. I read Wootton's explanation of accelerated motion three times and still came away thinking he believes speed proportional to the square of time elapsed. No: It is distance traversed, not speed, that is proportional to t^2.

The main point of fact on which the authors differ is the vexed question of how good an empiricist Galileo was. The difference of opinion is not great, though. Neither author is at the extreme of skep-ticism represented by the great historian of science Alexandre Koyré (*floruit* 1950s), who thought Galileo's empiricism consisted mostly of thought experiments.

Wootton is the more skeptical of the two, making a case that Galileo was a "reluctant" empiricist, especially in his earlier years. Of Galileo's unfinished 1590 study of dynamics, Wootton says that "the limited role assigned to experiment in *On Motion* . . . is the role that would have been assigned to it by any orthodox Aristotelian." This remark has more force if you know how blithely *un*-empirical Aristotle's physics was. It taught, for example, that a hurled object moves in a straight line for a while then drops vertically, and that ice is heavier than water.

Heilbron is more inclined to give Galileo the benefit of the doubt as an experimenter—and there *is* considerable doubt—though even he concedes what is plainly the case, that "Galileo could stick to an attractive theory in the face of overwhelming experimental refutation." Perhaps Galileo was by temperament less a scientist than a mathematician? If so, he was a very incurious one. He seems to have taken no interest in algebra, for example, a great mathematical growth point in his time, coming to full flower with Descartes's *Géométrie* (1637). Nor did he pay any attention to Kepler's 1609 book *Astronomia nova*, which contained the mathematical key to planetary motion.

My impression of these biographies is rather the one I get from well-nigh any reading on the history of science: that no other style of thinking comes less naturally to human beings than the empirical and that Galileo was all too human in this regard. Neither of the authors thinks that Galileo's 1633 abjuration was sincere; nor does either credit the tale about Galileo muttering *e pur si muove*—"and yet it [the earth] does move"—as he rose from his knees at the end of the proceedings. He had, both agree, been a convinced Copernican since 1597, his thirty-fourth year.

On the matter of Galileo's religious beliefs our two biographers take different approaches. Wootton gives over a whole chapter to the topic, arriving at a "very strong presumption that Galileo was not a Christian." He was not, however, an atheist or agnostic in the modern sense, more a Platonic deist, seeing God "as the Supreme Mathematician."

Heilbron shows less interest in Galileo's inner life. He portrays Galileo's occasional religious observances in cynical terms. Of the Venetian ambassador's noting in 1610 that Galileo "frequently takes the sacraments and is very much changed from what he was," Heilbron observes drily: "The probable etiology of this increased observance will soon be clear." (Galileo was planning to woo the Jesuits prior to publishing his Copernicanism.)

Galileo's 1610 book *Sidereus nuncius* appeared just a few months after Kepler's *Astronomia nova*, in which the notion of elliptical planetary orbits was first offered. Both books stand almost precisely midway in time between Copernicus's *De revolutionibus* (1543) and Newton's *Principia* (1687), the latter of which gives a sound mathematical explanation of *why* orbits are elliptical.

This 144-year period, with Galileo's book at its center point, saw the first great dethronement of humanity—the first clear evidence that an assumption carried forward from our most primitive paleolithic condition down to the seventeenth century, the assumption that all things were created for the sake of man, is false. Two centuries after Newton came the second terrible blow with the publication of Darwin's *On the Origin of Species* (1859).

We are still reeling. While acceptance of heliocentrism is now essentially universal outside the meeting rooms of the Hilton Garden Inn at South Bend, Indiana, still only forty percent of Americans believe in evolution. The idea of our utter insignificance—a smart ape dwelling on an inconsequential planet—is more than most of us can bear. "We do not doubt," wrote Descartes, in the year of Galileo's death, "but that many things exist, or formerly existed and have now ceased to be, which were never seen or known by man, and were never of use to him." It was the work of the troublesome Florentine that first forced this deeply unwelcome fact on our attention. Here in two fine scholarly books are the man and the work all laid out for inspection.

Doesn't Add Up

Claremont Review of Books

SPRING 2017

The following is a review of Cathy O'Neil's *Weapons of Math Destruction: How Big Data Increases Inequality and Threatens Democracy* (2016).

T HE AGE we live in, which is of course the Information Age, has presented us with great boons but also many problems. As an old Information Technology (IT) grunt—I wrote my first program in 1969 using the ALGOL language, now defunct—I habitually think of Information Age issues in a binary way, as pertaining either to data or to code.

In social and political commentary, it is data that gets most of the attention. What is the point of balance between privacy and national security in the collection of data? When a private corporation (Google, say) gathers data about me (from my internet searches, perhaps), what may they lawfully do with it? If a US company stores data on servers abroad, can they be compelled to repatriate it? (That is the gravamen of *Microsoft Corp. v. United States*, currently being litigated.)

Mathematician Cathy O'Neil's new book offers a welcome change of viewpoint, from data to code, that is, to the computer programs—she prefers "algorithms"—that analyze the great floods of data now washing over the world. These algorithms are the "weapons of math destruction" in her book's title.

Once they've analyzed the data, algorithms suggest decisions. The impact of those decisions may be trivial: which ads should appear on my Facebook page, perhaps. It may be middling: whether or not I should be given a loan. It may be life-changing: the sentence a convicted criminal should receive. It may even be historic: how many people in demographic X can be persuaded to vote for candidate A. Far too often, O'Neil tells us, these algorithms deliver unfairness, especially to poor and disadvantaged citizens.

She tackles her subject as a Social Justice Warrior, a description to which I don't think she would object. O'Neil holds conventional progressive opinions, and is active in the Occupy movement. This book's dedication is "to all the underdogs." She refers to illegal aliens as "undocumented migrants." (But then, in her chapter on work-scheduling algorithms, frowns that "[t]he trouble, from the employees' perspective, is an oversupply of low-wage labor.") She responded to Donald Trump's election victory with a sort of defiant incomprehension, telling readers of her blog, *mathbabe*, that "we are all activists now."

To a reader not of that parish, these inclinations give her book a rather peevish quality, a tone of relentless negativity. They also lead her into sins of both omission and commission: key facts left unstated, stock left-liberal fables repeated uncritically. It doesn't help that, as is quite normal nowadays, the book is not edited nor even spell-checked. There is no such place as "the British city of Kent"; there is no such word as "miniscule"; etc. All of which is a pity, because there are important issues to discuss here and O'Neil is very well placed to discuss them. She has years of experience as a quantitative analyst working with algorithms in the private sector, coding them up for financial and commercial firms. In *Weapons of Math Destruction* she casts her net wide, offering examples from education, law enforcement, employment, insurance, and politics.

I found chapter 2, "Shell Shocked: My Journey of Disillusionment," particularly engaging. In 2007 O'Neil left academia to work at a big hedge fund, searching out and capitalizing on market inefficiencies. This gave her a grandstand seat at the great recession of 2008. Disillusioned, she then moved to commercial work, tracking the habits of online shoppers, designing, for example, "an algorithm that would distinguish window shoppers from buyers." This broadened her awareness of the scope and power of algorithms in many walks of life.

> I wondered what the analogue to the [2008] credit crisis might be in Big Data. Instead of a bust, I saw a growing

> dystopia, with inequality rising. The algorithms would make sure that those deemed losers would remain that way. A lucky minority would gain ever more control over the data economy, raking in outrageous fortunes . . . I could barely keep up with all the ways I was hearing of people being manipulated, controlled, and intimidated by algorithms.

As it happens, I myself spent the years 1985–2001 working for a big Wall Street trading firm, mainly in Credit and Risk Management, with a concentration on mortgage-backed securities and their derivatives—the sparks that started the 2008 prairie fire. My recollections of that environment are at odds with some of O'Neil's. I don't, for example, recall the level of cynicism she claims to have seen.

> [T]he figures in my models at the hedge fund stood for something. They were people's retirement funds and mortgages. . . . For hedge funds, the smuggest of the players on Wall Street, this was "dumb money."

I never heard that expression. The Wall Streeters I knew uniformly believed that they were doing socially useful work, giving companies and individuals access to finance that would not otherwise be available to them. Nor did I see that, as she writes, "[t]he refusal to acknowledge risk runs deep in finance." To the contrary, my own directors were obsessed with risk. That's why they had staff working on Risk Management. It's true that the culture at hedge funds differs somewhat from that at older firms, but surely not *that* much.

Much more serious, O'Neil fails to acknowledge the *political* origins of the 2008 crisis. "After the recession that followed the terrorist attacks in 2001 . . . [a]nyone, it seemed, could get a mortgage."

It would have been more accurate to write: "After President George W. Bush's October 2002 speech on minority home ownership . . ." Bush was after the Hispanic vote and he calculated that homeowners were more likely than renters to vote Republican. Nor was Bush striking out into new political territory there. Efforts to increase minority home ownership went all the way back to the Carter administration's Community Reinvestment Act of 1977.

How do you increase minority home ownership? If you are a government armed with regulatory powers, one way is to browbeat mortgage lenders into relaxing credit standards. The federal government had been doing this for thirty years prior to the 2008 crash.

The abandonment of traditional credit standards for political ends was not the only cause of the 2008 crash, but it was a major contributing factor—a much bigger one, I'm sure, than faulty algorithms in the back offices of trading firms. A social justice warrior's account of these events really should include the fact that behind the crash lay thirty years of moon-booted efforts by the federal government to advance . . . social justice.

"In the run-up to the housing collapse, mortgage banks were not only offering unsustainable deals but actively prospecting for victims in poor and minority neighborhoods," writes O'Neil. Well, yes, that's what the government *wanted* them to do! . . . And then, after the crash, sued them for having done. With the feds, you can't win.

Programs for social justice, including O'Neil's, rather frequently display this damned-if-you-do, damned-if-you-don't, aspect. Here was Jesse Jackson complaining in 2012 about under-policing in poor Chicago neighborhoods: "More police have been dispatched to neighborhoods where the murders have spiked, but citizens there still aren't protected as well as our . . . uptown businesses are."[105]

On the other hand, O'Neil grumbles that policing algorithms such as New York's Comp-Stat and Los Angeles's PredPol send *too many* cops into poor, crime-prone neighborhoods. She writes:

> How about crimes far removed from the boxes on the Pred-Pol maps, the ones carried out by the rich? . . . We have every reason to believe that more such crimes [i.e., like those that led to the 2008 crash] are occurring in finance right now . . . Just imagine if police enforced their zero-tolerance strategy in finance.

How soon they forget! I refer Ms. O'Neil to Daniel Fischel's 1995 book, *Payback: The Conspiracy to Destroy Michael Milken and His Financial Revolution*, about the vengefully politicized arrests and prosecutions on Wall Street in the 1980s, when traders were led away from their desks in handcuffs.

The author herself notes a paradox embedded in the case she is making. Where so many decisions are being made today by, or with the aid of, algorithms, those decisions were, she writes, formerly made by human beings, their minds "occupied with human distortions—desires, prejudice, distrust of outsiders." Don't computerized algorithms remove those distortions?

O'Neil doesn't really manage to square this circle. After many pages of deploring those desires and prejudices and that distrust—in hiring, for example, and police work—she tells us that our algorithms "urgently require the context, common sense, and fairness that only humans can provide." Uh . . .

Much of her critique, in fact, amounts to little more than telling us that our algorithms are not very good. Probably they are not; but then, human judgment is often not very good, either, as she keeps reminding us . . . except when calling for more human judgment in our decision-making!

There is another paradox in O'Neil's case that she seems not to notice. She inveighs against the opacity of too many algorithms, the impossibility of knowing how they arrive at their results. Elsewhere, however, she complains that algorithms can be too easily gamed from knowledge of their workings—by colleges seeking to improve their rank on the *US News & World Report* listings, for example, or by job applicants faced with résumé-reading algorithms. "[I]n a digital universe touted to be fair, scientific, and democratic, the insiders find a way to gain a crucial edge." Wouldn't more opacity take care of that?

A book of this sort must end with a prescription. What, in the author's opinion, is to be done about the unfairness and inequality generated by our algorithms? The core problem, she tells us in her concluding chapter, is that algorithms have the wrong values built into them—*old* values.

> Big Data processes codify the past. They do not invent the future. Doing that requires moral imagination, and that's something only humans can provide. We have to explicitly embed better values into our algorithms, creating Big Data models that follow our ethical lead. Sometimes that will mean putting fairness ahead of profit.

Profit—*ugh!*

> The government, of course, has a powerful regulatory role to play.

Uh-oh. So the prescription is that algorithms should be built around "better values"—that is to say, the values of social justice warriors like Cathy O'Neil—and that government regulators should enforce this. Then unfairness and inequality will be eliminated from the outcomes, just as they were when government forced mortgage lenders to scrap those fusty, discriminatory, old credit standards for mortgage lending. What could possibly go wrong?

O'Neil's naïve progressivism, her blithe ignorance of what the road to Hell is paved with, mars what might have been a useful book. The Information Age is built of code as well as of data, and the code needs more attention.

Certainly the underdogs of her dedication deserve a hearing. Who, exactly, are the underdogs, though? Criminals, or the noncriminal residents of poor neighborhoods on whom the criminals prey? Welfare single mothers, or the gratification-deferring middle class whose taxes support them? "Undocumented migrants" or the low-skill Americans whose wages they depress? (Mathematicians are not much affected.) Poor-credit minorities seeking to buy a house, or the small investors whose savings were wiped out when rational credit standards were declared unlawful on minorities' behalf?

Perhaps last November's election results offer some clues as to what, in the opinions of several tens of millions of American voters, are the answers to questions like these.

CHAPTER NINE:

Pop Culture

Thug (Uncredited)

National Review

OCTOBER 15, 2003

F OR WEB column topics I have an "Ideas" file that I dip into when I can't be bothered with the actual news—a state of mind that I find comes upon me more and more often lately. A lot of these ideas have been suggested by kind readers.

This is one such. None of the following words or expressions occurs in the rest of this column: "Iraq," "Schwarzenegger," "WMD," "Hillary," "Wesley Clark," "Muslim," "Chirac," "Madonna," "Kim Jong Il," "CIA," "Kobe," "ICC," "gay bishop," or "omphaloskepsis." (Just kidding on the last—it's a word I have always wanted to use, but which has never fitted in with any diction I have been writing in.)

Everyone on board with this? Excellent.

A few months ago, I mentioned on The Corner that I had once been in a movie with the late great martial-arts star Bruce Lee. The movie has one Chinese name, *Meng Long Guo Jiang* (猛龍過江), and went through a couple of English names before settling as *The Way of the Dragon* (1972). I put up relevant clips from the movie on YouTube, with links from one of my "Virtual Attic" pages here.[106]

Well, this tiny revelation generated a huge burst of email, which still continues at a small but steady trickle today. A lot of readers think that having been in a movie with Bruce Lee makes me the coolest thing since Marlon Brando in *The Wild One* (1953). (*Old guy*: "You're a rebel, huh? What, exactly, are you rebelling against?" *Brando*: "Whaddya got?") Several readers computed my Bacon number,[107] which turns out to be 3. One got me established on that standard-reference movie database, where I am listed as an "(uncredited) . . . Thug."[108]

A lot of these readers follow up by asking me how this movie appearance came about, and what it was like to work with Bruce Lee. So here, for what it's worth, is my recollection of the event.

- ◆ ◆ ◆ -

THIS ALL HAPPENED in the *Wanderjahre* of my misspent youth—in the summer of 1972, to be precise, when I had been living by my wits for some months in Hong Kong. I had gotten involved in a business venture that was sinking fast, and also with a woman who, I had recently learned to my chagrin, was no better than she ought to be. I had, in short, come to one of the bumpier stretches on life's road.

Seriously broke and lying low, I was renting a room in a seedy guest house in downtown Kowloon. If I say "Chungking Mansions,"[109] old Kowloon hands will know exactly where we are here. I had struck up a friendship with another resident of that guest house, a Malaysian-Chinese guy whom I shall call Chang, whose circumstances were as straitened as my own. Chang actually had a decent job with one of the Hong Kong newspapers; his destitution was the result of an out-of-control gambling habit.

In the lounge of the guest house late one evening, in a brainstorming session over a dozen or so bottles of San Miguel beer, Chang and I identified the fundamental problem, the root cause of our wretched situations: Hong Kong was simply too backward, stuffy, small-minded, and constricting to contain intellectual and entrepreneurial genius on the scale possessed by such giants as ourselves.

We agreed that, in order to accomplish the next phase of our progress toward Mastery of the Universe, we should strike out for fresh woods and pastures new. Chang, who had lived all over Southeast Asia, said that Bangkok was the place. The living was cheaper, he said, the business climate easier, the weather balmier, the girls better behaved. We could settle in quickly, too. He knew people in Bangkok who would give us excellent jobs for the asking.

Our confidence thus fired up, we went to the Thai consulate the next day and filled out forms. Visas took ten days, we were told. Pooling our resources, we bought plane tickets for a date two weeks ahead. That left us with two weeks to kill. Chang killed them in his own style—at the mah-jong tables, mostly. I hung out in the guesthouse lounge, reading, playing solitaire, chatting with other residents, and watching TV.

Hong Kong TV in the early 1970s was nothing to get excited about. There were only three channels, either two English and one Cantonese, or (more likely) vice versa—I forget the details. I watched programs in both languages indiscriminately. I never did get very far with Cantonese, being linguistically incompetent, but I had picked up enough to follow what was happening.

A lot of the stuff on the Chinese channel, or channels, was imported from the States, anyway. You have not savored the full subtlety of *Bonanza* until you've seen it dubbed into Cantonese.

Hoss: "Mou dung! Ying-dak ngo ma?"

Villain: "Mou da! Mou da!"

. . . Etc., etc.

The rest was historical costume dramas from Taiwan, cheesy contemporary soaps with lots of weeping, shouting, and boom-mike shadow, quiz shows of astounding difficulty, news programs, and Cantonese opera.

The opera, I must say, was something I wish I had paid more attention to. The stories are very good, the librettos ingenious and often funny, and every one of the words is pronounced slowly and clearly, giving you a wonderful language lesson—which is not at all the case with other styles of Chinese opera.

And there were variety shows. These were low-budget affairs, with a great deal of chatter to fill the airtime. The people doing the chattering were drawn from a pool of twenty or so personalities who had established themselves in the hearts of Hong Kong's Chinese population as funny, wise, or endearing in some way.

Exactly *which* way was not always obvious to an observer from a different background. Cantonese culture is a lifetime study. It has that intimate, familial quality that comes from being a small language group nursing some serious territorial insecurities—like Israel, I imagine, or Hungary.

The only one of these people I can remember with any distinctness was a plump woman of thirty or so, who wore alarming substitute-teacher glasses with swept-up frames, and who was known to the entire Chinese population of Hong Kong as "Feifei," which is Cantonese for

"Fatty." (The Cantonese are a direct-speaking sort of people. The fat lady's last name was Shum, but I have forgotten her true given name, if I ever knew it.) Feifei's real-life attempts to get, and keep, boyfriends were a staple of Hong Kong showbiz gossip.

Bruce Lee was a sort of visiting member of this intimate little TV family, dropping in unexpectedly from time to time. The US TV show *The Green Hornet*, in which Bruce played the part of Hornet's valet, had only run for a single season in the United States (1966–67). It had been something of a breakthrough for Chinese racial pride, however, as Chinese actors had never been given decent roles in American films or TV up to that time. The movie and TV detective Charlie Chan, for instance, had been played by, successively, a Swedish-American (Warner Oland), a Scotchman from Missouri (Sidney Toler), and a German-Irish Bostonian (Roland Winters).

The Chinese people of Taiwan, Hong Kong, and the overseas communities had been thrilled to see Bruce in *The Green Hornet*, and the show had gone through endless reruns on Hong Kong TV. When Bruce arrived in the colony in 1971, after some years' absence, he found himself famous.

He promptly made the first movie he ever starred in, a fist-flick called *Tang Shan Da Xiong* (唐山大兄 . . . with the usual confusing plethora of alternative English names), which opened to frenzied interest in Hong Kong and broke all box-office records for the colony. In its first run, which lasted only three weeks, it grossed $3.2 million.

At the time I am speaking of, mid-1972, Bruce's second movie, *Jing Wu Men* (精武門), was showing to packed movie theaters.

(Here the English names get really confusing. *Jing Wu Men* was originally released with the English title *Fist of Fury*, though I think it ended up in the United States as *The Chinese Connection*. *Tang Shan Da Xiong* had already set sail in the English-speaking world with the title *Fists [sic] of Fury*. You can never get this stuff straight . . . which is why I am sticking with the original Chinese names. To further confuse things, though only very slightly, the Chinese written characters for those names sometimes have different, "simplified," forms in the mainland, the *men* of *Jing Wu Men*, for example, printed as 门, not 門. Still with me? It's OK; that's as deep into the Chinese-language weeds as I'm going.)

Bruce was a megastar among the Chinese all over Southeast Asia. In Singapore, *Jing Wu Men* had to be withdrawn from theaters because of the traffic jams it caused.

You would never have known the extent of Bruce's fame from the style of his appearances on Hong Kong Cantonese TV. He would amble on to the set of one of those corny variety programs in the middle of one of their air-filling chat-fests, or into a comedy sketch that was already underway, and tease people, and crack jokes, and pretend to be lost, or drunk, or belligerent. He stole the show every time, of course—he was a terrific natural performer, more fun to watch impromptu than most actors are after a week of rehearsals.

(Bruce came from a showbiz family. His father was a Cantonese-opera singer. Bruce had made his first film appearance at age three months.)

His charm, quick wit, good looks, and physical agility captured your attention at once, and held it for as long as he was on-screen . . . Which was never too long: He had an exquisite sense of how much of himself to give to his public.

There were a couple of occasions I had heard about—I can't recall having caught them in my own TV watching—when Bruce had been invited on TV martial-arts programs to discuss his own fighting style.

In the most talked-about of these, he had been confronted by a tra-ditionalist martial-arts master of one of the old Chinese schools, a fellow particularly proud of his defensive stance, who claimed that when he was in that stance, no one could push him over. He actually took up the infallible stance right there and challenged Bruce to push him over.

Bruce walked across and hit him with a highly unorthodox sucker punch. The guy fell over. Explained Bruce, helping the outraged master to his feet: "I don't push, I *hit*."

Bruce called his style of fighting "Jeet Kune Do" (截拳道, pro-nounced *jiequan dao* in Mandarin, *jit-kyun dou* in Cantonese)—"block-ing-fist style." It may as well be called "Bruce Lee Do," as it was a highly individual, very eclectic mix of styles that Bruce picked up at random from Chinese, Japanese, and Western sources (including boxing and ballroom dancing—he was the 1958 Hong Kong Cha-Cha Champion) and adapted to his own physique and inclinations.

Bruce's art was entirely physical. Though a martial-arts genius of the first order, he was no intellectual. His "philosophy" of fighting is a dull recycling of some commonplace clichés from Taoism and American self-help books.

You can sign up with instructors to study Jeet Kune Do, and I see there are a ton of websites, but my private opinion is that, as someone said of Gaullism after Charles de Gaulle died, Jeet Kune Do without Bruce Lee is like jugged hare in redcurrant jelly, minus the jugged hare.

- ◆ ◆ ◆ -

WELL, THAT WAS the extent of my acquaintance with Bruce Lee in mid-1972. Then, one afternoon, while waiting for my Thai visa, I was sitting in the guesthouse lounge reading a book. In that peculiar way the mind has of retaining the most trivial things while misplacing your children's names, your wife's office phone number, and which part of the supermarket lot you parked your car in, or perhaps just because of the coincidence of names, I remember the book: It was a collection of the short stories Bruce Jay Friedman had written for *Playboy* magazine.

So I was sitting there reading when a young Chinese guy came in. Seeing that I was the only person in the lounge, he addressed me. "Do you speak English?" I said I did. "Know any martial arts?" I said I had taken a few lessons. "Want to be in a movie?" I asked him if it paid. "Sure. Seventy bucks a day." (Hong Kong dollars, he meant—around 12 USD at that time.) I said I was game.

"Good. Be outside the Miramar Hotel front entrance tomorrow morning, seven-thirty."

There were half a dozen other ghost-heads (*gwai-tau*, the generic Cantonese term for a non-Chinese person) outside the Miramar. We must have looked an unsavory lot—the casting director had obviously just trawled around the low-class guesthouses for unemployed foreigners of a sufficiently thuggish appearance. One was a dead ringer for Jimi Hendrix. Another was a full-blood Maori from New Zealand, a huge fellow—an obvious rugby lock—who made a meager living as a nightclub singer in the colony's low dives.

A minibus arrived and drove us out to the New Territories—that is, the countryside that stretches out back of urban Hong Kong forty miles or so to the Chinese border. (Beyond which Mao Tse-tung's Great Proletarian Cultural Revolution was going through one of its nastier phases. Rafts of rotting corpses would occasionally float down the Pearl River past the colony.) Here there was a movie studio. We were led into a huge shed used for indoor sets, and spent the next two days filming fight scenes in that shed.

Bruce himself directed *Meng Long Guo Jiang*. He was on set all the time, setting up the fights, working out positions, talking to the lighting crews and the cameramen.

There was, by the way, no sound crew. Chinese movies at that time were shot without sound. The sound was dubbed in later. When you watch a Bruce Lee movie, you are not hearing Lee's voice, though I think they might have inserted his *qi-ai*—the intimidating yells, grunts, and howls he used when fighting—into the soundtrack of *Meng Long Guo Jiang*. The *qi-ai* sound like his, anyway.

In fact the first dubbing was always into Mandarin, and the on-screen lip syncing was to Mandarin words. Bruce, though fluent in English and Cantonese, could not speak Mandarin, so this was a constant vexation to him when filming, and probably the main reason he has very few speaking lines in his movies.

Bruce's presence was as striking in person as on screen. I have never seen a man who gave such an impression of concentrated energy. If he got animated when talking to you, he would make little springy skipping movements with his feet, as if warming up for a fight. When nothing much was happening, he would drop down and do one-arm finger-thumb push-ups[110] at one side of the set, or have someone hold up a board he could practice high kicks on.

Just as a skillful schoolteacher knows how to get the class's attention by speaking very softly, you were most aware of Bruce's presence, and he was most intimidating, on the rare occasions his body was dead still. In the relaxed state, he was in constant motion. Crouching tiger, indeed.

Movie fight scenes are a devil of a thing to get right. We did everything a dozen times, levels of frustration and discomfort rising each time.

This was summer in the tropics, and if the place had any air-conditioning, it wasn't adequate. There were huge electric fans everywhere, but they had to be switched off for filming, or the actors' hair would be streaming out horizontally from their heads. Yet through the entire two days I was on the set, I never saw Bruce lose his temper, or display any negative emotion stronger than momentary mild annoyance. He was just as I had seen him on TV: smiling, cracking jokes, smoothing out difficulties and differences, coaching, teasing, encouraging, cajoling.

I have a tall, lean physique, so he addressed me as "Slim."

"Hey, Slim, let's try that again—and this time look *mean.* You hate me, remember? I'm a runty obnoxious little Chink, just stole your woman, trashed your car, and pissed in your beer. Whaddya gonna do to me? Huh? *Whaddya gonna do?* Come on . . ." (He spoke perfect idiomatic American English the whole time.)

The fight scenes were all improvised out of his head. I can say this authoritatively, as I got a chance to read one of the scripts. The entire section I was involved in—two days filming, though of course less than five minutes in the finished movie—was encompassed by four Chinese characters in the script: *Li da xi ren*—"Lee strikes the Westerners."

We had some visitors on the set those two days. Chuck Norris showed up, though goodness knows why, as his scenes, later in the movie, were filmed on location in Rome.

Bruce's wife Linda also made an appearance at one point, with either one or both of the kids, I can't remember. (Brandon, whom Bruce described as "the only blond-haired, blue-eyed Chinaman in California," would have been seven and a half at this point; Shannon just over three.)

Other than us random *gwai-tau* hired as fist-fodder for Bruce, the other actors were all Chinese, as were all the set crews. The movie's female lead, Nora Miao, an accomplished Chinese actress with a sulky, icy kind of beauty—she was the only person Bruce ever kissed on-screen—spent most of her time in a lawn chair at one side of the set, being fussed over by a little bevy of Chinese grannies in old-style smocks and black pants. These chaperones kept everyone away; you couldn't get close enough to speak to Nora.

- ◆ ◆ ◆ -

I DID MY two days on the set, got paid, and left the colony a week later for Bangkok with Chang.

Bangkok was a comprehensive disaster. The night before we left— the actual *night before we left*—Chang sat in on our landlord's all-night mah-jong game and lost his shirt.

"Don't worry," he said. "Once we get to Bangkok we'll be all right. I know people there, it'll be fine."

He was, of course, a complete fantasist, as all chronic gamblers are. The people he knew turned out to be not at all keen on knowing him, much less any hippie stranger he had dragged along with him. His spirit cracked, he talked me into paying his train fare back home to his family in Malaysia, and I was on my own in Bangkok, a city I had never been in before, where I knew absolutely no one, and of whose language I spoke not a word, with around twenty US dollars to my name. That's another story, though.

Bruce died suddenly, probably from an allergic reaction to an unhappy combination of pain-killing drugs, a year later, on July 20, 1973. He was four months short of his thirty-third birthday. His funeral in Hong Kong was attended by twenty-five thousand people. The TV announcers were weeping so much they had to suspend their commentary. "White hair following black"—that is, the older generation walking behind the coffin of the younger in a funeral procession—is considered by the Chinese, and surely by the rest of us too, to be the most terrible of personal calamities.

A second ceremony was held in Seattle the following week. Bruce was buried there in Lake View Cemetery, where he still rests. At the funeral they played the Laura Nyro song "And When I Die":

> And when I die, and when I'm gone,
> There'll be one child born and
> A world to carry on.
> There'll be one child born to carry on.

Two of the six pall bearers were Steve McQueen and James Coburn, both of whom had studied martial arts with Bruce, as had Lee Marvin, James Garner, Kareem Abdul Jabbar, and Roman Polanski.

If my very brief acquaintance with Bruce Lee is any fair grounds for judgment, he was a lively, witty, charming man who thoroughly enjoyed life, a gifted natural stage and screen performer, liked by everyone around him and dedicated to his art—his martial art, I mean. It was a tragedy he died so young.

The death of his son Brandon just twenty years later in an absurd movie-set accident made a double tragedy for the family, and inspired a great deal of silly speculation about witchcraft and curses. An elderly Cantonese lady of my acquaintance put it all down to the fact that one of the scenes in *Tang Shan Da Xiong* had been filmed on location in an actual graveyard. "The dead people weren't happy about that . . ."

Bruce Lee left four movies behind, plus twenty-five episodes of *The Green Hornet* and a scattering of walk-on parts in TV shows and other people's movies. Martial-arts buffs still study his filmed fight scenes with intense interest. I made him a minor character in a novel.[111] The rest is silence.

Children of a Conservative God

National Review

FEBRUARY 21, 2003

I HAVE mentioned before in this space my fondness for the TV sitcom *Married . . . with Children*, which had a "reunion special" on Sunday. In case you never saw it, the show—it ran eleven years, 1987–97, on the Fox channel—featured the Bundys, a low-class family living in the Chicago suburbs. The husband, Al, worked as a sales assistant in a shoe store. Al's life had peaked with his high school football career and been pretty much downhill thereafter. The wife, Peg, was an empty-headed bimbo, who tottered around the house in high-heeled mules and tight pants, suffered from chronic sexual frustration, and occupied her time sitting on the sofa eating bonbons and watching *Oprah*. The daughter, Kelly, was a teenage slut with a shaky grasp of the English language—liable to describe herself as being "on the horns of an enema," for example, or to express a flash of insight by jumping up and shouting: "Urethra!" The son, Bud, was the only family member with any brains; but his brains were constantly being overruled by his raging hormones. The family dog, Buck, watched it all with a sardonic eye, and provided a sort of Greek chorus to the goings-on.

I was genuinely surprised, when I started getting hooked on *Married . . . with Children* in the early 1990s, to find that it was unpopular with a lot of conservatives. It poked fun at the nuclear family, these people told me, which, after all, is the basic building-block of a civilized society. It promoted parental irresponsibility and teenage promiscuity, they said. The Bundys were crude, antisocial, and occasionally criminal in a mild way. The show held up to ridicule all that we hold dear, etc., etc. (Some of these complaints look a little quaint up against, say, *South Park*. But this was network TV, remember.) Why didn't I watch *The Simpsons*, a much more wholesome show?

Well, I tried *The Simpsons* but (sorry, Jonah) just couldn't get on with it. Unless the two or three episodes I saw were untypical, *The Simpsons* never quite let go of the sentimental, moralizing tradition of American TV sitcoms. I was raised on the much more tart British variety—*Till Death Us Do Part, Steptoe and Son, One Foot in the Grave*, etc.—and prefer my comedy without the sugarcoating. I'm not claiming any particular superiority for the British product, it's just what I'm used to.

In any case, it seemed to me that *Married . . . with Children* was one of the most conservative shows on TV. I could make this case at some length, but I don't actually need to. The case was made for me sixty-one years ago by George Orwell, in an essay titled "The Art of Donald McGill."[112] Orwell was not, of course, writing about the Bundys. His subject was the "naughty postcards" that were a feature of low-class English life in the 1940s (and well into the 1970s, in my own recollection). These postcards were basically colored cartoons, populated by stock characters such as henpecked husbands, domineering fat wives, shrewish mothers-in-law, busty dumb blondes, lecherous young men, indefatigable newlyweds, red-nosed drunks, mean Scotsmen, crooked lawyers, and so on. The jokes are mostly about sex, and lean heavily on *double entendre*. Samples:

> Young man, to busty-blonde young female librarian: "I say, young lady, do you like Kipling?"

> BBYFL: "Oooh, I don't know, you naughty boy, I've never kippled."

> Young couple at seaside, standing very close together in the sea, which comes up to their chests. She: "Come on, George. The deeper in you go, the nicer it feels."

Orwell analyzes the world pictured in these postcards at length, and much of what he says applies equally well to *Married . . . with Children*. Here he is after describing one of the newlywed jokes.

> This is obscene, if you like, but it is not immoral. Its implication—and this is just the implication that *Esquire* or the *New Yorker* would avoid at all costs—is that marriage is something profoundly exciting and important, the biggest event in the average human being's life. So also with jokes about nagging wives and tyrannous mothers-in-law. [Al Bundy, after Peg has declared that her mother is a little shy: "Of what? A metric ton?"] They do at least imply a stable society in which marriage is indissoluble and family loyalty taken for granted.

A normal human being, Orwell points out, is a mix of the noble and the ignoble, of Don Quixote and Sancho Panza. One part of us wants to perform stirring deeds, to pursue noble causes, to commit heroic acts of self-sacrifice. Another part—the Sancho Panza part—wants "safety, soft beds, no work, pots of beer, and women with 'voluptuous' figures." We exist in a state of constant tension between the two sides of our personalities, between our soul and our belly. No society founded on just one of these aspects could possibly be stable. The people of China discovered thirty years ago that a society which demands constant acts of selflessness and public spirit is untenable. So is a *Brave New World* society founded on pure hedonism.

Married . . . with Children was a funny show because it showed us the Sancho Panza side of our natures in all its aspects: male and female, sexual and gluttonous, irreverent and work-shy. It showed it in proper social context, though, just as those seaside postcards did. Al hates his work, but he goes to work every day nonetheless. The Bundys' marriage is stale, but they stay married anyway. The kids are slaves to their own libidos, but it's hard to imagine them doing anything unkind or seriously illegal, or turning into dope addicts.

You might even stretch a point and say that the show was a celebration of marriage, as that institution has been experienced by most Western people through most of history. I am thinking of an exchange in one of Anthony Powell's *Dance to the Music of Time* novels. The narrator, Nick Jenkins, a sophisticated metropolitan type, has been commissioned in a Welsh regiment during World War Two. He is in conversation with one of his sergeants, a man with a working-class background, from a small town in Wales. The sergeant has mentioned a relative of his, who got married a few years previously. "And how are they now?" asks Jenkins. "Why, all right," replies the sergeant, somewhat puzzled. "Why should they not be?"

For the worldly, upper-crust Londoner it is natural to ask how a marriage is going; for the provincial proletarian, the question is baffling. *They met, they got married, that's the end of it. How could anything else happen to them now?* The sergeant has, to use Orwell's words again, "the working-class outlook which takes it as a matter of course that youth and adventure—almost, indeed, individual life—end with marriage."

You can take resignation too far, of course. There is a story about an old Vermont farmer whose wife died suddenly after fifty years of marriage. A neighbor, trying to console him, said: "Well, Zeke, I guess you'll be missing her." Zeke, after a few moments' thought: "Can't really say so. Never did get to like her much." I don't think Zeke's attitude has much to commend it; but without knowing more details, I hesitate to condemn him out of hand. My own parents were happy for the first four or five years of their marriage, I think, and thereafter miserable together. I have had a running argument with my sister, through all our adult lives, about whether they did the right thing in staying together, with me taking (approximately) the Don Quixote side, my sister speaking for Sancho Panza. My parents were both people who took their marriage vows seriously, though; and in any case, working-class English people in the mid-twentieth century had no culture of divorce. (They have since acquired one.)

For the principle underlying *Married . . . with Children*—it would be too much to say that the show actually *celebrated* it, but it was there anyway—was the principle of *duty*. This is not a very fashionable principle in an age like ours, an essentially hedonistic age; but without some widespread sense of duty, of selfless adherence to custom and principle and social obligation, no civilization could persist for long. Orwell:

> When it comes to the pinch, human beings are heroic. Women face childbed and the scrubbing brush, revolutionaries keep their mouths shut in the torture chamber, battleships go down with their guns still firing when their decks are awash. It is only that the other element in man, the lazy, cowardly, debt-bilking adulterer who is inside all of us, can never be suppressed altogether and needs a hearing occasionally.

I'd like to thank the producers, writers, and cast of *Married . . . with Children* for showing us that "other element" in all its unlovely and hilarious variety, in all its [Orwell again] "unredeemed lowness." I'm sorry the show ended, but in a way it doesn't matter. For as long as human beings exist, Al, Peg, Kelly, and Bud will always be within easy reach—sharing our skins with us, in fact.

A Dance to the (Disco) Music of Time

Claremont Review of Books

The following is a review of Louis Crompton's *Homosexuality and Civilization* (2003).

W E ARE, as everyone knows, living in the, or a, "gay moment." One of the consequences is that we have to put up with a great deal of homosexualist propaganda. (I favor the usage "homosexualist" for people who are activist about their sexual orientation, versus "homosexual" for people who are merely, and privately, homosexual. I admit, though, that my attempts to promote this—it seems to me, useful and noninsulting—usage have fallen mostly on stony ground.) Among homosexualists there are many whose devotion to what Christopher Isherwood famously called "my kind" is as intense as anything that can be shown by the followers of any religion or political ideology.

One aspect of this devotion is the urge to recruit long-dead historical names to the Cause—to comb through history seeking out gayness. Since history is, much more often than not, a very ambiguous affair, an explorer of this inclination can return with many trophies, which he will then display triumphantly to us dull-witted, unimaginative breeders, revealing to us that the human race is, contrary to our narrow brutish prejudices, a very ocean of gayness. Julius Caesar? Gay! Jesus of Nazareth? Gay! Leonardo? Gay! Frederick the Great? Gay! All of them—gay, gay, gay! I do not recall having seen it argued that George Washington was gay, but I have not the slightest doubt that the argument has been made by somebody, somewhere.

Louis Crompton's *Homosexuality and Civilization* belongs to this genre of homo-prop. It has, I should say here up front, many virtues. Crompton has done prodigies of literary and historical research across a wide range. His sources are for the most part secondary, but they could hardly be otherwise in a book of this scope. Nobody has real expertise on *both* ancient Greece *and* feudal Japan. He writes well for an academic (Crompton is Emeritus Professor of English at the University of Nebraska), and the book is beautifully produced, with a high standard of copy editing and many fine plates to please the eye.

Certainly Crompton has a bill of goods to sell, but there we come to matters of personal taste in reading. You either like didactic history, or you don't. I myself like it very much, to the degree that I even like it when an author writes contrary to my own prejudices. We—the readers of this fine periodical, I mean—are not gaping rubes, to be lured from the straight and narrow by a silver-tongued swindler. We have powers of judgment, which we can apply to an author's reasoning, and we have knowledge, which we can compare with the facts he presents. Crompton left me unconvinced on his main point, but he proved thoughtful, and entertained me along the way. As propaganda goes, this is a superior specimen.

His topic is, of course, homosexuality, and this raises a number of problems right away. What *is* homosexuality? The term is currently used in reference to those who find erotic fulfillment only with coevals of their own sex. A great deal of Crompton's book, however, deals with different matters. Much of it is about ephebophilia, or boy-love, a phenomenon whose connection to homosexuality is unclear. Indeed, many present-day homosexualist propagandists insist hotly that there is no connection at all.

And the matter of what people are *doing* contains all kinds of knotty sub-problems of language and interpretation. When George Russell tells us, "My intercourse with Jowett was not intimate," or when Dr. Johnson says, "I love Robertson, and I won't talk of his book," a person who had learned English as a second language might suppose—wrongly, of course—that these men are speaking about sexual enjoyment of the other party. How much more difficult to interpret recorded utterances from 2,500 years ago, in languages obscure, dead, or both.

Similarly, researcher J. Michael Bailey, in his recent book about effeminate men (*The Man Who Would Be Queen: The Science of Gender-Bending and Transsexualism* [2003]), notes the great difficulty of finding out about the sex lives of Americans today, even with our ability to conduct ambitious surveys costing millions of dollars and involving thousands of subjects. What proportion of the current US population is homosexual? We do not know, even to an order of magnitude. (Bailey's own estimate is from "less than 1 percent to more than 4 percent.") What, then, can we hope to understand about the sex lives of the Byzantine emperors—let alone of their subjects? As Sir Kenneth Dover says of Athenian slanders on the Spartans:

> If Spartans in the fourth century BC unanimously and firmly denied that their *erastai* and *eromenoi* [i.e., senior and junior partners in an ephebophilic bond] ever had any bodily contact beyond a clasping of right hands, it was not easy for an outsider even at the time to produce evidence to the contrary, and for us it is impossible.[113]

So on the things we really want to know, we have not much of a clue. What did members of the Theban Band actually *do* with each other in their leisure hours? Human nature being what it is, it would be surprising if nothing at all went on, but beyond that there is little we can say.

Reading Professor Crompton's book, I found that the most useful way of thinking about his topic was as a sort of dance—a "dance to the music of time," as it were. (Apologies to the late Anthony Powell.) The participants in this dance are not individual human beings but invariant components of the human personality, found in all times and places. Principal among those components I would list the following:

- Homosexual orientation. Some small proportion of people find erotic fulfillment only with members of their own sex.
- Ephebophilia. Some much larger proportion of adult men can be sexually aroused by contemplating the bodies of well-formed adolescent boys. Overt expression of this attraction has been approved in some societies (or among some social strata in some societies—this seems to be controversial), where it has led to open romantic bonding between adult men and boys. Some

similar, but much less historically significant, phenomenon is found among women.

- *Faute de mieux* homosexuality. In societies, or institutions in societies—monasteries, prisons, etc.—where social custom or institutional imperative severely constrains access to the opposite sex, some large proportion of adults, perhaps a majority, will find erotic satisfaction, or at least release, with members of their own sex, when there are not strong institutional prejudices against this (as there are, for instance, in elite combat units of the US military).
- Homophobia. (Note: This ugly and etymologically stupid word has entered general currency, so I use it here for convenience, though under protest.) The contemplation of homosexuality induces negative emotions—disgust and contempt, mostly, but also sometimes indignation, anger, and hatred—in many people.

The story told in *Homosexuality and Civilization* is in large part the story of a long dance among these four partners, with sometimes this one, sometimes that one taking the lead. The well-known proclivities of the ancient Greeks, for example, arose mainly from the union of the second and third of the factors I have listed.

Louis Crompton's position on some of these core topics is, I do not think it is unfair to say, controversial. On homosexual orientation, for example, consider the numbers again. So far as we understand the science of male homosexuality—which is further than most people realize, though nothing like far enough to make conclusive pronouncements—the orientation is congenital, with events in the mother's womb as causative factors, together probably with some slight effects from genetic predisposition (a perplexing thing in itself, considering the consequences for inheritance) and life events in infancy. On Bailey's estimate, from one to four percent of men are affected. Has this proportion been constant across other times and places? It is impossible to know. The science suggests, as a null hypothesis, that it has been. I am not aware of any evidence contradicting this.

Crompton's narrative contradicts that null hypothesis mightily, though. He has, for example, three of the six Stuart monarchs of England as homosexual in orientation. The probability of this on a four percent basis is one in 855. On a one percent basis it is one in 51,142. Even if you allow the possibility of that slight genetic factor, this is far out of range. Similarly with his catalogs of Chinese storytellers, Arab poets, and Elizabethan dramatists. Literary gents are not, to be sure, representative of the general population in their sexual preferences, but is Professor Crompton quite sure he has made all due allowance for flattery, stylistic fads, flights of fancy, and plain mischief? I once listened in on an e-list discussion among some Shakespeare experts, debating the question: Is there any character in the plays that can reasonably be taken as "gay" in the modern sense? The consensus was that there is not one. Considering the number of characters involved, this seems difficult to square with Crompton's speculations on the Sonnets and their author.

On homophobia, Crompton is emphatic: It is all the fault of "the Hebrew scriptures"—especially, of course, Leviticus. Those proscriptions infected Christianity via Saint Paul and then to a lesser degree tainted Islam. I should make it clear here that I see no signs of any anti-Semitic intent in Crompton's book, though I do think it is quite unpleasantly anti-Christian.

Is homophobia really all the fault of Leviticus and Saint Paul, though? I have said above that "many people" are repelled by homosexuality. How many? In present-day America, I would guess the answer to be: "A modest majority of men, a minority of women," though the numbers cut differently according to age, religion, education, and social class. The situation in other times and places is even less clear. However, there seems to have been, at a minimum, a widespread general repugnance, in all times and places, toward the passive partner in male-male buggery—"the man who plays the part of a woman." This repugnance may be sufficiently widespread to belong on anthropologist Donald E. Brown's list of "human universals," along with ethnocentrism, incest avoidance, jokes, and so on. It is not difficult to think of an explanation for it in terms of evolutionary biology, but so far as I am aware, the actual psychological status of homophobia is not known. It might be biologically "hardwired." Contrariwise, it might be socially conditioned—though if it is, there seems to have been no society that did not condition it to some degree.

In short, there is much more to homophobia than blind prejudice ignited by Hebrew scriptures. One of the most violently homophobic societies that ever existed was Mao Tse-tung's China. Bao Ruo-Wang's *Prisoner of Mao* (1973), for instance, includes a grisly eyewitness account of the execution of a labor-camp inmate suspected of having made homosexual advances. Yet practically nobody in that society had heard of Leviticus or Saint Paul. How does Crompton explain this? He doesn't; though he says that the turn toward homophobia in Meiji Japan was a result of "Western influence." Perhaps it was; perhaps Professor Crompton has misconstrued the openness of pre-Meiji times; perhaps the process of modernization anywhere excites homophobia for some reason; perhaps half a dozen other perhapses.

Crompton's explanations sometimes fall below the unconvincing down to the preposterous. "Abuse of sodomites [in the mid-eighteenth century] became a way for Englishmen to affirm their manhood and allay any suspicions about their own sexuality." This is only a more highfalutin version of the sneering retort often given by homosexuals to anyone who criticizes their activities: "What's *your* problem?" It has its roots in pop-Freudianism, which is to say, in a trivialized version of an exploded theory. Why did Englishmen at that particular time need to "affirm their manhood" in that particular way, rather than by, say, chasing women, fighting duels, or going to war?

Crompton's book also has odd omissions. Russia, for example, is left out altogether. Does he think that country not sufficiently civilized? Or just not sufficiently "gay"? (If the latter, he may be mistaken. One memoirist observed of the reign of Nicholas I that: "at that time buggery was widespread in high society.") The narrative ends rather abruptly, and early—the latest figure discussed at length is Jeremy Bentham. "Our story concludes here," says the author, "at the moment when executions finally cease in Europe." Why? It did not begin when executions started. Perhaps Crompton just got tired. One could not blame him, for the amount of sheer hard work he has put into his book is plain to see. The results, for this reader, were not altogether as intended, but I am glad to have read *Homosexuality and Civilization* anyway, and recommend it to anyone who likes this sort of thing.

Dancin', Yeah

National Review

APRIL 26, 2007

F OR PROPONENTS of the theory that everything in the world exists for some good reason, disco music must present a conundrum. What higher purpose could possibly be served by this vapid, thrumping, affectless sound, dragging in its wake a subculture of narcissism, pill-popping, promiscuity both straight and gay, cheesy light shows, and the worst male clothing styles since slashed doublets and neck ruffs went out? Disco was so mockable it had barely got started before it was mocking *itself*—remember "Disco Duck"?

The answer to the first of those questions will readily be given by any of us Seventies survivors. Disco came into the world so that producer Robert Stigwood and director John Badham could create *Saturday Night Fever*, one of the dozen or so best movies of all time.

THE RICHNESS OF THE MOVIE

THIS YEAR IS the thirtieth anniversary of *SNF*. Filming was wrapping up just about exactly thirty years ago as I write, and the movie premiered on December 7, 1977. By way of celebration I bought a DVD of the movie—a thing I rarely do. I have been sitting here in my study watching it on my computer. (It is *not* a family movie, certainly not in the nothing-spared DVD version). I can report that thirty years on, it is as good as ever—a beautiful, beautiful movie, a great movie.

Most movies are garbage. We try to have a family movie night once a week, on a Friday or a Saturday, playing some rented DVD from Netflix on the family TV. Dad likes a couple of glasses of wine with his dinner, and a couple of glasses of port afterward. The family joke is to open a book on how far the movie will get before Dad falls asleep. It's a rare movie that keeps me awake all the way through. (*The Devil Wears Prada* [2006] was the last one.) *SNF*, however, will never send me to sleep. I watched it all the way through three times before writing this, and I'll watch it again this weekend if I get time.

My high opinion was not shared by the Academy of Motion Picture Arts and Sciences. The 1978 Oscars (i.e., for movies released in 1977) were dominated by: *Julia*, a leftie swooner about anti-fascists in the 1930s; *Annie Hall*, the first of Woody Allen's 295 movies about Woody Allen's neuroses; and the original *Star Wars*. John Travolta got a Best Actor nomination for *SNF*, but no Oscar. So much for recognition of merit.

The first thing that struck me, watching *SNF* again after a lapse of years, was the *richness* of it. There is so much going on. How did they get it all into 118 minutes?

At its heart, the story is just boy-meets-girl. The boy, Tony Manero (John Travolta), is nineteen and works in a paint store. In his leisure hours he hangs out with a little group of coevals: Double J, Joey, Bobby C, Gus. These are all working-class youngsters in Bay Ridge, Brooklyn, a scruffy white-ethnic district at that time, although considerably yuppified since. On Saturday nights they go to the local disco, where Tony is the star dancer. The girl, Stephanie (Karen Lynn Gorney), is also an accomplished dancer. She shows up at the disco one night, catches Tony's eye, and the main plot line is under way.

The richness of the movie is in the other stories being told. Tony's brother, Frank Jr., leaves the Catholic priesthood, breaking his mother's heart. The father, Frank Sr., has been out of work for months and the family is having trouble making ends meet—a problem not helped by Frank Sr.'s incomplete acceptance of the situation. He is, for instance, angry at the idea that his wife might get a job herself. (These are second-generation Italian immigrants. The grandmother, who lives with them, speaks only Italian.)

Stephanie herself is struggling out of her working-class chrysalis, trying to give herself an intellectual, vocational, and elocutionary makeover, with mixed results. Tony's dancing partner, Annette, is afflicted with unrequited love for Tony, and is shattered when he takes up with

Stephanie. Bobby C, a hopeless loser, has a crisis of his own, which ends horribly. There is a turf war going on between Tony's friends and local Puerto Ricans. All this in 118 minutes! *Hamlet* doesn't get so much more into four hours.

A LEFT-SIDE-OF-THE-BELL-CURVE MOVIE

THE SECOND THING that struck me was that this is a movie about the left-hand half of the bell curve. Of the main characters, I would surmise that only Frank Jr. has an IQ over 100. A couple of the others—Bobby C, Doreen—come across as borderline retarded. All the rest are drawn from that big slab to the left of the mean: people with IQs of 80-something or 90-something. These are normal, unreflective working people who did not get much from their formal education, don't read books, and don't think in abstractions, or wish to.

In an age when most movies with any dramatic content at all are made for yuppies, by yuppies, about yuppies—an age in which nobody is supposed to go to work until age twenty-five, after that long soaking in a warm bath of political correctness that we call "college"—this is wonderfully refreshing. The only yuppie in *SNF* is Stephanie's slimy ex-boyfriend, a walk-on part. Political correctness? Fuhgeddaboutit. You can check off the violations: Homophobia? Check. N-word? Check. Hispanophobia? Check. Male chauvinism? Check, check, check, check, check. Everybody smokes, drinks, and cusses. (Tony's drink preference is the "7&7," i.e., Seagram's 7 whiskey mixed with 7 Up. He smokes Marlboros. His favorite cuss word is . . . well, use your imagination.)

It is true that Stephanie *aspires* to be a yuppie, but the script provides good and sufficient hope that she will never sell all her soul. You can take the girl out of Bay Ridge, Stephanie, but you can't take Bay Ridge out of the girl.

Thirty years on, with the white working class fast becoming an endangered species, their services no longer required, this second-quartile aspect of *SNF* is quite striking. White people with IQs around 90 are deeply uninteresting to our cultural content-providers, having no colorful ethnicity nor any anguished heritage of oppression to commend them. Our political and business elites find them bothersome, and are striving to replace them with cheaper, colorfully ethnic, and anguished-heritage-loaded immigrants. White American proles are not favorites with moviemakers.

The *SNF* characters even *look* like ordinary people—as opposed, I mean, to looking like movie stars pretending to be ordinary people.

Their teeth are not very white or very straight, they have bad haircuts and get bad shaves, they smoke cigarettes and eat crummy food, they wear cheap clothes and hang crucifixes on their walls, they are not very articulate or—away from the dance floor—graceful. They mumble, stumble, misunderstand each other, and tell little white lies.

SNF brings to mind Nathaniel Hawthorne's comment on Trollope's novel *Barchester Towers*:

> It is just as real as if some giant had hewn a great lump out of the earth and put it under a glass case, with all its inhabitants going about their daily business, and not suspecting that they were being made a show of.

Furthermore, the characters look exactly as they should look, each in his role. There is no Academy Award given for Best Casting Director, or *SNF*'s Shirley Rich would surely deserve one. The faces are just right, just right—and *memorable*:

- Stephanie breaking into giggles on realizing that what she has just said is pretentious psychobabble.
- Tony's warning look when Annette, whose affections he does not desire, puts her hand on his shoulder.
- Annette plunging into anguish when Tony tells her he has a new dance partner.
- Frank Jr. in the disco, grasping the hopelessness of Bobby C's situation, and his own utter inability to help, either as priest or ex-priest.

Any one of those could be framed and hung on the wall in an acting school. It's not the least bit surprising that, Travolta aside, none of these actors advanced into Major Celebrity status. They are too good, too human. Listen to their voices. Listen to Stephanie saying "delusions of grandeur"—pitch-perfect!

SNF was John Travolta's finest moment, too. His *only* moment, perhaps—if he has since made another movie that was half as good as *SNF*, I missed it. His speech, his movements, his mannerisms are all precisely right. The DVD has some "special features" showing Travolta rehearsing the dance sequences. It's clear that he didn't find them easy, and a credit to his professionalism that the end result was so polished.

(Travolta, by the way, was struck by a personal tragedy while filming the movie. He took a few days off, then came back and finished the job. If you can tell which scenes were shot before the calamity, and which after, you have sharper eyes than mine. The man is a true pro.)

THE MUSIC SO FINE

AND THEN, THE music. All right, it's disco music. Whaddya want?—it's a disco movie.

There is, after all, something to like about the disco craze. Dancing is a fundamental human activity. It is there in anthropologist Donald E. Brown's "list of human universals," in between "daily routines" and "death rituals." (Brown's entire list is given in an appendix to Steven Pinker's book *The Blank Slate* [2002].)

Dancing got lost somehow around 1965, though, like a great deal else. When I was at high school in the early 1960s, we all took ballroom dancing lessons as a matter of course. What were you going to do at a dance if you didn't know, at a minimum, the foxtrot, waltz, quickstep, and cha-cha? What kind of social life could you expect to have?

Then quite suddenly it was all gone, and solipsistic twitching took over as the preferred form of dance-floor display. All structure was lost: Formlessness and chaos took over. Ballroom dance steps? That's so *old*.

When disco came in, it was once again, for a brief while, cool to be able actually to *dance*, to dance *steps*. Far from being a kitschy joke, disco was a brief return to civilized social values before the darkness fell for good in the 1980s.

The disco crowd in *SNF* consists of people you would *not* likely bump into at Carnegie Hall or the Guggenheim. They have aesthetic impulses, though, just as much as any gallery or concert-hall patron, and those instincts are wakened by the sight of a skilful dancer doing his stuff. See how they applaud Tony! What he is doing is *beautiful*, and they know it. Having a 90 IQ does not mean that you are an esthetically challenged clod. Personally, I'll take Bay Ridge aesthetic sensibilities any time over those displayed by admirers of Robert Mapplethorpe, Eve Ensler, or Karlheinz Stockhausen.

And the music is—dare I say it?—not bad.

> What you doin' on your back? (Aah.)
> What you doin' on your back? (Aah.)
> You should be dancin', yeah.
> Dancin', yeah.

Or how about:

> Here I am,
> Prayin' for this moment to last,
> Livin' on the music so fine,
> Borne on the wind,
> Makin' it mine . . .

And of course:

> Feel the city breakin'
> an' ev'rybody shakin'
> An' we're stayin' alive, stayin' alive.
> Ah, ha, ha, ha, stayin' alive.

All right, it's not Cole Porter, but then, hardly anything is. As late-twentieth-century pop music goes, this is pretty superior stuff. Furthermore, if you pay attention, you will notice that the lyrics are loosely keyed to the movie's plot line. Someone here really knows what he's doing.

CONFUCIUS TAKES THE "R" TRAIN

TONY MANERO IS what used to be called a diamond in the rough. Crude and classless (as Stephanie tells him bluntly), he is nonetheless a natural gentleman, with all the right instincts (as Stephanie grasps, at some less conscious level).

- After losing it with his mother, Tony at once feels terrible and tries to comfort her, his voice cracking for the only time in the movie.
- Having decided to break with Annette, he tells her directly, with a proper apology.
- After telling Stephanie one of those little white lies, he is immediately ashamed, as a gentleman should be, and covers with the truth. "I'm twenty." (Stephanie gives him a skeptical look.) "Well, I'm nineteen at the moment, but I'll be twenty very shortly."

This fundamental decency comes out plainly in the scene where Mr. Fusco, Tony's boss at the paint store, gives him a raise.

FUSCO: I gave you a raise.
TONY: A what?
FUSCO: A raise.
TONY: You kiddin' me?
FUSCO: Come on, look, see how much it is.
TONY: You gave me a raise? Thank you! [Extends hand to shake.] I can't believe this!
FUSCO: [Embarrassed at the not-yet-revealed smallness of the raise.] Hold on, you better look first.
TONY: I don't gotta look, it makes no difference. You gave me a raise, that's the important thing.
FUSCO: [Somewhat shamed by Tony's reaction.] It's only two fifty.
TONY: So what?

Tony understands instinctively that to what Confucius called the *jūnzi*, the "superior man," honor, recognition, and right conduct mean everything, money nothing.

Most memorably, Tony's strong sense of natural justice and fair play lifts him above his gang's ethnic squabbling with the Puerto Ricans, prompting him to fierce anger when he and Stephanie are awarded a dance prize unfairly, out of flagrant ethnic favoritism. He walks over to the Puerto Rican couple and thrusts the prize trophy and cash envelope into their hands—"Congratulations! I'd like to give you *this*, and I'd like to give you *that*, because I think you deserve it, all right?"—then walks right out of the dance hall, fuming.

Tony's character includes a proper component of manly tenderness, too. Driving Stephanie back from Manhattan, they have a shouting match. Stephanie, wounded by his words, breaks down and cries. Tony repents at once, and does his best to soothe and heal: "It's all right . . . Don't worry about nothin'." His reward at last is Stephanie's first tentative kiss, on his cheek.

Everybody is drawn to this instinctive decency. To be a natural gentleman like this is to be a natural leader. Tony controls his little clique effortlessly, directing their activities ("We ain't droppin' nothin' till I say so"), trying to prompt them to his own innate standards of manliness, scolding them for their pill popping ("Can't you guys get off on dancin'?"), instructing Annette in the rudiments of female honor: "That's the thing a girl's gotta decide early on. You gotta decide whether you're gonna be a nice girl or a c***."

With that solid moral framework to support him, Tony is acquiring wisdom rapidly. He has a long way to go, to be sure, but you don't doubt he'll get there. Did Bobby C kill himself? the investigating cop asks. Tony: "There's ways of killin' yourself without killin' yourself." Indeed there are, Tony—many, many ways.

AT TWENTY, YOU'RE DONE

AMONG ALL THE other things it is about, *SNF* is about being twenty. It is hard to watch it at any much greater age without a painful twinge of nostalgia.

Here it all is—all the vanity, foolishness, and excitement of twenty-dom. Here is the vigor: "I feel so wild! I got all this energy!" The narcissism: "He hits my hair!" The tribal bonding: "We got 'em . . . Italian style!" Here is the intense awareness of in-group status rankings, and the keen importance of maintaining one's own at the top: "Now shape up, you assholes, we're the *faces*."

Here is the *urgency* of being twenty, the *immediacy*.

> FUSCO: You can save a little, build a future.
> TONY: Fuck the future.
> FUSCO: No, Tony, you can't fuck the future. The future fucks you. It catches up with you and it fucks you if you ain't planned for it.
> TONY: Look, tonight is the future, and I am planning for it. There's this shirt I gotta buy, a beautiful shirt . . .

And of course there is the wonderful, terrible affliction of romantic love. Cupid's arrow can strike at any time of life, to be sure; but it never pierces so deep, nor with such pain, as at twenty.

SNF is a romantic movie, a celebration of love. Just watch Tony's second sighting of Stephanie, when she is in the dance studio doing exercises at the barre. (And not to disco music, either: Her choice is Chopin's *Nocturne*, Op. 9, No. 2—a piece that is not merely romantic, but Romantic, in the precise and technical sense.)

Judith Rich Harris, in one of her books, tells of dealing with her aged mother, who suffers from severe Alzheimer's. On one particular day, Judith tries to get her mother to focus on the fact that this day is actually her eightieth birthday.

"Do you know today is your birthday, Mom?"

"Is it?"

"Yes. How old do you think you are?"

Dimly aware that something really important is being asked of her, the mother summons up all the powers of concentration she has left. At last she says: "Twenty?"

This is exactly right. We are all twenty, even when we're eighty. At twenty we are cooked right through, we are done. Later changes are nothing but "walking north on the deck of a southbound ship." Your essential character is formed at twenty, and will not change.

SNF is very good on this sad fact of our essential immutability. There is no uplifting flapdoodle here about self-transformation. Bobby C praises Tony's dancing.

TONY: You could do as good as me if you practiced.

BOBBY C: Yeah? Think I'd be a good dancer?

TONY: Sure, why not? No.

Tony is right, of course. Bobby C will never be a good dancer, or a good anything. Poor Bobby!

BOBBY C: If you had to make a choice between getting an abortion and having to get married to somebody, what would you do?

STEPHANIE: Well, who'd I have to marry?

BOBBY C: You'd have to marry me.

STEPHANIE: I think I'd get an abortion.

At twenty, these young men are all pretty much done, and you can practically hear the doors of opportunity clanging shut around them. Not that it is impossible for them to get somewhere in life from this point on, but now it will need more courage, determination, and luck with every passing year. This is the thing that Tony grasps at the very end of the movie: "I'm an able person. I can do these things." (Unspoken: *But I better get moving.*)

"I KNOW EVERYTHING ABOUT THAT BRIDGE"

FOR SEEKERS OF symbols, *SNF* is dominated by bridges. You could get a PhD thesis out of the bridge symbols in this movie. Someone probably has.

The very first shot in *SNF* is of the Brooklyn Bridge. That is also the bridge Tony and Stephanie drive over when moving her furniture to Manhattan. Then there is the Verrazzano-Narrows Bridge, whose construction would have dominated Tony's childhood. (He was six when it opened in 1964.)

And beyond the bridges—the city! From Bay Ridge you can see lower Manhattan—including, in *SNF*, the dear old Twin Towers. Manhattan shimmers there in the background of the movie—a fairytale place: near, yet somehow hard of access. In Manhattan you can be *free*, no longer cumbered by ties of tradition, family, neighborhood.

This freedom is of course a mixed blessing. Manhattan is no place for children or old folk. What do Tony and Stephanie care? They are twenty! (See above.) Manhattan is the land of Cockaigne, where everything is possible and you don't have to be home in time for dinner. Freedom and opportunity—Manhattan is *America*.

A cynical middle-aged conservative might frown at that, and point out that Manhattan, with its bossy mayor and feather-bedding unions, its five-hundred-word parking signs and "rent control" rackets, is the least free stretch of real estate in the country.

Again, Stephanie and Tony don't see that, and wouldn't care about it if they *could* see it. Manhattan is for them the great finishing school, the place of new experiences, the place where you shuck off that chrysalis and dump it in the East River.

Any number of movies have romanticized Manhattan, of course, but none so deftly, so lightly, as *SNF*. Even the subway comes out well: I have never felt the same about it since watching Tony's long solitary ride near the movie's end.

> Stephanie: You've got no idea how it changes, just right over there, right across the river. Everything is different, really different. It's just beautiful. The people are beautiful, the offices are beautiful . . .

Yes, they are, Stephanie. Don't let any cynical old farts tell you otherwise.

BORNE ON THE WIND

SNF ISN'T FLAWLESS. There is a list of continuity bloopers at the IMDB site.[114] The lighting strikes me as somewhat erratic. Soft-focus shots look corny nowadays outside TV commercials for geriatric medications. And what *is* it that Double J says at 1:49:16 on the DVD, just after Bobby C has removed himself from the gene pool?

These things aren't important, though. *SNF* is not the production of some tortured genius striving for immortality through perfection. It was created by a bunch of capable professional people pooling their talents in the hope of pulling down some overtime and making a bit of money.

In this respect, *SNF* reminds me of the *bel canto* operas I love—those early nineteenth-century Italian operas thrown together in a hurry by journeyman composers trying to catch the public taste, with implausible librettos, recycled overtures (Rossini used the same overture for *three* different operas), and arias written for tenor A in city X, then hastily rewritten for tenor B in city Y, the opera house manager drumming his fingers impatiently as the composer reaches for another sheet of music paper.

Most work produced on the fly like this is ephemeral, but now and then everything comes right. The hasty scribbler, the harassed director, the struggling actor, are kissed with genius. Then all is lifted out of the common plane, into the light of beauty and glory, up into the realm of true art—borne on the wind!

CHAPTER TEN:

Q and A

Interview with Richard Hoste

HBD Books

SEPTEMBER 2009

Y OU STARTED *out as a computer programmer. That's certainly not a typical background for a political writer. How did you end up working at* National Review?

I'm a chronic writer, always been writing something—Letters to the Editor, for example. If you are like that, eventually you will get stuff published. By the time I reached that point, I was a middle-aged conservative living in the United States, so *NR* was my natural home.

You weren't always a race realist. Can you talk about your journey from a sort of soft culturalism to biologism?

It was gradual. Landmarks were reading Jared Taylor's *Paved with Good Intentions* (1992) in the mid-1990s (and becoming an *American Renaissance* subscriber shortly afterward), and being signed up in Steve Sailer's Human Bio-Diversity listserv later that decade, and hobnobbing with actual biologists, anthropologists, etc. Then a lot of reading and cogitation. My scientific interests prior to that had been entirely physical and mathematical.

Did you hesitate before coming forward at NRO with your views on the black/white achievement gap?

No. I have always said exactly what I think at *NR/NRO*, and they have hardly ever spiked me. (Every contributor gets spiked *some* of the time.)

Did you ever feel that your job was in danger?

Yes, but not for race realism.

Why do you think you continue to be a regular NR *contributor when other politically incorrect thinkers such as Peter Brimelow and Steve Sailer were, at least according to the alternative right, purged?*

No idea. I've heard all the theories about what happened in 1997, but don't know which one is true. I was hoping Rick Brookhiser's latest book would shed some light, but it really doesn't—Rick is too much of a gent.

That change of editors and direction (i.e., away from strong articles on immigration policy, and articles with an openness toward human bio-diversity topics) seems to have been driven by whims of Bill Buckley's. He was still very much in charge at that time, even though no longer editor, and inclined to sudden changes of favor, as Rick's book does make clear.

Bill must always have had his doubts about the O'Sullivan/Brimelow/Sailer immigration line. He was sentimentally inclined to Hispanics—his first language was Spanish, remember—and always sensitive to the feelings of his Jewish peers, who of course were all fanatically pro-immigration. The story favored by paleos—that Bill was just taking out extra "Jew insurance"—seems to me simpleminded. You have to factor in his age, character, part-Spanish childhood, friendships, and lifelong strategy toward ideas and people he perceived, with varying degrees of accuracy, to be in or beyond the outer borderlands of conservatism.

I myself don't actually write much about race and HBD topics. I am engaged (for a couple of years now!) in porting over all my web archives from the horrid old FrontPage format to something crisper and more manageable. I have written VB* routines to do the grunt work, but they don't catch everything, and each piece needs to be hand polished. So I am reading my way through my entire output since the 1990s. Very little of it even touches on these topics. Yes, I am a race realist. It's not a big part of what I want to write about, though.

In Doomed *you talk about meeting a conservative academic who argued for the noble lie when it comes to religion. You don't seem to believe in it. But isn't it true that for a person with an IQ of, say, 90, the religious view can give him something that a bunch of theories about bell curves and selfish genes that he doesn't even understand cannot?*

Yes, I agree with you. I don't know that *Doomed* contradicts that. The stories offered by religions are very comforting and consoling, and taken together the stories of one particular religion can offer a good overall framework for helping you through life, if you don't have a strongly empirical way of thinking. (Most people don't.) That by no means only applies to the bottom IQ quartile either. Far be it from me to remove those consolations from anyone. *Doomed* does not try to.

Something is always owed to truth, though. The human race as a whole only gets ahead by figuring out true things about the world. Ghosts, demons, angels, magical impregnations and resurrections, the Afterlife, are not true things. If you are writing a book trying to orient people toward a darker, more pessimistic view of the human situation, that is something you want to point out.

You list the six nations (the United States, Canada, Australia, Switzerland, Sweden, and New Zealand) out of 152 that existed in 1911 which have survived to the present day.† Notice they're all countries founded by Germanic peoples. While nonwhites have been making inroads, Northern Europeans still make up a majority in each country (except America maybe, which still has a white majority). Do you think that there's a human biodiversity explanation for that?

---

*   Visual Basic, or VB, is a high-level, object-oriented computer programming language.

†   In Derbyshire's 2009 book, *We Are Doomed*, the author cites his 1911 *Encyclopaedia Britannica*, observing that only six nations—Australia, Canada, New Zealand, Sweden, Switzerland, and the United States—survived the 20th century without revolution, civil war, foreign occupation, or major territorial dismemberment. He explicitly excludes Britain due to the secession of Ireland.

My guess would be that there is, though the evidence to date is circumstantial. Why do some peoples do so much better than others? That's the great central problem of the human sciences. There are some fascinating ideas in the air, often supported by good data and elegant writing (for example, Gregory Clark's *A Farewell to Alms* [2007]) but we don't at present really know.

Kevin MacDonald for example thinks that Northern Europeans were selected for traits that lead to societal stability (at least when their nations stay homogenous).[115]

Hmm. Eighteenth-century France, seventeenth-century England, nineteenth-century America—were they really so "stable"? Try checking off some countries NOT in that list you quoted from *Doomed* . . . Kevin's written some interesting stuff, but always with a whiff of crankiness and confirmation bias. Not icily empirical enough for me.

You talk about being fascinated by the problem of consciousness. You've read books on the topic and attended a conference but don't feel any the wiser for it. I've also taken an interest in the topic but have been unable to find any kind of explanation of what consciousness is or why it exists. An interesting thing that you once said was that you believed that the human mind hasn't evolved to understand itself (you had a name for the philosophical position, though I can't remember it now). Do we simply wait for genetic engineering to make us smart enough to figure it all out?

New Mysterianism, yes. Whether or not humanity is smart enough to crack what they call "the hard problem of consciousness," I don't know. I feel pretty sure that *I* am not smart enough though, and will go to my grave not understanding any more than I do now. The fascination with consciousness is a bit regrettable, like a nicotine habit. It does you no good and ends in frustration. I should swear off it.

You initially supported the Iraq war but now have turned against it. I remember during the run up to the war everybody and their mother who opposed it was denounced by mainstream conservatives as a traitor.[116] *Do you think you could've survived at* National Review *if you took the position you hold now from the start? I don't believe a single writer at the magazine opposed the war at the time, correct?*

Well, as I say in *Doomed*, it depends what you mean by "war." I wanted revenge and was very happy to see Iraq get smashed up. I wasn't shy about saying so, which kept me on side *NR*-wise. I never supported "nation-building" though; and when it became obvious that was what Bush was trying for, I complained. I certainly don't remember holding back at any point.

My basic approach to terrorism, though, was the one I expressed on the morning of 9/11—lots of covert ops—"small teams of inconceivably brave men and women, working in strange places, unknown and unacknowledged."[117] That's never changed. That's the War on Terror I'd like to see. Perhaps I was naive to think I'd see it, though. Any modern American administration would demand a good quota of lawyers in among those "small teams" to make sure nobody's human rights got violated, or feelings hurt.

NR-wise, mine is more of a science/culture/China beat, so my opinions about a war probably wouldn't get me fired in any case, since that's not the stuff I write about.

You've said elsewhere that you're a believer in Steve Sailer's citizenism, where the government ignores race and simply favors citizens over noncitizens.[118] *My main problem with that is that there's no rational reason for Non-Asian Minorities (NAMs) to support the idea. They benefit from the Affirmative Action/diversity state, don't they? Surely Michelle Obama would've never earned $300,000 a year doing real work.*

Yes; but non-NAM liberals (that tag includes a lot of conservatives in this context) have to enable the NAM preference, since NAMs are a minority. That NAMs support race-guilt policies is not the least bit surprising. That non-NAMs throw in their lot with them is nuts. Mrs. Obama got that $300K diversity-enforcer job because lots of non-NAMs thought it was a great idea to give it to her. Why on earth did they think that? Beats me. The attitude of non-NAM—can I say "Ice People," please?—liberals toward NAMs seems to be a mix of fear and contempt. "Oh, give 'em a few high-salary make-work jobs with fancy titles because (a) then perhaps they won't break our windows, and (b) they're too stupid to do much harm, so what's it matter, long as it keeps 'em off the streets?" Attitudes like that, if I am right, are not conducive to a harmonious society.

You end your book on a pretty hopeless note. You say that you're not a white nationalist, but you have had respectful dialogues with Jared Taylor. Could you see a point where minority activism and the racial double standards become so bad that you'd advocate white nationalism to counter it?

The United States I would like to live in would be one in which White Nationalism is not necessary, because (a) nonwhite nationalisms are not pandered to (removing the WN argument: "*They* have identity politics, why shouldn't *we*?"), and (b) whites are a big, fat, and permanent majority, confident in their culture and proud of their ancestry, but tolerant and helpful toward their minority fellow-citizens.

To get to (a) we have to scrap multiculturalism and the "Diversity" dog poop; to get to (b) we need rational, restrictive immigration policies, prefaced by expulsion of all illegal residents and revocation of "anchor baby" citizenships.

I admire Jared tremendously—a fine American gentleman of the kind we English brats heard about when growing up, from Louisa M. Alcott and Mark Twain, and saw on screen in that wonderful crop of mid-twentieth-century American-gent movie stars (Gable, Grant, Cooper, Stewart . . .). A dying breed now, alas. Jared may be the best-mannered person I know. He is certainly one of the most intelligent.

Break some news to ya though: There are *not* a lot of Jareds in the white nationalist movement. Way too few. Way, way. A real, science-based WN movement that wanted to get somewhere in public life would begin by cloning Jared.

Healthcare is currently dominating the political debate in America. You've lived under socialized medicine in the United Kingdom and under the American system. Which do you view more favorably?

Hard for me to judge, as I'm too darn healthy (touch wood). I was pretty continuously sick—often hospitalized—through my childhood, but since then have interacted very little with any healthcare system. Hardly ever think about my health. My basic attitude is to just run my body as long as it'll go, then die gracefully. (I treat cars the same.) I like Saint Francis apologizing to his body at the end: "Poor donkey!" There have been no valetudinarians in my family, and I don't plan to break the run.

As a self-employed, I have a "plan" to cover me and my family, costing over $1K per month, which seems to me far too much, but other people tell me is cheap around here (i.e., New York). We no way run up $12K bills a year, so it's basically just catastrophe insurance, which it seems to me I could get much cheaper in a rational system. Pegging healthcare to employment is *NUTS*—who on earth thought *THAT* up?

When I was a kid and using the NHS a lot, it was good to me. My English friends and relatives seem to like it. It's way cheaper than our system [in the United States]. People get denied things, but so do they here—hell, my policy is all premised on denial-of-service. You have to argue a case; and I think all policies are like that.

The big question seems to me: Can a nationalized system work in the United States? That it works, to the satisfaction of most, in small European countries, doesn't tell us much. We're not them. We are SIMPLY TERRIBLE at socialism. Something about our system, and those "profound demographic divisions."

Do the Tea Bag movement and opposition to Obama's centralizing plans give you hope or do you believe it will all come to naught?

Not to utterly naught, perhaps. Noisy movements like the Teabaggers can slow things down, perhaps change direction here and there. In the end, though—after two more administrations—we shall be at European levels of public spending as proportion of GDP, with or without socialized medicine (though of course a bit sooner with it).

Does the fact that the fall of Western civilization is happening at the hands of a bunch of diversity bureaucrats and feminist scholars make it more depressing than if it were being destroyed at the hands of, say, a superior military force?

Oh yes. Isn't civil war always a lot uglier than international war?

Endnotes

1   Deborah Solomon, "Head of the Class: Questions for Charles Murray," *New York Times Magazine*, September 19, 2008.

2   Christopher Jackson, "A White Teacher Speaks Out," *American Renaissance* 20, no. 7 (2009).

3   See George Orwell, "Notes on Nationalism," in *England Your England and Other Essays* (London: Secker and Warburg, 1953).

4   See John Derbyshire, "An Arctic Alliance?" *New English Review* (October 2007).

5   See John Derbyshire, "Sing, con allegria!" *National Review Online*, November 22, 2001.

6   See James Fulford, "Quote Of The Day: 'Mostly Involving Big, Big Beachballs,'" *VDARE*, September 3, 2009.

7   John Derbyshire, "The Single Talent Well Employed," *National Review Online*, January 4, 2002.

8   John Derbyshire, "The Futility of Dissidence," *Taki's Magazine*, February 2, 2011.

9   Adam Rutherford, "Why racism is not backed by science," *Guardian*, March 1, 2015

10 Madison Grant, *The Passing Of The Great* Race, New York: Charles Scribner's Sons, 1923.

11 John Derbyshire, "Diversity Graphic," JPEG image.

12 See John Derbyshire, "The Husks of Dead Theories," *National Review Online*, April 24, 2009.

13 John Derbyshire, "Is HBD Over?" *VDARE*, January 10, 2013.

14 John Derbyshire, *We Are Doomed* (New York: Crown Forum, 2009).

15 John Derbyshire, "The Datanaut," *National Review*, December 22, 2003.

16 In the *Washington Post* Book World, July 9, 1989, Charles Sheffield described Apollo as, among other things, "Rich, densely packed and beautifully told. . . . Filled with cliffhangers, suspense and spine-tingling adventure."

17 Sam Harris, host, *Making Sense*, podcast, episode 73, "Forbidden Knowledge: A Conversation with Charles Murray," April 22, 2017.

18 *By the People: Rebuilding Liberty Without Permission* (2015) and *In Our Hands: A Plan to Replace the Welfare State* (2016).

19 Real Education: Four Simple Truths for Bringing America's Schools Back to Reality (2008).

20 *The Curmudgeon's Guide to Getting Ahead: Dos and Don'ts of Right Behavior, Tough Thinking, Clear Writing, and Living a Good Life* (2014).

21 Katharine Q. Seelye, "Protesters Disrupt Speech by 'Bell Curve' Author at Vermont College," *New York Times*, March 3, 2017.

22 Stephanie Saul, "Dozens of Middlebury Students Are Disciplined for Charles Murray Protest," *New York Times*, May 24, 2017.

23 For more on Neo-Lysenkoism, see Bernard D Davis, "Neo-Lysenkoism, IQ, and the press," *National Affairs* (Fall 1983).

24 Deborah Solomon, "Head of the Class: Questions for Charles Murray," *New York Times Magazine*, September 19, 2008.

25 Steven J. Rosenthal, "Academic Nazism."

26   See Robert Plomin, *Blueprint: How DNA Makes Us Who We Are* (Cambridge: MIT Press, 2018).

27   Nicole Hemmer, " 'Scientific racism' is on the rise on the right. But it's been lurking there for years," *Vox*, March 28, 2017.

28   Kathryn Paige Harden, "Why Progressives Should Embrace the Genetics of Education," *New York Times*, July 24, 2018.

29   Eric Turkheimer, Kathryn Paige Harden, and Richard Nisbett, "Charles Murray is once again peddling junk science about race and IQ," *Vox*, May 18, 2017.

30   "Racial groupings match genetic profiles, Stanford study finds," *Stanford Medicine News Center*, January 27, 2005.

31   James J. Lee et al., "Gene discovery and polygenic prediction from a genome-wide association study of educational attainment in 1.1 million individuals," *Nature Genetics*, July 23, 2018.

32   Richard Haier, "VOX Goes from 'Junk' to 'No Good': That's a Bit of Intelligent Progress," *Quillette*, June 21, 2017.

33   David Reich, "How Genetics Is Changing Our Understanding of 'Race,'" *New York Times*, March 23, 2018.

34   Michael Schiavo's Terri: The Truth (2006), Mary and Robert Schindler's A Life That Matters: The Legacy of Terri Schiavo—A Lesson for Us All (2006), and Jon B. Eisenberg's *Using Terri: The Religious Right's Conspiracy to Take Away Our Rights* (2005).

35   William Johnson Cory, "Mimnermus in Church."

36   Alexis de Tocqueville, *Democracy in America*, vol. 2, trans. Henry Reeve as revised by Francis Bowen (New York: Random House, 1990), 318–19.

37   Zev Chafets, "Late-Period Limbaugh," *New York Times*, July 6, 2008.

38   As quoted in James Bowman, "Rush Limbaugh: The Leader of the Opposition," *National Review*, February 17, 2021.

39   Christopher Buckley, "My Brush With Rush," *Daily Beast*, October 27, 2008.

40   E. J. Dionne Jr., "Civil War on the Right," *Washington Post*, October 23, 2008.

41 Ron Paul, *The Revolution: A Manifesto* (New York: Grand Central Publishing, 2009).

42 See Alan Zeichick, "Zeichick's Take: With mobile, it's all about the installed base," SD Times, July 11, 2012.

43 Tom Wolfe, "Sorry, But Your Soul Just Died," Forbes ASAP: *The Big Issue*, December 2, 1996.

44 Neela Banerjee, "25 Blacks at Texaco Sue for Arbiters," *New York Times*, November 28, 2000.

45 Adam Nagourney, "THE 2000 CAMPAIGN: THE OVERVIEW; Bradley and Gore Trade Jabs in Fiercest Campaign Debate," *New York Times,* February 22, 2000.

46 Jeffrey Goldberg, "The Color of Suspicion," *New York Times Magazine*, June 20, 1999.

47 As quoted in Randall Kennedy, "Suspect Policy," *The New Republic*, September 13, 1999.

48 "Red Light on Racial Profiling," *Washington Post*, January 26, 2000.

49 *United States v. Montoya De Hernandez*, 473 U.S. 531 (1985).

50 For the best short counter-blast against the drug legalizers, see Ann Coulter, "The Drug Shills," *Human Events*, September 22, 2000.

51 Randall Kennedy, "Suspect Policy," *The New Republic*, September 13, 1999.

52 Robert Burns, "To a Mouse" (1785).

53 Leonard Greene, "Trayvon Martin tragedy brings focus to 'the talk' for black parents," *New York Post*, March 30, 2012.

54 KJ Dell'Antonia, "Trayvon Martin and 'the Talk' Black Parents Have with Their Teenage Sons," *New York Times*, March 26, 2012.

55 Darryl Owens, "Treyvon Martin: Revisiting 'The Talk' that black parents give to keep their children safe," *Orlando Sentinel*, March 23, 2012.

56 See Razib Khan, "Genetic Variation Among African Americans," *Discover Magazine (GNXP blog)*, May 5, 2010.

57 JeFreda R. Brown, "Law of Large Numbers: What It Is, How It's Used, and Examples," *Investopedia*, June 27, 2025.

58 Moriah Balingit, "Racial disparities in school discipline are growing, federal data show," *Washington Post*, April 24, 2018.

59 John Bresnahan, "Racial disparity: All active ethics probes focus on black lawmakers," *Politico*, November 3, 2009.

60 "The Color of Crime," *American Renaissance*, undated.

61 See Gregory Kane, "Racist Democrats always get free passes," *Washington Examiner*, August 10, 2011.

62 Ron Guhname, "Interracial murder," *Inductivist* (blog), March 25, 2012.

63 See James Barron, "Gunman Fires into a Crowd at Jersey Park," *New York Times*, April 20, 1987.

64 Philip L. Roth, et al., "Ethnic Group Differences in Cognitive Ability in Employment and Educational Settings: A Meta-analysis," *Personnel Psychology*, December 7, 2006.

65 See John Derbyshire, "On the Voter Demographic That Dare Not Speak Its Name," *VDARE*, August 7, 2013.

66 Eugene Genovese, *Roll, Jordan, Roll: The World the Slaves Made* (New York: Random House, 1974).

67 Katherine Heintzelman, "Oprah Winfrey, Forest Whitaker Talk Lee Daniel's The Butler, Racism, and the N-word," *Parade*, July 31, 2013.

68 Vietnam War casualty statistics.

69 "Why We Profile," *Those Who Can See* (blog), August 6, 2013.

70 Darryl Fears, "Hue and Cry on 'Whiteness Studies,'" *Washington Post*, June 20, 2003.

71 See Steven Erlanger and Elvire Camus, "In a Ban, a Measure of European Tolerance," *New York Times*, September 1, 2012.

72 Steve Bird, "How to crush a gypsy camp French-style," *Daily Mail*, August 28, 2012.

73   Erlanger and Camus, "In a Ban, a Measure of European Tolerance."

74   See Ann Corcoran, "Sweden! One Djiboutian to Another, Come On Over—The Living Is Easy!," *Refugee Resettlement Watch*, September 1, 2012.

75   See John Derbyshire, "Somali's All Over," *Taki's Magazine*, August 18, 2011.

76   See Brenda Walker, "Ramadan Muslims Fill Moscow Streets," *VDARE*, September 2, 2012.

77   For more on this episode, see John Derbyshire, "Kings of the Deal."

78   The first two of the three books are, *A People That Shall Dwell Alone: Judaism as a Group Evolutionary Strategy, With Diaspora Peoples* (Praeger, 1994) and *Separation and Its Discontents: Toward an Evolutionary Theory of Anti-Semitism* (Praeger, 1998).

79   Nick Paton Walsh, "Solzhenitsyn breaks last taboo of the revolution," *Guardian*, January 25, 2003.

80   See Eric P. Kaufmann, *The Rise and Fall of Anglo-America* (Cambridge: Harvard University Press, 2004).

81   "World Population to Increase by 2.6 Billion Over Next 45 Years, With All Growth Occurring in Less Developed Regions," *United Nations*, February 24, 2005.

82   See Norman Podhoretz, *World War IV: The Long Struggle Against Islamofascism* (New York: Doubleday, 2007).

83   Richard Lynn and Tatu Vanhanen, IQ and the Wealth of Nations (Westport, CT: Praeger, 2002).

84   John Derbyshire, *We Are Doomed* (New York: Crown Forum, 2009).

85   2008 Nobel Prize in Literature, 2008.

86   Amy Chua, "Why Chinese Mothers Are Superior," *Wall Street Journal*, January 8, 2011.

87   Kate Zernike, "Retreat of the 'Tiger Mother,'" *New York Times*, January 14, 2011.

88   Milton Friedman, "The Role of Government in Education," 1955.

89   John Derbyshire, "Chinese Junk," *National Review Online*, May 28, 2009.

90   Robert Fortune, *Three Years' Wanderings in the Northern Provinces of China: Including a Visit to the Tea, Silk, and Cotton Countries; with an Account of the Agriculture and Horticulture of the Chinese, New Plants, Etc.* (London: J. Murray, 1847), 110.

91   Duke Xiang of Song.

92   Rodney Gilbert, *What's Wrong with China* (New York: Frederick A Stokes, 1926), 118.

93   Arthur Henderson Smith.

94   Évariste Régis Huc.

95   Demetrius Charles Boulger, *History of China* (London: W.H. Allen, 1881).

96   Luo Guanzhong, *Romance of the Three Kingdoms*.

97   See Steven W. Mosher, *Bully of Asia: Why China's Dream Is the New Threat to World Order* (Washington, DC: Regnery, 2017).

98   John Derbyshire, *Prime Obsession: Bernhard Riemann and the Greatest Unsolved Problem in Mathematics* (Washington, DC: Joseph Henry Press, 2003).

99   James Thompson, "World IQ 82," April 10, 2019.

100   Total fertility rate.

101   Long nineteenth century.

102   See John Derbyshire, "A Barbarian's Barbarian," *National Review Online*, January 13, 2003.

103   George Orwell, "Rudyard Kipling," *Critical Essays* (London: Secker and Warburg, 1946).

104   Detlef Laugwitz, Bernhard Riemann 1826–1866: Turning Points in the Conception of Mathematics, translated by Abe Shenitzer (Boston: Birkhäuser, 2008).

105 Jesse Jackson, "We Must Choose Nonviolence," *HuffPost*, May 29, 2012.

106 John Derbyshire pictured appearing in "The Way of the Dragon."

107 Bacon Number.

108 John Derbyshire's IMDB profile.

109 John Derbyshire, "Fire from the Sun," John Derbyshire (website). Last modified October 2011.

110 "Amazing 2 Fingers Push Up by Bruce Lee," YouTube video, posted Sep 19, 2012.

111 John Derbyshire, "Fire from the Sun," John Derbyshire (website).

112 George Orwell, "The Art of Donald McGill," in *The Collected Essays, Journalism, and Letters of George Orwell*, vol. 2, *My Country Right or Left, 1940–1943* (London: Secker & Warburg, 1968).

113 Kenneth Dover, *Homosexuality in Ancient Greece* (Cambridge, MA: Harvard University Press, 1978), p.193.

114 IMDB "Saturday Night Fever (1977) - Goofs." IMDB.

115 Kevin MacDonald, "The Culture of Critique: Toward a True Understanding of the 1965 Immigration Act," The Occidental Quarterly.

116 See David Frum, "Unpatriotic Conservatives," *National Review*, April 7, 2003.

117 John Derbyshire, "Steel and Fire and Stone," *National Review Online*, September 11, 2001.

118 Steve Sailer, "Citizenism" vs. White Nationalism (II): Sailer Sums Up," *VDARE*, November 20, 2005.

Index